PETER THE GREAT

. . . . .

PETER THE GREAT

M. S. Anderson

Second Edition

LONGMAN
London and New York

Longman Group Limited,
Longman House, Burnt Mill,
Harlow, Essex CM20 2JE, England
and Associated Companies throughout the world.

*Published in the United States of America
by Longman Publishing, New York*

First published 1978 by Thames and Hudson Limited
Second edition published 1995 by Longman Group Limited

ISBN 0 582 08412 1 CSD
ISBN 0 582 08411 3 PPR

British Library Cataloguing-in-Publication Data

A catalogue record for this book is
available from the British Library

Library of Congress Cataloging-in-Publication Data

Anderson, M. S. (Matthew Smith)
 Peter the Great / M. S. Anderson. — 2nd ed.
  p. cm. — (Profiles in power)
 "First published by Thames and Hudson LTD 1978" —CIP t.p. verso.
 Includes bibliographical references and index.
 ISBN 0–582–08412–1. — ISBN 0–582–08411–3 (pbk.)
 1. Peter I, Emperor of Russia, 1672–1725. 2. Russia—History—Peter I,
1689–1725. 3. Russia—Kings and rulers—Biography.
 I. Title. II. Series: Profiles in power (London, England)
DK131.A49 1995
947'.05'092—dc20
[B]   94–44378
                                             CIP

Set by 5 in 10½ Baskerville
Produced by Longman Singapore Publishers (Pte) Ltd
Printed in Singapore

CONTENTS

CONTENTS

GENEALOGICAL TABLE
AND MAPS LIST

PREFACE TO THE FIRST EDITION

The complexities of Peter the Great's character and achievements, coupled with the immensity of the historical literature on every aspect of his reign, make the writing of a short biography of him a somewhat intimidating challenge. In meeting it I have been greatly helped by the encouragement and criticism provided by Professor Ragnhild Hatton, the editor of the Thames and Hudson series Men in Office in which the first edition of this book was published in 1978. I am also deeply indebted to Dr Isabel de Madariaga, whose careful and expert reading of the typescript has much improved and strengthened it. For the errors and inadequacies which must inevitably remain I alone am responsible. I also wish to thank Mrs N. E. Walsh for her skilful typing of the final draft, while it is a particular pleasure to acknowledge the help I have received, not merely in the preparation of this book but over the whole course of the last quarter-century, from the library of the London School of Economics.

It has seemed appropriate, in a book which hopes to reach a relatively wide and non-expert public, to give personal names frequently used in the text in their English rather than their Russian form, e.g. Alexis rather than Aleksey, and to refrain from italicizing a few Russian terms, e.g. boyar, which may be considered as to some extent familiar to the reading public.

M. S. Anderson
London School of Economics

PREFACE TO THE SECOND EDITION

The changes made for this edition have not been extensive. Apart from minor and purely verbal alterations I have expanded and amplified the text at a number of points to take advantage of work published since the first edition appeared. I have also recast the list of suggestions for further reading by limiting it to books and articles in the main west-European languages, particularly in English, and excluding the references, numerous in the first edition, to the enormous Russian literature. I hope that this may both keep the list within reasonable limits of length and make it more useful to the students and members of the general reading public for whom this book is primarily intended. I am grateful to Dr. Hamish Scott, of the University of St. Andrews, who first suggested the appearance of a second edition, and to Longmans, whose agreement to republish the book marks one more stage in a long and fruitful association.

M. S. Anderson
London

Chapter 1

RUSSIA BEFORE PETER: MODERNIZATION AND RESISTANCE

The Russia into which Peter was born, on 9 June 1672,[1] was already in some ways a part of Europe, or rapidly becoming one. It differed radically, none the less, from the states and societies to be found further west. Though much smaller in terms of territory than it was to become under Peter and his successors, it already covered a huge area. In the west it was severed from the Baltic by Sweden's possession of Finland, Ingria and Estonia. The great fortress-city of Smolensk, only 150 miles west of Moscow, bitterly contested for many years, had been finally wrested from the Poles as recently as 1654, and not until 1667 was the Polish Republic forced to surrender Kiev. Moreover, Russia had no outlet on the Black Sea, from which it was separated by hundreds of miles of largely uninhabited steppe as well as by the Moslem Nogais and Tatars of the Khanate of the Crimea, a vassal-state of the Ottoman empire since the later fifteenth century. Its only usable coastline, on the White Sea in the far north, where the new port of Archangel had been established at the end of the sixteenth century, was blocked by ice for much of the year. In the Caucasus, though its influence was growing, Russia as yet held no territory. It had nevertheless, in spite of these still restricted European frontiers, already shown both the desire and the capacity for territorial growth on a great scale. In the 1550s Ivan IV (Ivan the Terrible) had made a gigantic forward step by conquering the Tatar khanates of Kazan and Astrakhan, thus gaining control of the whole course of the river Volga. From the 1580s onwards the exploration and conquest of Siberia had been pushed ahead with remarkable speed, so that by the 1630s Russian adventurers had already reached the shores of the north Pacific. Long before Peter's birth, therefore,

1

his country had become, in mere size, a giant who dwarfed all the states of Europe.

This enormous territory was as yet undeveloped or only inadequately developed, and almost everywhere very thinly populated. In the north, vast tracts of tundra and forest supported only hunters, fur-trappers and a little primitive and precarious agriculture. The potentialities of Siberia, in the main still peopled only by native tribes, were almost completely unexploited, as indeed they were to remain until the present century. Even in central Russia, in the area around Moscow whose expansion had produced the huge territorial aggregation which Peter inherited, the population was scanty and the level of economic development low by west-European standards. It is impossible to say with any accuracy what the total population was; perhaps a figure of 10–12 million for the second half of the seventeenth century is the most plausible. Some signs of economic growth were visible. From the sixteenth century onwards, with the emergence of larger and to some extent unified internal markets, a tendency for different areas to specialize in the production of particular commodities had become more marked. Thus iron was smelted and worked in the north-west and around Tula, south of Moscow; linen and canvas were also produced in the north-west, grain most abundantly in the middle Volga valley and the area south of Moscow; and salt was an important product on the White Sea coast, in the Perm area and on the lower Volga. But the overwhelming impression is still one of potentially enormous resources exploited very inadequately if at all.

To some extent this was a matter of geography. Great distances and an extreme 'continental' climate, with severe winters, burning summers and a shorter growing season for crops than in western Europe, were in themselves barriers to economic progress. For each grain of wheat or rye sown only three or four were harvested; this was far lower than the standard yield in the more advanced areas of western Europe. Such a scanty yield meant that the overwhelming majority of the population had to till the ground if any kind of organized society were to survive. These natural obstacles, however, were reinforced by man-made ones. The rulers of Russia had forged a form of government more completely autocratic, in both form and substance, than any to be found elsewhere in Europe. The services rendered to the country by the autocracy were real. From the time of the Grand Duke Ivan III of Muscovy (1462–1505), a line of rulers had struggled, with considerable success, to unify Russia, to extend its territory and to defend it against the enemies – Poles, Tatars, Swedes – who confronted it across exposed and badly-defined frontiers. Military defence and territorial growth demanded strong and centralized, if necessary ruthless, government. But rule of this kind involved an increasingly complete monopoly by the ruler and the central government of initiative and decision-making of all significant kinds. New decrees in the seventeenth century still began with the traditional formula, 'the tsar has decreed and the boyars have assented'; but in fact members of old boyar families and the 'feudal' influences they represented were by the later part of the century becoming less important than an inner ring of personal advisers of the tsars. Many of these were drawn from relatively minor landowning families, though they were often promoted to the rank of boyar. The disappearance under Peter of the Boyar Council (*Boyarskaya Duma*) was merely the culmination of a development which had begun a good deal earlier. The obsequiousness which even the greatest nobles showed to the tsar, describing themselves as his 'slaves' and prostrating themselves before him, together with their acceptance of humiliating corporal punishments, showed how little they possessed the outlook of a west-European *noblesse*, with all that this implied in terms of a sense of personal honour. In the first decades of the century it had seemed that the Assembly of the Land (*Zemskii Sobor*) might become a permanent feature of Russian government and even a check on the tsar's autocracy. This was a representative body made up mainly of representatives of the service class, the 'serving men' (*sluzhilie lyudi*) who provided the tsars with most of their army and their rudimentary administration and who were normally rewarded for their services with grants of land. It also included, however, spokesmen of the town merchant class, and for a moment seemed to be on the point of gaining real power. But after the early 1650s the Assembly ceased to be called together; instead the government, for its own purposes and at its own convenience, summoned only occasional meetings of particular and limited social groups – merchants, 'serving men', or the representatives of Moscow. From this quasi-parliamentary direction no effective tempering of tsarist autocracy was to be hoped for. Even the officials through whom the tsar ruled were kept under continual scrutiny, guided by meticulous instructions and deprived as far as possible of all powers of initiative. Seventeenth-century Russia was thus a society in which there was no secular institution able or even willing to challenge the autocracy of the monarch. In it any display of independence or initiative, whether on a class or an institutional basis, was distrusted and discouraged.

It was largely through the landholding service class that the tsars, ruling an overwhelmingly agrarian society, made their authority effective. Whether as officials, as soldiers, or in a few cases as diplomats, it was members of this group who staffed the state-machine. Often poor, very often uneducated, they frequently depended heavily on government service for a livelihood. The tsar in his turn could not govern without their help. The result was a partnership which, although not always easy, proved lasting and for centuries gave a distinctive flavour to almost every aspect of Russian life. Most landlords still held their estates only on a life tenure in return for service. In practice, however, the traditional distinction between an estate held on these conditions (*pomestie*) and one held by the more prestigious hereditary tenure (*vochina*) was now becoming increasingly formal and unreal, since service was exacted irrespective of the type of tenure. More important, the government by the second half of the seventeenth century was in effect guaranteeing to the landlord, by the extension of serfdom, a secure supply of peasant labour. In 1649 a new law-code (*Ulozhenie*) bound the peasant holding land from a lord permanently to the estate on which he worked. Henceforth it was impossible for him legally to move without a certificate of permission (*otpusknaya*) from the lord. This legislation, the climax of a long process of cutting down peasant freedom of movement which had begun in the fifteenth century, consolidated the position of serfdom as the most fundamental and pervasive of all Russian social institutions. Free peasants still existed in considerable numbers; and even the many affected by the *Ulozhenie* retained significant rights – they could sue in the law-courts and own movable property. Their legal position was still much superior to that of the slaves (*kholopy*) who formed the lowest stratum of society. Nevertheless by the second half of the century the largest single element in the population of Russia was made up of unfree peasants paying dues to their lord in labour or kind. Given the situation in which Russia found itself, the need to pin down a scanty population in a huge undeveloped country and force it to support the service class of soldiers and officials essential for defence and the workings of even a primitive administrative machine, some development of this kind was perhaps inevitable. Heavy losses of population in the later sixteenth and early seventeenth centuries, and perhaps also the territorial growth of the Russian state from the 1550s, were powerful forces tending in this direction. In a sense, it can be argued, the peasant was enserfed not to the land or to the person of the landowner but indirectly to the state. In the last analysis he worked for the state, with the landlord as an intermediary; and Peter's policies and the thinking behind them intensified this aspect of the situation. But serfdom, however inevitable, was being extended and made more rigid in Russia at a time when it was contracting and becoming less important in much of the rest of Europe. It therefore tended to mark the country, in the eyes of foreigners, as backward and semi-barbaric; and in the long run serfdom was to become one of the most intractable obstacles to constructive change.

Nothing showed more clearly the social and economic gulf which separated Russia from the more developed parts of western Europe than the weakness and unimportance of its towns. Even if settlements of as few as 1,000 inhabitants are regarded as towns, it is probable that less than a twentieth of the population was urban. Moscow was an exception. It had a population of 150,000–200,000 and impressed foreign visitors as one of the greatest cities in Europe (though their admiration when they saw it at a distance often turned to disappointment when they could study it at closer quarters); the German Adam Olearius, who saw it in the 1630s, thought it numbered as many as 40,000 houses. No other city except Astrakhan, hundreds of miles away on the Caspian, held even a tenth as many people. But townsmen were slowly coming to make up a larger fraction of the total population. An enumeration of 1678 showed an increase of 24 per cent in their numbers over an earlier one of 1652, though the figures are unreliable and hard to interpret. Yet the urban population remained proportionately much smaller than in western Europe. It was subject not merely to the epidemics which afflicted towns everywhere in this period (plague is said to have killed almost 80 per cent of the taxpaying population of Moscow in 1654–55) but also to devastating fires which frequently ravaged towns built almost entirely of wood. Moscow, for example, suffered great fires in 1626 and 1648; the old and still important provincial city of Yaroslavl in 1658, 1659 and 1680.

The smallness and vulnerability of Russian towns partly explain the complete subjection to the central government which had for long been characteristic of them. This also owed much to the fact that many of them, probably at least a third, were primarily or exclusively military settlements which had been placed on the country's southern or eastern frontiers for defence against the Crimean Tatars or non-Russian tribes such as the Bashkirs. In the seventeenth century as much as half of the whole urban population of the country may have been made up of people whose functions were military or governmental. The social structure of even small Russian towns was complex: but even the richest merchants, the *gosti* (of whom there were in all no more than 300–400), did not enjoy the relative independence of the bourgeois of western Europe. Unlike his equivalent in the west, the Russian townsman enjoyed no taxation privileges. In so far as he was called on to take any share in local administration he did so under the control of the provincial governor, the *voevod*, and not as a member of a self-governing urban community. When he acted in this way he was performing, usually reluctantly, a service to the state, not exercising a right. Nor had he much more freedom of movement than the serf in the countryside. The increasingly inflexible structure of Muscovite society demanded that, to ease the collection of taxes, he should remain as bound to his town as the serf was to the estate upon which he worked. In 1665 a new searching-out of runaway townsmen was ordered by the government; and in 1674 Yaroslavl and Vologda petitioned successfully for the forcible return to them of former inhabitants now living in Moscow. Not until 1699, as a result of Peter's rather unsuccessful effort of that year at urban reform, did the town population acquire, at least for a time, the right to move freely. Moreover, although Russian merchants showed a certain amount of enterprise as far as trade with foreign countries was concerned, their efforts during the seventeenth century to branch out into industry were nearly always unimportant and small-scale.[2] Nor do we find any contributions to Russian cultural life from the merchant class of the kind made in western Europe. Even the wealthiest Russian

6

traders owned few, if any, books; and those they did possess seem largely to have been conventional works of religion.[3]

Seventeenth-century Russia was thus a highly rigid and restrictive society; and at the same time it was singularly lacking in institutions through which men might exercise some initiative and some control of their own lives. It was a society still in many ways unformed, disjointed, full of contradictions. Side by side with increasing official efforts to immobilize more and more of the population and end free movement went large-scale flight to the frontier areas of the south and the east, where the effective authority of Moscow was slight or non-existent. Among the Cossacks of the Ukraine (semi-independent communities made up originally of refugees from Russian or Polish rule) or in the largely non-Russian areas of the Urals, fugitive serfs, religious dissidents, anyone in flight from the oppressive authority of Moscow, might hope for refuge. While the central government sought to assert its control by minutely detailed legislation, and opposition was severely punished, there was a stubborn undercurrent of popular resistance which often expressed itself in anarchic violence. It is significant that the brigands, who created one of the most intractable of the problems facing the tsar's government, were the heroes of many folk-tales; oral epics (*byliny*) often credited them with magical powers such as invulnerability to bullets.[4] And Peter himself had to issue frequent decrees (for example, in 1699, 1714, 1716, 1719 and 1724) forbidding the giving of shelter to bandits and prescribing severe punishment for those who did. Resentment of bondage, of government exactions, of oppressive administration, broke out most spectacularly in the revolt which, under the leadership of Stenka Razin, set aflame a great area of south-east Russia in 1667–71. Razin, a Cossack, dreamt of introducing the free Cossack form of government into the tsardom itself; but in practice this amounted merely to a desire 'to take Moscow and to beat to death all you boyars and landlords and the government men'. In spite of its lack of constructive or well-defined objectives, however, this famous rising (which was also sympathetically reflected in the folk-songs and tales of the period) showed with frightening clarity the potentially explosive popular grievances and anger which simmered, barely concealed, under the surface of seventeenth-century Russia.

The greatest and most far-reaching of all conflicts in the two decades before Peter's birth was, however, a religious one. From a remarkable churchman, the Patriarch Nikon, came the one serious effort of the age to create a power able to counterbalance the autocracy of the tsar. Head of the Church in Russia in 1652, at the early age of forty-seven, Nikon introduced over the next fifteen years a series of liturgical and ritual reforms – making the sign of the cross with three fingers instead of two and singing three hallelujahs instead of two were the most important – which had the effect of aligning Russian Orthodoxy with that of Constantinople. These changes, which also involved the repudiation of ancient and revered liturgical works if they differed from Greek originals, horrified and infuriated a great body of nationalist religious conservatives in Russia. Nikon, a learned man and a passionate reformer, stood for a more critical and intellectually questioning attitude than that hitherto dominant in the Russian Church. His reforms implied a recognition that, as Russia's contacts with the outside world developed, its religious life must be put on a firmer intellectual basis than the blind acceptance of tradition. Nevertheless his opponents were often sustained by a fanatical loathing of 'Greek innovations' and a determination to adhere to practices felt to be sanctified by time. (In fact, the making of the sign of the cross with two fingers, the most emotionally charged of all the points in dispute, had been prescribed only as late as 1551, by a church council held in Moscow.) The result was a deep and unbridgeable cleavage between different aspects of Orthodoxy in Russia.

Simultaneously Nikon put forward far-reaching claims on behalf of the church against the ruler. For several years after his appointment as Patriarch he dominated the young Tsar Alexis (1645–76), receiving the title of 'Great Sovereign' (*Velikii Gosudar*) which was normally reserved to the ruler alone, and asserting the supremacy of ecclesiastical over secular power and the derivation of the latter from the former. Conflict soon followed. The growing subjection of church to state in non-ecclesiastical affairs and efforts (in the *Ulozhenie* of 1649) to prevent the accumulation of still more land in the hands of clerics aroused his particular anger. In 1658 Alexis deprived Nikon of his title of 'Great Sovereign'; but it was not until the end of 1666 that an ecumenical council in Moscow, attended by representatives of the patriarchates of Alexandria, Antioch,

Constantinople and Jerusalem, finally deprived him of the patriarchate. This council reiterated the traditional subjection of the church to the tsar in all secular matters, thus clearly rejecting Nikon's claims in this sphere; but in 1667 it confirmed his ritual and liturgical reforms and excommunicated those who refused to accept them. This decision formalized and made permanent the schism (*raskol*) which had been developing for many years. The adherents of the old practices (*raskolniki* or *starovertsy*) were henceforth driven increasingly to regard the tsar and his ministers not merely as mistaken in their policies but as the very agents of Antichrist himself.

The schism was thus more than a religious or even spiritual struggle. Its outcome marked the victory of an attitude to church affairs which was critical, and at least to some extent rational, over one which was traditionalist and essentially uncritical. The effects of this victory spilled over from the purely religious sphere into other aspects of Russian life, slowly eroding old conservative certainties and accelerating the pace of change. It is true that these effects were felt in full only by a small segment at the top of society; but that segment was strong enough to change the course of the country's history, in spite of the adherence of a great mass of ordinary folk to the intense and narrow pieties, the traditional values and certainties, of the past. It is an exaggeration to say that the *raskol* marked the end of the old Russia; but it was the beginning of the end.

Seventeenth-century Russia was thus a society in many ways profoundly different from those of western and even central Europe. Yet contacts of many kinds – political, economic, cultural – with Europe were already of long standing. In the later decades of the century particularly they were increasing in frequency and importance.

Foreign policy, and above all relations with Russia's western neighbours and with the Ottoman empire to the south, were coming to assume, as the century went on, an importance hitherto unprecedented in the Russian official scheme of things. The *Posolskii Prikaz* (Office of Embassies), the chief government organ for the conduct of foreign affairs, had roots going back to the early days of the Muscovite state. It had first been given definite form under the Tsar Ivan IV in 1549. But the growing scale and significance of Russia's foreign relations in the seventeenth century can be seen in a tendency for its functions to expand and its official importance to increase. Until 1667 it was normally controlled by a senior official with the high rank of *dumnyi dyak*; but in that year A. L. Ordin-Nashchokin, who had just been raised to the higher rank of boyar, became its head. The rise in its status can be seen more strikingly in a growing tendency in the later years of the century for the official who directed it to be also keeper of the seals of state, required to give validity to decrees or orders of the tsar. Its functions, moreover, were much wider than the mere conduct of foreign policy in a strict sense. Foreign trade, the post office (postal services between Moscow and several other European capitals had begun in the 1660s), the import of foreign newspapers and books, were all under its control. It kept records of all the European reigning families. It was also well provided with experts in foreign languages; in the later seventeenth century it could normally muster perhaps twenty *perevodchiki* (translators) and twice as many *tolmachi* (interpreters). In the 1660s it began the regular compilation and circulation of *kuranty*, handwritten digests of information obtained from foreign newspapers. Its officials were chosen for their education and specialized knowledge and not on the basis of favouritism or social standing (a school for the training of young recruits was set up in 1660), and from their ranks were invariably selected the heads of Russian missions to foreign rulers. Before reaching the rank of *dyak* (that most frequently held by the head of a Russian mission abroad) an official of the *Posolskii Prikaz* would normally have served in such missions in a subordinate capacity on numerous occasions, sometimes for as long as a year at a stretch. In other words the *prikaz* was not merely an agency for the conduct of foreign policy whose efficiency has perhaps been rather underestimated in most conventional accounts of seventeenth-century Russia: it was also a channel for the entry of foreign ideas, techniques and culture in general. Many west-European terms relating to diplomacy and international law, for example, had entered the Russian language and were in use by the *Posolskii Prikaz* long before the reign of Peter and the 'Europeanization' with which it is conventionally associated.[5]

Throughout the seventeenth century, however, there were no permanent Russian diplomatic missions stationed in the capitals of western and central Europe. Instead such missions were sent only intermittently, often merely when some crisis or turn of events made them necessary; and it was quite normal for the same mission to visit a series of courts in turn, staying only briefly in each. Apart from their intermittent and impermanent character, diplomatic missions from Moscow suffered from other difficulties. The almost total ignorance of the Russian language in the courts and capitals of Europe sometimes created problems. Thus in 1673, after Prussian protests, the Russian government had to agree to provide in future Latin or German translations of any documents which its envoys might bring to Berlin. The not uncommon Russian practice of paying diplomats in kind, by providing them with furs and other goods to sell abroad, sometimes inspired condescending amusement, or even outright contempt, in the capitals of western Europe. When in 1687 a Russian embassy to Paris and Madrid publicly sold goods in this way in France, the diplomats concerned were accused by an official observer of 'forgetting, so to speak, the quality of ambassadors to act as retail traders, and preferring their individual profit and interest to the honour of their masters'.[6]

Nevertheless, minor difficulties of this kind could not conceal the fact that the international significance of Russia was perceptibly increasing. In the first half of the seventeenth century, in the aftermath of the 'Time of Troubles' (the period of internal collapse and foreign occupation which in 1605–13 temporarily destroyed the country as an effective political organism), its weight in the affairs of Europe had been slight indeed. Gustavus Adolphus, the warrior-king of Sweden, had seen as early as the 1620s Russia's potentialities as an ally against Poland and the powers of the Counter-Reformation. In 1630 he had established a Swedish resident in Moscow to exploit these potentialities. No other major ruler or statesman of the period, however, found it necessary to pay Russia much attention. In the Treaty of Osnabrück, one of those which in 1648 ended the Thirty Years War in Germany, it was referred to merely in passing as one of the states 'allied and adhering' to Sweden. (This fact, unknown to the Russian government at the time, was later, under Peter, made a grievance against Sweden during the Great Northern War.) But by the later decades of the century Russia's growing military strength and more active interest in the politics of Europe had made considerable changes in this position. In particular its accession to the Holy League of 1686, which united it with Poland, Venice and the Habsburg Emperor Leopold I in a long struggle against the Ottoman empire, meant its formal emergence, more clearly than ever before, as a factor in international affairs, and the recognition of this fact by other states. The following year saw the despatch of an unprecedented group of simultaneous embassies (all of them still short-lived) to most of the states of western Europe. Besides the French government, whose sensibilities were so outraged, those of Prussia, Holland, England, Venice, Florence, Denmark and Sweden were all favoured in this way. Though hardly anyone in the west realized it, this foreshadowed the emergence of a new and potent force in European international relations.

History and geography confronted Russia with different and competing foreign policy objectives. Its inability to achieve them all simultaneously compelled it to choose between them. Ordin-Nashchokin, perhaps the most intelligent and open-minded figure in Russian foreign policy during the seventeenth century, was throughout his career (after successfully holding a number of provincial governorships he was head of the *Posolskii Prikaz* in 1667–71) a strong advocate of alliance with Poland, which he regarded as Russia's natural ally against Sweden and the Turks. To him the most important of all possible acquisitions was that of a secure outlet on the Baltic, the outlet which Ivan IV had sought unsuccessfully and at great cost during the long Livonian war against the Swedes and Poles in 1558–82. But other views were equally possible. It could be argued (as by his successor as head of the *Posolskii Prikaz*, A. S. Matveev) that the gaining of territory in the Ukraine at the expense of the Poles was more significant than that of a coastline and ports on the Baltic; while in the 1670s and 1680s the need to defend Russia against a partially rejuvenated Ottoman empire and its vassal-state, the Khanate of the Crimea, and perhaps to overrun the latter and obtain an outlet on the Black Sea, came to bulk larger than ever before in the thinking of statesmen and officials in Moscow. The traditions of Russian external relations were, however, until the last decades of the century, much more anti-Polish and anti-Swedish than anti-Turkish. Ottoman dominance of the Black Sea littoral was not resented as a bridling of Russia's economic development and a seizure of territory formerly Russian, or at least Russian-held, in the way that Swedish possession of Ingria and Livonia was. Nor (in spite of devastating raids by

12

the Crimean Tatars, during one of which Moscow was taken and burned in 1571) had an Ottoman army ever threatened the permanent conquest of much of Russia as the Poles did during the later years of the Times of Troubles. Yet by 1686 Russia was a partner in a great anti-Turkish alliance; and in 1687 and 1689 it made unsuccessful efforts to invade and conquer the Crimea, so long a thorn in its flesh. The last quarter of the century, in other words, made it increasingly clear that Russian expansionist energies would in future be directed in the main either westwards against Sweden, in a renewed effort to force an entry to the Baltic, or southwards against the Turks. Poland, so formidable a threat for so long, was now much too far gone in decay to be in itself a serious danger. The treaty of 1686, which gave Russia final possession of Kiev and much of the Ukraine, marked the end of the Russo-Polish struggles which for two centuries had been the most permanent feature of international relations in eastern Europe. But both Sweden and the Ottoman empire remained dangerous antagonists. To fight them simultaneously with any hope of success was impossible. Russia, if it were to expand and end the isolation from which it still suffered, must decide at whose expense this was to be achieved.

The economic as well as the diplomatic relations between Russia and the European states were growing in scale and importance in the later seventeenth century. From early in the century the importance of the English merchants who, since the 1550s and the beginnings of trade with western Europe via the White Sea, had been the most active element in commercial relations between Russia and the outside world, declined sharply. But this was more than compensated for by a growth of trade with other parts of western Europe, notably with the Dutch Republic, now commercially the most advanced and successful state in the world. Russian raw materials – pitch, tallow, leather, grain, furs – formed the basis of a rapidly growing Dutch trade carried on both directly through Archangel and indirectly through such Swedish Baltic ports as Narva and Riga. By the 1690s there were over 300 Dutch merchants in Russia; while the whole foreign merchant colony in Moscow numbered over 1,000. The later years of the century saw a considerable expansion of commercial contacts with the outside world (for example, in the signature of a trade agreement with Prussia in 1689). All over Europe merchants and governments continued to be attracted by the century-old hope that through Russia it might be possible to develop a lucrative trade in luxury goods with Persia and perhaps even with China. Nor should it be forgotten, as it often tends to be, that Russia was to some extent an active partner in these commercial contacts with the outside world. Its merchants had travelled and traded abroad, at least in Sweden, Livonia, and Denmark, since the sixteenth century. The peace of 1661, which ended a sharp five-year struggle with Sweden, increased their numbers, so that twenty years later there were about forty Russians trading in Stockholm.[7]

Underlying and accompanying the growth of political and economic relations between Russia and Europe was a corresponding expansion of European influences of many kinds – military, technological, artistic, intellectual – in Russian life. These influences already had a long history. In the later fifteenth century there had been a considerable influx into Russia of Italian artists and experts of various sorts: an Italian was for some time in charge of the Russian coinage, and Italian architects such as Fioravanti, Ruffo and Solario designed churches and palaces in Moscow. A hundred years later the country was host to a number of foreign mercenary soldiers; the first European work on military affairs to reach Russia, the *Kriegsbuch* of Leonhard Fronsperger (first published in Frankfurt-am-Main in 1566), made its appearance there during the Time of Troubles. The seventeenth century, especially in its second half, was marked by a rapid growth in these military influences. In 1648, in what seemed a potentially revolutionary situation, the Tsar Alexis thought of placing his personal bodyguard under the command of a Dutch colonel; and during the great struggle with Poland in 1654–67 there was a rapid formation of new regiments organized on more or less west-European lines. By 1663 some 60,000 men were in units of this kind. Such a development was made possible only by the large-scale import of foreign officers. The imperial ambassador, Mayerberg, spoke in 1661 of an 'innumerable multitude' of foreign soldiers in Russia: he knew of over a hundred generals and colonels from different parts of Europe who were serving there. An official list of 1696 gives the names of 231 foreign cavalry officers and 723 infantry ones (down to and including the rank of ensign).[8] In the 1630s the first

14

large-scale production of arms in Russia began in a new foundry at Tula built by Dutch experts.

Perhaps the most convincing index of the spectacular growth in the numbers and importance of foreigners in Russia is the fact that, whereas the law code of 1589 mentioned them in only one of its articles, the more famous (and admittedly much more extensive) one of 1649 referred to them in over forty. European influences on material life and in the provision of expert professional knowledge generally were concentrated in and symbolized by the German (or Foreign) Suburb (*Nemetskaya Sloboda*) of Moscow. The establishment of this foreign settlement just outside the capital, in 1652, was the result of a marked growth of anti-foreign feeling in the middle years of the century. Unable, as they would have preferred, either to expel foreigners from the country altogether or to convert them forcibly to Orthodoxy, religious conservatives had to be content with the modified victory represented by confining them to a limited area of the capital. Marked out as strangers and therefore dangerous by being forbidden to wear Russian clothes, forbidden also to sell wine, beer or tobacco to Russians, the inhabitants of the Sloboda (who in the 1670s and 1680s numbered in all perhaps some 1,500) lived largely cut off from the life around them. Nevertheless, they were the one substantial element of relatively advanced technical and professional knowledge in the country: the Sloboda included workshops, mills, a paperworks, an iron-works and a glassworks.

Technology, new industrial methods and techniques, new forms of tactics and military organization, came from western Europe, above all from the Dutch Republic and Germany. From Poland in the later decades of the seventeenth century came other influences, less material but, for some time at least, equally important. The union of a large part of the Ukraine with Russia in 1654, and the acquisition of much former Polish territory in 1667, greatly strengthened such influences. These conquests were followed by a considerable movement of Polish and Ukrainian craftsmen to Moscow and the production there of large quantities of Polish luxury goods, while in the last quarter of the century well over a hundred Polish books were translated into Russian – a degree of cultural borrowing from Russia's western neighbour never before approached. From the Polish-Lithuanian Commonwealth there was even some infiltration into Russia of foreign, above all Italian, musical influences, notably with the arrival in Moscow in about 1681 of Nicholas Diletskii from the University of Vilna. It was at the top of society that the influence of Polish culture showed itself most clearly. In the 1660s the Tsar Alexis began to sit on a new Polish-designed throne which, significantly, bore a Latin inscription. His successor, Feodor, ordered the wearing of Polish dress at court, was a patron of Diletskii and in 1680 married the daughter of a Polish nobleman from Smolensk. From Poland the Russian nobility acquired a taste for the western sciences of heraldry and genealogy and began to equip itself for the first time with coats of arms of the kind which had for so long been a preoccupation of the nobility of Europe.

More important was the pronounced Ukrainian influence which was developing within the Orthodox Church in Russia by the middle of the century. Through scholars from the Ukraine who had been exposed to Catholic and Uniate[9] influences (above all those educated at the great Kiev Academy, where all teaching was in Latin) foreign and even to some extent secular forces entered Russian religious life on an unprecedented scale. So marked was the leading role of the Ukrainians that in 1686 the Patriarch of Jerusalem, Dositheus, was moved to urge that 'in Moscow the old order of things should be preserved, so that there should not be igumens [i.e. abbots] or archimandrites of the Cossack people [i.e. Ukrainians], but Muscovites'.

Ukrainians were also very prominent as teachers and as tutors of the sons of the greater Russian nobles; from their ranks were drawn most of the orators who, on holidays and festivals, made speeches praising traditional heroes and well-doers. Simeon Polotskii, who came to Moscow from the Ukraine in 1663 and was by 1667 teaching several members of the ruling family, was the greatest scholar of the age in Russia. A prolific writer, he composed stage plays, wrote speeches for the tsar and high officials and produced polemical works on religious subjects, as well as carrying on an extensive correspondence on literary questions with other scholars in Moscow and the Ukraine. In his works can be seen the first reasonably clear statement in Russia of the idea of the state as a secular institution, one originating not merely in the divine will but in a natural human tendency to associate in groups and communities. The ruler, whom the need for security compelled these communities to choose for themselves, was not merely to lead his subjects to virtue but to safeguard their material welfare in this world.[10] This emphasis on the tsar's inescapable secular responsibilities was one which was later to appeal strongly to Peter, though there is no evidence that Polotskii or any other theorist influenced him much on this point. Ukrainian intellectual influences, however, were always deeply suspect in the eyes of devout Russians as likely to be tainted with Catholicism. The result was an effort to weaken them by importing Greek scholars who could provide Russia with the modern teaching which was now clearly needed but whose orthodoxy was not open to the same suspicions. The statute for a college which would combine the study of Latin and Greek with the teaching of religion along orthodox lines, the Slavo-Greek-Latin Academy, was approved by Tsar Feodor and the Patriarch Joachim in 1682; but it was only in 1687, after suitable Greek scholars, the brothers Ioanniki and Sofroni Likhud, had been brought to Moscow to run it, that it began to function. Kievans and their Russian pupils were excluded from it, and it soon became the main focus of the struggle between Greek and 'Latin' (Ukrainian) intellectual influences which was to be a feature of the next decade.

It is easy to see these widely differing stimuli from the west mainly in terms of the material and the external. It is tempting to describe them in terms of trivialities such as the placing for the first time of weathervanes on Russian churches, or even of more significant developments, such as the building by Tsar Alexis in 1666–68 at Kolomenskoe, outside Moscow, of a new palace whose design and decoration showed many western characteristics. Yet this would be to take a superficial and short-sighted view. As has already been seen, the great schism of the 1650s and 1660s had strained as never before the spiritual and psychological unity of Russia. Henceforth, individuals were no longer to be submerged as in the past in an all-pervasive structure of impersonal unanimity and anonymous piety. A great scholar has spoken of an 'emancipation of personality' in Russia during the second half of the seventeenth century; and it now becomes possible for the first time for the historian to receive, from letters, autobiographies and similar materials, the impression of distinct and recognizable individuals.[11] Ordin-Nashchokin; A. S. Matveev; F. M. Rtishchev and G. K. Kotoshikhin, two of the most interesting and original of the statesmen of the period; Prince V. V. Golitsyn, the

17

favourite and chief minister of the Tsarevna Sophia during her years as effective ruler of Russia in 1682–89: all these are examples. One of the most striking testimonies to the new feeling for the individual, the new willingness to consider him in his own right and not merely as a member of a social order or a religious communion, is the beginnings of portrait painting. An interest now begins to be visible, for the first time in Russian history, in the realistic representation by the artist of an individual sitter. Nikon himself sat for his portrait to the Dutch painter Daniel Vukhters, who in 1667 was engaged as official artist to the tsar and his family. A few years later the officially sponsored *Book of Titled Figures* was published. This contained sixty-five portraits of rulers, foreign as well as Russian, which in their relatively lifelike character mark a clear break with the impersonal and non-realistic representation of saints which had hitherto dominated Russian painting.

Allied with this new secular individualism was the birth of the modern theatre in Russia. As early as 1660 Alexis had shown his eagerness to obtain from western Europe experts skilled in the production of plays. A decade later Matveev was maintaining a private theatrical troupe led by a German, Johann Gottfried. The first secular dramas to be staged in Russia were probably those written and produced in the autumn of 1672 by Johann Gregory, the pastor of one of the foreign churches in Moscow. The first performers, not surprisingly given the extreme conservatism which still pervaded Russian life, were boys from the foreign colony. Two years later, without arousing any popular protest, Alexis attended a performance of a 'comedy' on the Biblical story of Esther (though he took the precaution of consulting his confessor beforehand on the permissibility of his behaviour). This court theatre remained in existence for more than three years; and during that time it presented nine different plays and one ballet, some more than once. Most of these were based on biblical themes. Nevertheless the dancing, costumes and sometimes comic interludes which they involved made them totally without precedent in Russian history. They were a striking though limited indication of the way in which the iron grip of tradition and habit was beginning to be loosened. Even within the church a slowly growing willingness to give more freedom to the individual and more scope to his talents can be seen in the tentative introduction of preaching of the type normal in western Europe. The duty of a pious Orthodox man, according to centuries-old assumptions, was not to glorify his petty individual abilities by delivering sermons of his own concoction but to submit absolutely to the great stream of unchanging tradition of which the church was the guardian. Any weakening of this attitude was a sure sign of intellectual and psychological change.

The Russia of Peter's childhood, adolescence and early manhood was thus rapidly developing. The great territorial gains made during the 1650s and 1660s and the ending of the Polish threat pointed to a future of further growth and increasing power. Though peasant agriculture, unchanging in its techniques and based on a labour-force increasingly made up of serfs, was overwhelmingly the most important form of economic activity, foreign technology was beginning to reveal possibilities of industrial growth on a scale hitherto unknown. The grip of the church on intellectual life, hitherto almost total, was still complete as far as the ordinary man was concerned. But it was slowly beginning, at least in the capital and among the upper ranks of society, to relax. The old Russia, isolated, self-sufficient, fearing and despising foreigners, dominated by traditional pieties, hostile to individualism and incapable of conceiving of real change, was far from dead. The attitudes which it embodied were still unchallenged among the vast majority of the population. But some of its foundations were now, if not undermined, at least partially eroded by new ideas, new potentialities and widening horizons. To see Peter, as many of his contemporaries came to and nearly all writers of the eighteenth century did, as bursting upon a Russia still languishing in medieval obscurantism and hopeless stagnation, is a gross error. Long before his birth, forces of change and possibilities of new growth had been evident. He strengthened these forces and in some cases diverted them into important new channels; but he did not create them.

. . .

NOTES

1. All dates are given in the New Style, i.e. that of the Gregorian Calendar. Until the revolution of 1917, Russia used the Julian Calendar, which was ten days behind the New Style in the seventeenth century and eleven in the eighteenth.

2. For details of these see J. Kaufmann-Rochard, *Origines d'une bourgeoisie russe (XVIe et XVIIe siècles)* (Paris, 1969), pp. 124–30.

3. M. I. Slukhovskii, *Bibliotechnoe delo v Rossii do XVIII veka* (Moscow, 1968), p. 106.

4. Denise Eeckaute, 'Les brigands en Russie du XVIIe au XIXe siècle, mythe et réalité', *Revue d'histoire moderne et contemporaine,* XII (1965), 165–7.

5. P. P. Shafirov, *A Discourse concerning the just Causes of the War between Sweden and Russia: 1700–1721,* ed. W. E. Butler (Dobbs Ferry, 1973), Introduction, pp. 14–16.

6. *Sbornik Imperatorskogo Russkogo Istoricheskogo Obshchestva* (St Petersburg, 1867–1916), XXXIV, 17.

7. J. Kaufmann-Rochard, *Origines d'une bourgeoisie russe,* p. 99.

8. S. F. Platonov, *Moskva i Zapad* (Berlin, 1926), p. 132.

9. The Uniate Church, whose adherents were numerous in the eastern parts of the Polish Republic, used a Slavonic liturgy but acknowledged the authority of the Pope.

10. A. Lappo-Danilevskii, 'L'idée de l'Etat et son évolution en Russie depuis les Troubles du XVIIe siècle jusqu'aux réformes du XVIIIe', *Essays in Legal History,* ed. P. Vinogradoff (Oxford, 1913), p. 361.

11. Platonov, *Moskva i Zapad,* p. 115.

Chapter 2

THE YOUNG TSAR

From the moment of his birth, Peter was caught up in a complex dynastic and political situation dominated by brutal conflicts between different factions and personalities. His father, the Tsar Alexis, had married as his first wife Maria Miloslavskaya, a member of a minor noble family. By her he had no fewer than thirteen children; but of the sons of this first marriage only two, Feodor (Theodore) and Ivan, survived him, and both of these were in poor health from birth. Feodor, though he was officially recognized as having come of age in 1674, was so delicate that he was not expected ever to reign. Ivan was an even more pathetic creature, almost blind, mentally deficient and with a speech defect. Six daughters of this marriage also survived; of these, Sophia was to prove one of the most remarkable figures in the whole of Russian history. As a result of Alexis's first marriage, the Miloslavskiis, a family hitherto obscure and with no significant record of state service, achieved for a number of years a leading position at court which aroused the envy and dislike of older and more prominent noble houses. This was lost, however, upon the death of Maria Miloslavskaya in 1669 and the remarriage of the tsar to Natalia Naryshkina, also a member of a relatively unimportant landowning family. Peter was her first child. Unlike his half-brothers he was lively and healthy from birth. The tsar's second marriage meant that the Naryshkin family used its newly won importance, as the Miloslavskiis had done earlier, to further the interests of its members. The two families thus formed competing court factions or at least provided the nuclei for them. It would be a mistake, however, to assume that they stood in any significant way for differing policies. It is true that the foster-father of Natalia Naryshkina, Artamon Matveev,

21

who had become head of the *Posolskii Prikaz* in 1671, was one of the most progressive and westernized figures in Russia. His wife was the daughter of a Scottish officer in Russian service. His substantial library, his interest in the theatre now just beginning to take root in Russia, his responsiveness to innovations of many kinds, mark him out as quite untypical of his class even in an age of accelerating change. Yet to identify the Naryshkin party with progress and the Miloslavskii one with resistance to it would be an oversimplification. The Miloslavskiis, for example, were stronger supporters than their rivals of the Polish and Ukrainian influences which, as has been seen, were in many ways the most important leaven at work in late seventeenth-century Russia. The factional struggle was for position, for power and ultimately for the physical survival of the contestants rather than over policies or ideas.

Nevertheless, with Alexis still only in middle life and in good health, these rivalries (for which there were plenty of precedents in the earlier history of Russia) seemed unlikely to become seriously disruptive. It was his sudden and completely unexpected death in February 1676, when he was only forty-seven, which opened the door to over a decade of bitter factional struggle. Feodor, who succeeded to the throne, brought back to court his uncle, Ivan Miloslavskii, who had been for some time in virtual exile as *voevod* of Astrakhan and who was regarded as the leader of the Miloslavskii faction. He also exiled Matveev, the most important figure in the Naryshkin party, to Pustozersk, a small and remote town in the far north of Russia. Nevertheless the position of the Naryshkins, in a situation so much influenced by dynastic considerations, was fundamentally strong. Nothing could alter the fact that they had incomparably the better of the two available candidates for the succession. Feodor could not live for long. By the first months of 1682 he was clearly dying. The principles which governed the succession to the throne were less clear-cut in Russia than in most west-European states; but there was no doubt that, had he been competent to rule, Ivan would have succeeded. But a helpless invalid as tsar offered an unpromising prospect, especially by comparison with the physically and mentally vigorous young Peter. Feodor seems in his last weeks seriously to have considered naming his half-brother as his successor, though he died without having done so. Irrespective of who succeeded, in any case, there would have to be a regency. Ivan, though sixteen years old, was totally incapable of ruling alone, while Peter was still a child of nine. This situation inevitably meant domination of the government by either the Miloslavskii or the Naryshkin party.

Feodor's death in May 1682 was followed by an easy and apparently complete victory for the latter group. A so-called *Zemskii Sobor* (it was one in no more than name, for its membership was in effect limited to those nobles who happened to be in Moscow at the time) chose Peter, largely at the urging of the Patriarch Joachim, as sole tsar. Matveev was recalled from exile. Government posts and court rank and offices were showered upon members of the Naryshkin family. Yet within a few weeks this victory had been nullified as the result of a dramatic and bloody episode in which the leading role was played by regiments in one of the major branches of the Russian army, the streltsy (from *strelets*, a shooter; the name originated from their being equipped chiefly with firearms). These were a powerful corps, numbering about 50,000, which had originated during the second half of the sixteenth century. Membership was hereditary, and members enjoyed important privileges, since they could live in their own houses rather than in barracks, engage in trade and produce alcoholic drinks for their own use. For almost a century after their creation they performed a useful function, acting in wartime mainly as an infantry force in the field and helping to garrison Russian cities. By the 1670s, however, their position was threatened by Russia's need for more modern fighting forces and by their own increasing inefficiency. Under Feodor they had already shown themselves discontented and even potentially rebellious. Some regiments had genuine grievances against their colonels, who often delayed or embezzled the men's pay, punished them harshly and sometimes forced them to work on their estates. The commander-in-chief of the corps, Prince Yury Dolgorukii, was generally disliked. The streltsy as a whole were deeply hostile to innovations and foreign influences, and to anything which seemed to threaten their traditional position and privileges. Old Believers, bitter enemies of Nikon's reforms, were numerous and influential in their ranks; this intensified their deeply-rooted conservatism. They also feared and suspected the boyars, and their discipline and morale had become, at least in Moscow, extremely poor. By the end of May 1682 it was widely believed among them that the Naryshkins had poisoned Tsar Feodor and meant to kill the Tsarevich Ivan: the Miloslavskiis seem deliberately to have encouraged these beliefs in the hope of using the streltsy regiments to destroy the newly created Naryshkin ascendancy. 'Great calamities are feared', wrote the Dutch resident, 'and not without cause, for the might of the Streltsi is great and redoubtable, and no resistance can be opposed to them. Their grievances should be corrected so as to avoid bad consequences.'[1]

This explosive situation culminated in a streltsy attack on the Kremlin on 25 May. The Tsaritsa Natalia tried vainly to calm the rioters by appearing on the Red Staircase hand in hand with Peter and Ivan and giving the streltsy a chance to satisfy themselves, by talking to and even touching the latter, that he was still alive. In spite of her efforts, there were appalling scenes of brutality that day and the two following. Matveev, hurled from the staircase into the courtyard below, was hacked to death by the halberds of the streltsy. Several members of the Naryshkin family and a number of leading boyars were murdered; in several cases the bodies were dragged to the Lobnoe Mesto, the traditional spot for the holding of popular assemblies of the citizens of Moscow, and there cut into small pieces. Throughout Moscow indiscriminate murder and looting continued for at least a week. The government was helpless; it had at its disposal no forces capable of resisting the streltsy and their demands. The result was that on 26 May the *Zemskii Sobor*, now even more obviously a sham than a few weeks earlier, agreed that Ivan and Peter should reign jointly, with the former as 'first tsar' and the latter as 'second'. Real power, however, rested with the Tsarevna Sophia, though it is almost certain that she was never formally declared regent and her decrees were issued, at least at first, in the names of her brother and half-brother. For the next seven years this remarkable woman was to dominate the government.

Her régime undertook a series of important constructive achievements – the conclusion after long negotiations of a treaty with Poland (1686) which confirmed Russia in possession of Kiev; the sweeping away in the following year of the customs barrier between Great Russia and the Ukraine; an unprecedented effort to develop diplomatic relations with western and central Europe (embassies were sent to eleven European capitals between 1684 and 1688). There was even a Russo–Chinese treaty, signed at Nerchinsk in 1689, the first ever made by the Chinese government with any European power. Sophia's lover and chief minister, Prince V. V. Golitsyn, was the greatest reformer of his day in Russia, a man whose breadth of view and accessibility to new ideas were greater than those which Peter himself was later to show. He had already, in 1681–82, played an important role in the abolition of *mestnichestvo*, a complicated system of precedence among Russian noble families which had for long hampered the efficient working of both the army and the administrative machine. As chief minister he lived in strikingly western style. He freely met and exchanged ideas with foreigners. In Moscow he had a great house with European furniture, portraits of both Russians and foreigners, mirrors (seventy-six of them, an unprecedentedly large number for Russia), clocks, maps, thermometers and even paintings of the planetary system on the ceilings of some of the chief rooms. A French observer thought this resembled the palace of an Italian prince rather than the usual dwelling of a Russian boyar.[2] When it was confiscated on Golitsyn's fall from power in 1689 the inventory made of its contents filled an entire book. Golitsyn's large library contained books and manuscripts in Polish and German as well as Russian; and, equally significant, about half of these were on secular, not religious, subjects. Perhaps most striking of all is the fact that women were sometimes present at banquets in his palace on a more or less equal footing with men. Nor was this enlightenment a matter merely of his own way of life. He did something to make legal procedure more humane and the punishments meted out for some offences milder. He planned to send large numbers of young Russians abroad for education and training, to raise a regular army of the west-European type and even to relax the control of the landlords over their serfs. Some, though by no means all, of his objectives parallel those afterwards aimed at by Peter; but his methods were quite different from those of the tsar. Throughout his years in power he showed a mildness and humanity which impressed both foreign and Russian observers. The brutality, the uninhibited use of coercion, which marked so many of Peter's policies, as well as his furious energy, were quite foreign to Golitsyn.

It was against this background that Peter passed the formative years of his life. In spite of his status as co-ruler he spent relatively little time in Moscow, especially after 1684, and took no part in the work of government. With his mother he lived in various villages and estates in the neighbourhood of the capital, above all at Preobrazhenskoe on the river Yauza, and came to Moscow only when it was unavoidable. This exile was, however, self-imposed. There is no evidence that Sophia, as has often been claimed, deliberately kept her half-brother away from the capital. The events of 1682 and the disorder and uncertainty which had pervaded the summer and autumn of that year in Moscow left a deep mark on the young tsar. His dislike of the Kremlin was to persist for the rest of his life. Years later he admitted that he still shuddered at the memory of the streltsy and could not 'smother the thought of these days'.[3]

Peter's political outlook during his adolescence (and indeed for many years after that) was limited. He feared and hated his half-sister, the Miloslavskii faction and the streltsy; but of the great questions and opportunities facing Russia he had no grasp, and of Golitsyn's reforms and the spirit which underlay them he knew little. His remoteness from politics and court life, however, had an important positive as well as a negative significance. It made possible, during these years, the sort of training which he was receiving, or rather giving himself, one quite unlike that of any previous ruler of Russia. Up to the age of ten or so his education had been of the type traditional in the ruling family. He was taught to read by a middle-ranking official, Nikita Zotov, using the Prayer Book, the Gospels and the Psalter as textbooks: Peter's knowledge of the Bible and fondness for quoting it in later years probably owed something to this early and highly conventional schooling. After 1682, in the freedom and irresponsibility of Preobrazhenskoe, the situation was different. Even as a young child he had been given military toys, wooden models of cannon and firearms, to play with. Now, left largely to his own devices, his tastes and inclinations found free expression in elaborate military games and mimic warfare. On his eleventh birthday, in 1683, he was allowed for the first time to have some real guns, small brass and iron cannon. When he moved from one village or monastery to another in the environs of Moscow, as he frequently did, his arsenal, which became considerable, went with him by the cartload. 'He has such a strong preference for military pursuits', wrote the Dutch minister in 1685, 'that when he comes of age we may surely expect from him brave actions and heroic deeds.'[4] Four years later the Prussian representative reported that 'The great application of the

Tsar Peter is much commented on, especially to war and horses.'5 From varied sources – court chamberlains, huntsmen, equerries, even serfs – he recruited young men and boys to form his toy regiments, the *poteshnie polki*, with which he staged parades, manoeuvres and mimic battles and sieges. As time went on, the dividing line between pretence and reality in these games became increasingly blurred. By the later 1680s his regiments, the Preobrazhenskii and Semenovskii, had a strength of several thousand men (exact figures are not available) and were becoming a genuine military force. Henceforth, until the collapse of the entire imperial structure in 1917, they were to remain the most famous and influential units in the entire Russian army. Barracks and stables were built at Preobrazhenskoe, the soldiers clothed in dark green uniforms and rigorously drilled and exercised. Noblemen with an eye to the future, when Peter would be tsar in fact as well as name, began to join the new regiments; and, indeed, to have served in them proved the starting point for more than one successful career. In particular the young Alexander Menshikov, born in the same year as Peter though of obscure parentage, was later able, through the personal acquaintance with the tsar begun in this way, to acquire a position of immense power.

In all this activity book-learning played little part. Yet the organization and command of an effective fighting force involved technical knowledge, a grasp of gunnery, engineering and the science of fortification. This the young tsar acquired from a small number of foreigners in the German Suburb of Moscow, most of them men of little formal education. Such were the German Theodor Sommer, who taught Peter gunnery; Franz Timmerman, who in 1687 was teaching him the use of the astrolabe and from whom he learnt the elements of ballistics and fortification; and the Dutchman Karsten Brand who repaired for him an old English boat and thus laid the foundations of an intense and lifelong interest in everything maritime. The young tsar's urge to be doing, his feeling for craftsmanship, his passion for the concrete, showed that in tastes and aptitude he was quite different from any of his predecessors. Even in his liking for loud noises and his intense enjoyment of fireworks (another western innovation which he had discovered in the Sloboda), he was a change from the tsars of the past, hemmed in by ceremonial and a rigid code of conventional behaviour. Whereas his half-brothers and half-sister had studied Latin, rhetoric and theology with Polotskii, Peter learned to write late, and always wrote badly; one historian, after much experience, confessed that 'nothing could be uglier than his handwriting'.[6] His spelling, even by the standards of that age, was erratic. Though he acquired some grasp of Dutch and German and of the simplest forms of mathematics from his foreign contacts in the Sloboda, he was never in any formal sense a well-educated man. Yet he boasted, no doubt with some exaggeration, that he had mastered fourteen different trades; and his taste for handicrafts and skilled manual work never left him. In 1711 during the Pruth campaign, at one of the most critical moments of his reign, he sent to Moscow for a lathe in order to divert himself by wood-turning, one of his favourite occupations.

By the later 1680s Peter, tall, healthy, with a will of his own and plenty of intelligence, was becoming an important and active element in the political situation. In January 1689 he married Evdokia Lopukhina, a young noblewoman who had been chosen for him by his mother and for whom he never felt any affection. He was beginning to show at least intermittent interest in affairs of state and in 1688 began to attend meetings of the *Boyarskaya Duma*, the council of magnates and high-ranking officials which, at least in theory, advised the ruler. It was becoming impossible to claim that he was any longer a minor. Moreover, two mismanaged and unsuccessful campaigns against the Crimea in 1687 and 1689 had shaken the prestige and self-confidence of Sophia's régime. It was clear, however, that she would not surrender power without a struggle. She had already assumed the title of 'Autocrat' (*Samoderzhitsa*), thus placing herself ostensibly on a footing of equality with Peter and Ivan. In January 1684 she had arranged the marriage of Ivan with a member of the important Soltykov family, almost certainly in the hope that it might quickly produce a son, thus destroying Peter's hopes of succession and prolonging her own power. In 1687 there were even proposals by some of her supporters for a coup d'état to make possible her coronation as ruler.

By the summer of 1689 a trial of strength between Sophia and her half-brother seemed inevitable. After midnight on 7 August Peter was suddenly roused from sleep by the news that streltsy were on the way from Moscow to seize and kill him. In an access of terror he leapt from his bed, took refuge in a nearby wood where he hastily dressed, and then made for the security of the great Troitsa-Sergeev monastery some forty miles away. For almost a month the Naryshkins and their adherents, with their base at the monastery, increased in strength. The streltsy, on the other hand, were now divided and uncertain in their attitude. Gradually Sophia began to lose their support, along with that of her other adherents. Early in September she was forced to retire to the Novodevichii convent outside the Kremlin, handing over to Peter's party the advisers who had been most closely associated with her régime. Golitsyn's fate was to be exiled to the far north where he spent a quarter of a century, unpardoned in spite of constant pleading, until his death in 1714.

Peter, still only seventeen, had played little active role in this struggle. In it he had been a symbol, a rallying-point for one of the contending parties, rather than a real participant. He now reigned in Russia without challenge (Ivan, though his half-brother had a real affection for him, counted for nothing). But he still did not rule, essentially because he did not wish to. For the next five years the government remained in the hands of his mother, a woman of mediocre abilities, and of a number of conventionally minded boyars. Of these, Peter's uncle, Lev Naryshkin, and Prince Boris Golitsyn, a distant relation of Sophia's fallen minister, were the most important. The change of régime had brought, in many respects, a decided conservative reaction, a movement away from the genuine striving for progress under Sophia and Golitsyn. The Jesuits were almost at once expelled from Russia. When the Patriarch Joachim, himself no friend to change or to foreigners, died in March 1690 he was succeeded, against Peter's will, by the ignorant and highly conservative Adrian, metropolitan of Kazan. Russian contracts with the outside world, notably with Poland, now began to be controlled much more strictly than in the 1680s.

State affairs, however, still meant little to the young tsar by comparison with the military and, even more, the naval hobbies and experiments which fascinated, indeed obsessed him. In 1688 he had begun, with wild enthusiasm, experiments in shipbuilding at Pereyaslavl on Lake Pleshcheev, about 200 miles from Moscow. Such was his passion for this work, in which he took a large personal share, labouring with his own hands, that in the spring of 1689 he deserted his young wife without the slightest compunction to indulge in it. Though he soon had to return to Moscow for a memorial service on the anniversary of Tsar Feodor's death, he spent as little time as possible in the capital; when he got back to Pereyaslavl he was delighted to find that the three small ships under construction there were almost ready. At this, he told his mother, 'I rejoiced as Noah did over the olive branch.'[7] From 1691 onwards his shipbuilding experiments grew in scale. Soldiers of one of his 'toy' regiments, the Preobrazhenskii, were used as ordinary carpenters for this work. Russian specialists in this field did not yet exist, but Timmerman and a Dutch merchant, Adolf Houtman, recruited shipwrights in the Netherlands – Peter's first deliberate import of foreign technicians into Russia. Such was his preoccupation with shipbuilding, and so slight his interest in political questions, that in 1692 he refused to return to Moscow to receive an important Persian embassy. Only a special journey by Naryshkin and Boris Golitsyn to the rather makeshift house in which Peter was living outside Pereyaslavl to supervise work on his ships could make him change his mind. In 1693 and 1694 he paid two visits to Archangel and for the first time saw the sea and the life of a seaport. This experience was one of the turning points of his life. It confirmed irrevocably the determination which had long been forming in his mind to create a Russian navy. In 1693 he laid with his own hands the keel of a warship at Archangel and gave orders for the purchase of a large frigate in Holland. Its arrival in the following year led to intensified efforts to recruit craftsmen of various kinds for a substantial programme of shipbuilding. From now on Peter lost interest in his earlier small-scale efforts on Lake Pleshcheev. He was setting his sights higher and aiming at the creation of a seagoing fleet. As yet he had little or no clear idea of how such a navy might be used or how it might benefit Russia. To him it was still no more than a gigantic and costly toy; but it was a toy which he desired almost frantically to possess. This passion, largely irrational and in a sense childish, was henceforth to be one of the dominant aspects of his life.

As admiral of his fleet, when it was built, Peter proposed to appoint the man who, more than anyone else, was close to him during the 1690s, the closest friend of his entire life. This was Franz Lefort. A native of Geneva (where a street close by the Orthodox church still bears his name), Lefort had lived in the German Suburb of Moscow since 1676. He was a man of little intellectual depth. He had nothing which could be called political ideas, no plans for the reform or modernization of Russian life. Nevertheless his social qualities, his open and engaging manner and his capacities as a drinker and womanizer, made him popular with the Sloboba. From 1690 his influence over Peter became very great. As well as making him an admiral, the tsar built for him in Moscow a palace which, with its rich decorations, its gilt leather, silks, damasks and Chinese rarities, and even in its size, anticipated the displays of conspicuous luxury which were indulged in by rulers of Russia during the eighteenth century. Lefort seems to have been genuinely attached to Peter; and his own good nature inspired in the tsar an affection stronger and more sincere than he was to feel for any other of his associates.

Nor was Lefort the only foreigner to influence Peter in these years. A much older man and a staider and more responsible personality, the Scot Patrick Gordon, since 1661 an officer in Russian service, was also important in his life. In the crisis of 1689 it had been the desertion of Sophia by Gordon and other foreign officers which helped to turn the tide in favour of Peter; and in March of the following year Peter paid Gordon the unprecedented compliment of dining with him in his house in the Sloboda. No previous tsar would have contemplated such a step; the fact that Peter took it is a good indication of his indifference or active hostility to custom and tradition.

Gordon, who received in Moscow the *Transactions* of the Royal Society in London, was a man of some intellectual pretensions. In this he was hardly typical of the foreigners with whom Peter consorted during his adolescence and young manhood. The shipwrights and other craftsmen who so much aroused his interest, his mistress Anna Mons (the daughter of a German wine merchant), even Lefort himself, were narrow and limited in their interests and range of knowledge. The higher reaches of European intellectual or artistic life were still far away. Drinking, smoking, crude jesting and practical jokes were at least as typical of Peter's day-to-day contacts with foreigners as the acquisition of new knowledge and ideas. What he wanted from these contacts, now as throughout the greater part of his life, was information of direct practical use, mechanical devices, ways of achieving specific material objectives, rather than new ideas or a new outlook in any deep sense. All the men with whom he came into contact in the Sloboda were in some sense adventurers. Luck, ambition or simply the need to survive had brought them to Russia in search of the success which had eluded them elsewhere. Over his entourage during the early 1690s there hangs an atmosphere of freebooting and insecurity. Peter's associates, Russian as well as foreign, were well aware of their direct personal dependence, not merely for their position but even for their physical safety, on the young tsar. Should he die, the verdict of 1689 might well be reversed, with deeply unpleasant consequences for them. At the end of 1692, when Peter was seriously ill, Lefort, Boris Golitsyn and others known for their close personal relations with him, kept horses in constant readiness to flee from Sophia's revenge should he fail to survive.

By his absorption in his military games and shipbuilding, by the time he spent in horseplay and heavy drinking, by his refusal to interest himself in many aspects of government and its problems, Peter was turning his back on the obligations of his position and selfishly indulging purely personal tastes. One of the mock battles in which he still delighted, fought in the autumn of 1694 outside Moscow, may have involved as many as 30,000 men, twenty-four of whom were killed. On the other hand, he had by now formed an outlook and ambitions which, however limited and incoherent, ensured that Russia's future would be different from its past. Intimate with foreigners and preferring to meet them on their own ground in the Sloboda, on the move since the middle 1680s from place to place (though as yet his journeys to Archangel were the longest he had undertaken), passionately interested in technology and craftsmanship and in mastering all the processes they involved, he was a tsar of a totally new and individual stamp. Nothing could have less resembled the traditional Russian ruler, a remote and hieratic figure hardly ever visible to his subjects, rigidly bound by convention and ceremonial and seldom leaving Moscow – or even the Kremlin itself – except for highly-organized and largely formal hunting parties. As yet this young iconoclast had little idea of what he wanted to make of his country. Concepts later to be of fundamental importance to him – his responsibility for the well-being and progress of Russia, his duty to serve that well-being and progress and to force all his subjects to serve it also – were still unformulated in his mind.

Events, however, were now forcing upon him a more active interest in government and the assumption for the first time of an active and undivided responsibility for it. In January 1694 his mother died. Peter was emotionally moved; but for long he had had little in common with her and had paid little attention to her wishes. Her death did nothing to alter his own attitudes and scale of values. A letter to Feodor Apraksin, now one of his most trusted associates, written soon after receiving the news, begins with a mention of his grief, 'about which my hand cannot write in detail', but goes on almost at once to give elaborate orders about a ship to be built at Archangel.[8] Nevertheless it was hardly possible for the young tsar, now matured to manhood, to behave with the carelessness and self-absorption which he had so often displayed for the last decade. His enthusiasms were as powerful and compelling as ever; but they were now being tempered by a new sense of responsibility and by widening horizons. In February 1696, when his half-brother Ivan died, this process was carried a stage further. Ivan had never been more than a helpless invalid absorbed mainly in the performance of those traditional ceremonies in the Kremlin for which Peter cared little. His death, however, left Peter as sole tsar. Twenty-three years old, in rude health, contemptuous of tradition, he was full of unfocused and half-formulated ambitions. He was now poised to launch Russia on a long course of essentially unplanned change, exhilarating to some of his subjects, incomprehensible and even tormenting to many more, which was to alter drastically almost every aspect of its life.

• • •

NOTES

1. Quoted in E. Schuyler, *Peter the Great, Emperor of Russia* (New York, 1884), I, 48.
2. Foy de la Neuville, *Relation curieuse et nouvelle de la Moscovie* (The Hague, 1696), pp. 15, 177–78.
3. S. F. Platonov, *Moskva i Zapad* (Berlin, 1926), p. 148.
4. Quoted in E. Schuyler, *Peter the Great*, I, 106.

5. Quoted in K. Forstreuter, *Preussen und Russland von den Anfängen des Deutschen Ordens bis zu Peter dem Grossen* (Göttingen-Berlin, 1955), p. 174.
6. Platonov, *Moskva i Zapad*, p. 150.
7. Quoted in N. Ustryalov, *Istoriya tsarstvovaniya Petra Velikogo* (St Petersburg, 1858–63), II, 29–30.
8. *Pisma i Bumagi Petra Velikogo* (St Petersburg-Moscow, 1887–), I, No. 21.

Chapter 3

THE FIRST INITIATIVES: THE CAPTURE OF AZOV AND THE 'GREAT EMBASSY' TO THE WEST

The exact reasons for the Russian campaign which began in the spring of 1695 against the port of Azov, at the mouth of the Don, remain obscure. In particular it is doubtful whether Peter himself had much to do with the decision to attack the Turkish fortress, for as yet he had hardly begun to play a leading role in the government. A new outburst of fighting between Russians and Turks, however, was to be expected. The war between them, though quiescent since Golitsyn's second failure against the Crimea in 1689, was still in being. The Tatars of the Crimea continued to carry out occasional destructive raids against Russian territory; in 1692, for example, they burnt part of the town of Nemirov in the Ukraine and carried off a considerable number of prisoners. There was a real danger that, if Russia did not play a more active part in the struggle, its allies, the Holy Roman Emperor and the king of Poland, would neglect Russian interests when peace was made. A Turkish agreement in the summer of 1694 to open negotiations with the Austrians and Poles aroused fears of Russia being relegated to a position of inferiority in the alliance and perhaps even denied the representation expected at a peace congress. Religious feeling and tradition, a certain crusading impulse, also provided a significant part of the background to the attack on Azov; it is noteworthy that the army which captured it in 1696 bore at its head a flag which had been carried, almost a century and a half before, by the army of Ivan IV when it took the great Tatar and Muslim fortress of Kazan in 1552.

After years of mimic fighting Peter enthusiastically welcomed the chance to experience war. 'Although for five weeks last autumn we practised in the game of Mars at Kozhukhovo', he

35

wrote to Apraksin, 'with no idea except that of amusement, yet this amusement of ours has become a forerunner of the present war. . . . At Kozhukhovo we jested. We are now going to play the real game before Azov.'[1] With the ostensible rank of a bombardier sergeant of the Preobrazhenskii regiment (a striking indication of his unwillingness to accept high rank in either army or navy until he felt he had earned it by training and experience), he accompanied the army which besieged Azov from July to October. This campaign, however, was a complete failure, only partly counterbalanced by the considerable success of a second Russian army under B.P. Sheremetiev, which took two Turkish forts at the mouth of the Dnieper. A cumbersome system of divided command (a council of three generals, none of whose decisions could be carried into effect without Peter's consent), a marked lack of technical skill in the conduct of the siege and the inability of the Russians to prevent Turkish seaborne reinforcements from reaching the town led to a costly and humiliating defeat.

Peter never for a moment contemplated accepting this defeat as final. A larger army was raised, and put under a single commander, the boyar A. S. Shein, for a new campaign against Azov in 1696. More significant, however, was the great effort made to construct a naval force able to bar access by water to the town. A Dutch galley of 32 oars was brought overland from Archangel to Preobrazhenskoe, to be used as a model for others to be built there; and with great difficulty 27 small ships were transported overland from Moscow to be launched at Voronezh on the Don. There and at other places on the river – Dobry, Sokolsk and Kozlov – no fewer than 1,400 barges were also built to carry the army down to Azov. In addition to the mass of small craft, two ships of 36 guns, the *Apostle Peter* and the *Apostle Paul*, were launched on the Don – the first sizable ships of war to be built in Russia. In all this Peter played a very active part in the most direct and physical way. 'According to the commandment of God to our ancestor Adam', he wrote from Voronezh in March 1696, 'we are eating our bread by the sweat of our face'; and certainly at least one of the galleys built at this time, the *Principium* launched in the following month, was worked on by the tsar in person.

The building of this huge flotilla of barges and other vessels was the first of the great series of demands, in men, labour and materials, which Peter was to make upon his subjects almost incessantly for the next generation. Like its successors it aroused, because of the sacrifices and sufferings it involved, much passive resistance. The peasants drafted for work often failed to appear or ran away after a short time. Thus, of the 4,743 men allocated to the yards at Dobry 1,244 never turned up and 1,878 fled as the task progressed. Yet in spite of such difficulties 360 barges were built at this one site.[2] Here, in the very first days of Peter's effective reign, we see the characteristics of much of his work – bold and far-reaching plans put into force with little or no detailed preparation and brought to fruition, in the face of suffering and opposition, by ruthless, driving energy. Inevitably a shortage of skilled seamen and technicians made itself felt. Some shipwrights were brought from Archangel. The Emperor and the Elector of Brandenburg were asked to send miners and engineers for the conduct of the second siege of Azov. An effort was made to obtain detailed information about the Venetian galley-fleet, which might be used as a model – the different officer ranks and their duties, the number of oars to a galley and of men to each oar, the punishments meted out for various offences.[3] The 4,000 men who were to serve on board the newly-built ships were, however, soldiers drawn mainly from the increasingly indispensable Preobrazhenskii and Semenovskii regiments. They were commanded by Lefort who, in spite of his title of admiral, had no naval experience and who also commanded one of the four divisions of the army. Under him as vice-admiral and rear-admiral served two other professional soldiers, the Venetian Colonel Lima and the French soldier of fortune Balthasar de l'Oisière. It was this improvised force which entered the Sea of Azov at the end of May 1696.

It proved remarkably successful in isolating Azov from the sea and Turkish reinforcements. After a two-month siege the town surrendered. It was Peter's first victory. He celebrated it on his return to Moscow in October by the first of the great ceremonial parades, full of pompous display and classical allusions, to which he was to become so attached. This also showed the tsar's rejection of tradition and the past. Under the triumphal arch erected for the occasion he walked in the guise of a mere captain in the suite of Admiral Lefort; and he wore not Russian traditional dress but the costume of western Europe – a plain black coat and a plumed hat. A few years later the first Russian commemorative medal, a medium for self-advertisement long exploited by the rulers of western Europe, was devoted to the taking of Azov.[4]

The victory meant to Peter more than prestige and an opportunity for display. He now possessed a stretch of coastline which, though it gave him access only to the Sea of Azov, presented new opportunities for increasing Russian naval power. It might be used as a jumping-off point for entry into the Black Sea proper and even into the Mediterranean. Azov itself, abandoned by its Turkish garrison and largely in ruins, was repopulated by the compulsory migration of peasants from the Kazan area, and refortified. Peter clearly hoped, quite unrealistically, that it would become a major Russian port. He took a close personal interest in the extensive new building work which at once began there; and of the foreign technicians and specialists who took service in Russia in the following years a high proportion were employed in the development of the new conquest. Thirty miles west, at Taganrog, the building of a new naval base was ordered. In the years which followed, thousands of conscripted peasants were to labour on its dockyards and defences: 20,000 were summoned from the Ukraine in 1698 for this purpose. Above all, a systematic effort was made, the first in Russian history, to construct a powerful fleet of large and heavily armed vessels of the west-European type. A series of edicts in November–December 1696 ordered the formation of companies of secular and clerical landowners, each of which was to be charged with the building, equipping and arming of a man-of-war. Every secular landowner, or group of such, controlling 10,000 peasant households, and every monastery or group of monasteries or clerics with 8,000, had to provide a ship. Landlords with less than 100 peasant households were to be exempted from this obligation in return for a money payment. This rather crude expedient produced significant results, at least in the short term. At least sixty-one companies were formed (nineteen of clerical and forty-two of secular landlords),[5] and a considerable fleet was constructed at Voronezh over the next three years. Peter himself laid the keel of one of the new ships, the 58-gun *Predestinatsiya* (the foreign name is significant), in November 1698. During the first half of 1697 about fifty foreign shipwrights – Dutch, English, Danish, Swedish, Venetian – arrived for work at Voronezh. Almost simultaneously about the same number of young Russians were sent abroad to learn the crafts of shipbuilding. More than half of them went to Venice, still regarded as the greatest centre of galley technology, the rest to the Dutch Republic and England. These formed the first batch of what was to become, as the reign progressed, a steady and growing stream of Russian students of various kinds sent by Peter to western and central Europe.

But the lasting achievement of the initiatives of 1696–97 was disappointing. Ships were built; but built badly. The new programme had been embarked upon (this was typical of the young Peter) with hardly any detailed consideration of how it would work or how it could be used to produce the kind of fleet that was wanted. Because of runaway workers labour was often scarce: in July 1698 orders had to be given to surround Voronezh and its dockyard with soldiers so that neither Russian workers nor foreign specialists might leave without official permission.[6] Disputes among different groups of foreign experts hampered progress. Administration was generally inefficient. The result was ships of bad proportions and shoddy construction which did not last well and were often more or less unseaworthy from the moment they were launched. To the fifty-two envisaged in 1696 another twenty-five were added in 1698, apparently because so many of the first batch were unsatisfactory: the tsar himself thought them 'rather fitted to bear mercantile burdens than do military service'. As early as 1701 at least ten of those launched only a year or two earlier had to be rebuilt.[7]

One reason for the defective administration of the scheme was Peter's absence from Russia. In March 1697 he left the country, and did not return until September 1698. In those eighteen months he travelled through Courland and Brandenburg to the Dutch Republic, thence to England and, on his return journey, to Vienna. He did not see France and had to abandon an intended visit to Italy. But with these important exceptions he made the acquaintance of the most advanced regions of Europe. Ostensibly he travelled merely as 'Peter Mikhailov', a member of the 'great embassy' of which Lefort was the formal leader. This easily penetrated incognito deceived no one; but it was carefully maintained throughout the journey. It reflects Peter's deeply held belief that what really mattered was a man's innate worth, a compound of knowledge, energy and public spirit, not titles, ceremonies or outward appearances. The feeling which had led him to serve as a sergeant-bombardier and work as a shipwright now forbade him to travel abroad in the role of a tsar. The journey was the supreme illustration of his contempt for tradition and of his wide-ranging though somewhat superficial curiosity about the contemporary world. No Russian ruler had ever visited a foreign land; and apart from a few diplomats and merchants very few Russians of any kind travelled abroad. Now Peter was seen to be throwing down the barriers which had hitherto separated his country from the rest of Europe.

The dominant motives behind the embassy, as far as he himself was concerned, were almost certainly the acquisition of a deeper knowledge of shipbuilding and everything maritime, and the recruitment of foreign experts in these fields on a much larger scale than hitherto. He was unwilling to contemplate the possibility that the young Russians now being sent abroad for training might return with a knowledge of naval matters superior to his own, even though the 250-strong embassy included thirty-five 'volunteers' destined for the study of maritime affairs. It recruited, mainly in the Netherlands and England, about a thousand technicians and instructors – shipwrights, officers, navigators, even a few teachers of mathematics – some of whom were to play important roles in the carrying-out of Peter's plans.

At the same time, however, there were important political and diplomatic considerations underlying the great journey to the west. Peter hoped to press further the victories he had won over the Turks. In particular he was anxious to obtain, if possible, the fortress of Kerch and with it free passage for his ships through the Straits of Kerch into the Black Sea. If this could be achieved the entire relationship between Russia and the Ottoman empire would be tilted, perhaps decisively, in favour of the former. It seemed possible, from the perspective of Moscow, that an enlarged and more effective coalition of the Christian powers against the infidel might be created; for the war of the Grand Alliance, which had absorbed the energies of France, England and the Dutch since 1689, was clearly drawing to its close. Already in February 1697 Peter's agent, Nefimonov, who had been sent to Vienna over a year earlier, had signed with the emperor and the Venetian Republic an agreement by which the three states undertook a three-year offensive alliance against the Turks and promised to concert their military efforts to that end. Three months after the tsar left Russia a new and more directly important international complication forced itself on his attention. The death of John Sobieski, the last great king of Poland, in June 1697, led inevitably to a struggle over the succession (since the Polish monarchy was elective) in which the rival candidates were supported by competing foreign powers. Should France succeed in establishing its nominee, the Prince de Conti, on the Polish throne and defeating the Elector Augustus of Saxony, who was backed by Russia and the Habsburgs, this would be a very serious defeat for Russia. It would almost certainly mean the withdrawal of Poland from the anti-Turkish league and possibly a Polish–Turkish alliance.

The great journey to the west, in other words, was much more than a matter of the acquisition of technical knowledge. This element, so far as Peter was concerned, was very important; and he used to the full the opportunities of this kind which now presented themselves. In Holland he worked for over four months (September 1697–early January 1698) in the docks of the East India Company in Amsterdam. In England he spent almost as long (February to early May 1698) in the dockyard at Deptford. His curiosity about technical processes and even, to a limited extent, scientific discoveries was boundless. Detained for three weeks at Pillau in East Prussia in July 1697 by the need to observe events in Poland after the death of Sobieski, he occupied the time in a serious study of gunnery and won a certificate of progress from the chief engineer of the fortress. At Zaandam in Holland he made a sheet of paper with his own hands. A little later he became competent in another art in which the Dutch were pre-eminent – etching and engraving. He met the two greatest Dutch scientists of the age, the doctor Boerhaave and the microscopist Leeuwenhoek, though the real significance of their work largely escaped him. In London he visited the Tower, the arsenal at Woolwich, the Mint and the Royal Society. Everywhere museums, cabinets of curiosities, factories and even theatres attracted his attention and provoked his incessant questions.

However the political aspects of the embassy, the need to win allies for Russia, to strengthen its international position and pave the way for its future expansion, were not neglected. A treaty of friendship with Prussia was signed at Königsberg early in July 1697. Though this had little significance in itself, Peter

41

and the Elector Frederick probably gave each other, during the sea journey to Pillau which followed, verbal promises of support against all enemies.[8] In Utrecht Peter had an interview with William III, whom he had long admired and with whom his personal relations became very cordial. (He was delighted by the present of William's best yacht, the newly-built *Transport Royal*.) In Vienna he discussed international affairs at some length with the Imperial Chancellor, Count Kinsky. None of this political activity had much result. The promises exchanged with Frederick of Prussia were a long way from constituting a treaty; and Prussia's energies and attention were in any case soon to be absorbed once more by a renewed struggle with France after the outbreak in 1701–2 of the war of the Spanish Succession. The Dutch and English governments had not the slightest intention of becoming involved in a conflict with the Turks of the kind for which Peter still hoped. On the contrary, they were now secretly doing their best to mediate between the Ottoman empire and the Habsburgs in the negotiations which were to bear fruit in the peace treaty of Carlowitz in January 1699. Austria was increasingly preoccupied by the imminent death of Charles II of Spain and the crisis over the Spanish inheritance which was likely to follow, and correspondingly more inclined to a peace with the Turks which would free its hands for action in Italy and on the Rhine. The Habsburg government therefore proved unresponsive to Russian pleas or demands that it should continue the war with the sultan, as agreed in the Russo–Austro–Venetian treaty of February 1697, until the Porte agreed to cede Kerch to Russia. The whole configuration of international relations was, at least for the time being, unfavourable to Peter's hopes. This fact was strongly borne in upon him as his travels proceeded and his grasp of the situation improved.

Reactions to the 'great embassy' and to Peter personally differed considerably. In the Swedish fortress-city of Riga (the first western city to be visited by the young tsar), through which the embassy passed to reach Prussian territory, his reception was polite and formally correct rather than warm. Peter's efforts to inspect the fortifications produced an incident trivial in itself but destined to have considerable consequences, when he was rudely ordered away by a sentry. Lefort, as formal head of the embassy, admitted that the soldier had merely done his duty. But the insult rankled in the tsar's mind and the memory of it grew with the passage of time. More than three years later it was the only specific reason given for the Russian declaration of war against Sweden; and when the Russian siege of Riga began in 1709, Peter rejoiced that 'The Lord God has enabled us to see the beginning of our revenge on this accursed place.' Whatever his virtues, easy forgiveness of an injury, real or imagined, was not among them.

Nor did his passage through Prussian territory arouse great interest or enthusiasm in ruling circles. The official charged with the reception of the embassy in Königsberg was told by the elector that 'we should prefer it if he [Peter] wishes to pass through entirely incognito without speaking with us or coming to our court, so that we may remain free from the embarrassments which we should otherwise have with him.'[9] In Holland and England the official attention paid to him was as much a matter of curiosity as the result of any feeling that this bizarre individual, a visitor almost from another world, was a figure of real political importance. In Vienna disputes over ceremonial meant a delay of over a month before the ambassadors could present their credentials to the Emperor Leopold I. The most active official interest taken in the tsar there was probably that of the papal nuncio, who hoped for his conversion, to be followed by that of his subjects, to Roman Catholicism.

If the 'great embassy' introduced Peter to Europe it also gave Europeans their first glimpse of a Russian ruler. Their reactions, like those of their governments, were mixed and often lukewarm. The tsar's energy and curiosity, together with his obvious native intelligence, aroused admiration. On the other hand, the uncouthness of his manners, his heavy drinking (striking even by the standards of that uncritical age) and the facial spasms that afflicted him at moments of strain (and were to do so for the rest of his life), all made him seem something of a savage, however powerful and interesting. 'The tsar is very tall, his features are fine, and his figure very noble,' wrote the widowed electress of Hanover after meeting him in Germany. 'He has great vivacity of mind and a ready and just repartee. But, with all the advantages with which nature has endowed him, it could be wished that his manners were a little less rustic.' She was amused when the Russians, in dancing, took the whale-bones of the German ladies' corsets for their ribs 'and the tsar showed his astonishment by saying that the German ladies had devilish hard bones'.[10] In England the bishop of Salisbury thought Peter 'designed by nature rather to be a ship-carpenter, than a great prince', and went on to comment that 'after I had seen him often, and had conversed much with him, I could not but adore the depth of the providence of God, that had raised up such a furious man to so absolute an authority over so great a part of the world.'[11] Hoffmann, the Austrian representative in London, reported to Vienna that 'They say that he intends to civilize his subjects in the manner of other nations. But from his acts here, one cannot find any other intention than to make them sailors; he has had intercourse almost exclusively with sailors, and has gone away as shy as he came.'[12] Certainly it would be an error to imagine that this famous journey fundamentally changed Peter's ideas or even greatly widened his intellectual horizons. The science and political ideas of western Europe, even its forms of government and administrative methods, received little of his attention. But its wealth, its productive power, its military and still more naval strength had, by direct personal acquaintance, impressed themselves on his mind most forcibly. His determination, confused but unwavering, to win for Russia some of the same advantages by a programme of change imposed from above, was now stronger than ever.

Peter had meant to go on from Vienna to Italy, perhaps also to France. But all plans of this kind were shattered when, at the end of July 1698, a letter was received from Prince Feodor Romodanovskii, whom he had appointed governor of Moscow on his departure, with the alarming news of another revolt of the streltsy. Peter, still in the dark as to the true situation in his capital, at once set out for home, travelling day and night. Not until he was more than halfway across Poland was he reassured by news that the rebellion had been suppressed and that his throne was safe. Early in September he entered Moscow once more.

The background to the renewed unrest among the streltsy was the widespread and deep-rooted dislike in Russia not only of Peter's policies but of the style and atmosphere of his rule. His desire to build a navy, his friendships with foreigners and in particular the immense influence wielded by Lefort, his European dress, the journey to the west, in a word his wholesale and brutal rejection of the traditional behaviour proper to an orthodox tsar, aroused the deepest misgivings and resentment.

During the months before he set out on the great journey to the west there had been several manifestations of this. The monk Avraam of the Andreevskii monastery had presented to the tsar a written protest against the novelties being introduced into Russia; this resulted only in his being despatched to a more distant monastery, while his associates were flogged and exiled to Azov. More serious was the conspiracy led by a streltsy colonel, Ivan Zickler, which came to light in February 1697. This was joined by representatives of two old boyar families, A. P. Sokovnin and F. M. Pushkin, as well as by a Don Cossack leader, Lukyanov, and a number of streltsy officers: the conspirators may have hoped to kill Peter and put a leading boyar such as A. S. Shein or B. P. Sheremetiev on the throne.[13] Peter was never in any serious danger from this ineffectual plot. Nevertheless it revived his dislike of the streltsy and still more his fear and hatred of the Miloslavskii family, the foes of his childhood and youth. The corpse of Ivan Miloslavskii, dead for twelve years, was taken from its grave and dragged on a sledge drawn by swine to the place of execution of Zickler and his associates, so that when the executioner hacked off their arms, legs and finally heads their blood flowed over it. This savage in incident is the best of all indications of the lasting traumatic effects on Peter of the events of 1682 and the following years.

Besides a general conservative dislike of the turn of events in Russia the streltsy were influenced by a feeling, only too well justified, that they were now an obsolescent fighting force threatened by new military developments. They also had specific grievances. They were well aware of Peter's dislike of the corps; and there was bitter resentment at the use of a number of Moscow streltsy regiments to garrison Azov and other distant places such as Velikie Luki. The lack of success of representatives of these regiments, sent to Moscow to present their case in the spring of 1698, was followed by open revolt in June. This disorganized and leaderless explosion of helpless resentment was quickly suppressed, with little bloodshed, by loyal forces under Shein, Gordon and a minor military commander, Prince Koltsov-Massalskii. Yet Peter was alarmed by this continual source of danger and disloyalty, and in particular by the suspicion that Sophia, still immured in her Moscow convent, might have been in touch with the rebels in the hope that their victory would restore her to power. He determined to crush the streltsy for ever.

Even before he was able to return to Moscow he had ordered Romodanovskii to treat the rebels with great severity and to intensify the surveillance of Sophia.[14] On 17 September systematic investigation of the background and inspiration of the revolt began. It was conducted with appalling cruelty, indeed with a sustained brutality which Peter was never again to display to the same extent. Hundreds of the captured streltsy were tortured, normally by being beaten with the knout (a thick and hard leather thong) and then having their raw and bleeding backs roasted slowly over a fire. Fourteen separate torture-chambers established for the purpose, most of them at Preobrazhenskoe, were used to interrogate about twenty men a day each: the tsar took part occasionally in person. Torture was followed by execution. In three weeks in October 1698, 799 streltsy were put to death; and then after a gap of three months another wave of over 350 executions followed in February 1699. It is unlikely that Peter himself took part in these executions. A famous book, the *Diarium Itineris in Moscoviam* by Johann-Georg Korb, the secretary of the Austrian minister in Moscow, which appeared in Vienna in 1700, alleged that he had; and the allegation was widely believed in Europe. Korb, however, did not write as an eye-witness; and there seems to be no proof that the tsar himself ever handled the headsman's axe. It is clear, nevertheless, that some of Peter's close associates helped on occasion to put the condemned streltsy to death, among them Menshikov. It was claimed by Korb that the evening before one batch of executions he rode through Moscow in an open carriage, showing 'by the exceedingly frequent flourishing of a naked sword how sanguinary a tragedy he expected next day'.[15]

These months were perhaps the most strained and tense of Peter's reign. During them he found respite from the torture and execution of the rebels in unrestrained feasting, drinking, revelry and violent horseplay with his boon companions. On at least two occasions during these entertainments he kicked and struck Lefort himself. A note of wildness, even of desperation, is perceptible in Peter's actions during this period. The death of Lefort in March 1699 must have increased his feeling that he was struggling, with all too little support and encouragement, against a world hostile to his dreams and hopes. At the funeral he 'showed many tokens of grief: fixed sorrow was in his face', while he 'shed tears most abundantly' and gave the last kiss to

46

the corpse. He had lost the closest friend of his life; and he was angered by another demonstration of the unsympathetic atmosphere which surrounded him when, on the return of the mourners to Lefort's house after the funeral, the boyars attempted to leave sooner than Peter thought appropriate.[16] In February–March 1699 both the Austrian and Prussian ministers remarked to their governments on the general feeling of confusion and tension in Moscow; they felt there was a real danger that the tsar and his unpopular innovations might be swept away by a new upsurge of resentment.[17]

Peter had no intention of giving in to the opposition which he sensed around him. He was determined to consolidate his power, however ruthless the means, and then to use it to change Russia. The Moscow streltsy regiments were abolished. Their members lost their houses and lands and were sent into exile in the provinces. Wherever they went, however, they carried resentment of Peter's rule and the seeds of sedition. Both the rising in Astrakhan in 1705–6 and that of the Cossacks of the Ukraine in 1707–8 were to owe something to their influence. As for Sophia, even torture and the most searching interrogation, including the flogging of a number of her serving-women and attendants, and her questioning by Peter in person, failed to prove that she had instigated the revolt. If it had succeeded, however, the rebels, as well as destroying the foreign suburb of Moscow, killing many of the boyars and breaking up Peter's new regiments, might well have recalled her to power as regent. She and one of her sisters were therefore forced to become nuns; and any threat she presented to her half-brother was thus much reduced. Outside her window in the Novodevichii convent were hanged three streltsy, one of them holding in his lifeless hands a paper representing the petition for redress of their grievances which the discontented regiments had presented before their revolt.

The punishment of the streltsy was accompanied by other signs, less bloodthirsty but none the less significant, of Peter's refusal to compromise with the forces of conservatism in Russia. His dull and traditional-minded wife, of whom he had for some time wished to be rid, was despatched to a convent at Suzdal where she too was forced to become a nun. There were even rumours that the young tsar wished to marry Anna Mons, in spite of her humble and foreign birth. The Tsarevich Alexis, only eight years old, was handed over to Peter's favourite sister

Natalia, the only member of his family with whom the tsar's relations were close.

Peter's return to Moscow in September 1698 meant, in addition to the punishment of the streltsy, the first systematic efforts to force at least the upper classes in Russia to conform to the manner and appearances of western Europe. The shaving of beards and the adoption of foreign dress, in place of the long coats and long sleeves of traditional boyar costume, were not in themselves of great importance. Their effect was largely confined, at least in the short run, to courtiers and officials (though after 1705 the yearly payment exacted for the wearing of beards, the amount of which varied as between different classes, became notably heavier). But they made visible, as few other things had done, Peter's continuing insistence on change and readiness to reject the weight of tradition and routine which blanketed Russian life so heavily. The same is true of the decree of December 1699 which provided that in future the years should begin on 1 January, not on 1 September as hitherto in Russia, and that dating should be as in western Europe, from the birth of Christ and not from the alleged creation of the world. The next year, in other words, was to be 1700 and not 7208. Almost simultaneously, moreover, there appeared the first serious administrative reform which the tsar had hitherto attempted, the establishment of the *Ratusha*.[18]

It was during 1698 and 1699, therefore, that in domestic affairs there was a marked extension and speeding-up of a process of enforced change which hitherto had been confined to the creation of the new navy and the anticipation, in the new guards regiments, of a reformed army. In foreign policy the change of course, the beginning of a new era, was even more distinct. During his travels in Europe Peter had still been thinking almost entirely in terms of a renewed struggle with the Turks. The vague verbal agreement he seems to have made with the elector of Brandenburg had anti-Swedish overtones; but these were as yet of little importance. In the Dutch Republic, in England, in Vienna, it was the hope of support against the enemy in the south which had inspired his advances to foreign governments and rulers. By the time he left Vienna it was clear that the Austrians were likely to make peace soon and had no intention of prolonging the war to give Peter the chance of capturing Kerch, for which he hoped. In January 1699 the treaty of Carlowitz, mediated by

England and the Dutch, brought peace between the Ottoman empire on the one hand and the Habsburgs, Poland and Venice on the other. This completely destroyed any chance of gaining Kerch. P. B. Voznitsyn, the Russian representative at the congress, fought hard to obtain it; but he found himself largely disregarded by Russia's allies while the Turks, once sure of peace with their most dangerous enemy, were reluctant to agree even to a Russian retention of Azov. All that could be obtained was a Russo–Turkish truce of two years. Peter felt, with some reason, that he had been badly let down by his allies, above all by Austria. Without Kerch the fleet built with such effort and expense from 1699 onwards was confined to the Sea of Azov and of little use. His resentment was bitter and lasting. Even twelve years later he told the British minister to Russia that, 'In my lifetime I shall never forget what they have done to me, I feel it, and am come off with empty pockets.'[19]

But there was little to do but make the best of a bad job. In September 1699 E. I. Ukraintsev, a high official of the *Posolskii Prikaz* and one of the most experienced Russian diplomats, arrived at Constantinople to negotiate a peace treaty. He held some good cards in the tedious haggling over terms which followed. The Ottoman empire was exhausted by a long and disastrous war. Moreover Ukraintsev arrived in the Turkish capital on board a frigate of forty-six guns, a clear and deliberate indication of Russia's new status as a naval power. The implications of this unprecedented event were not lost on the Turks. The Russian ship aroused great interest and not a little uneasiness, and was carefully inspected by the sultan himself. The treaty signed in Constantinople at the end of June 1700 was therefore in some ways relatively favourable to Russia. The fortresses taken by Sheremetiev on the lower Dnieper in 1695 were to be destroyed and the territory on which they stood returned to Turkey; but Azov and the surrounding area were to be retained by Russia. Ukraintsev also won important successes on two specific points: henceforth there was to be no more payment of Russian tribute to the Tatars of the Crimea, and Russia was to have a minister in Constantinople with the same rights and privileges as the representatives of other Christian powers.

Almost two years earlier, however, Peter had begun to think in terms of expansion to the north-east, towards the Baltic and at the expense of Sweden, as a substitute for the renewed southward movement which the international situation made so difficult. In August 1698, during his hasty return from Vienna to Moscow, he spent four days in talks at Rawa, a small village in Galicia, with Augustus, the new king whom he had helped to place on the Polish throne. Much of the time was spent in drinking; and the two rulers, both young and given to self-indulgence of this kind, at once took to each other. During the meeting there was certainly talk of cooperation against Sweden. Indeed, in return for a promise to support the king if necessary against his notoriously intractable nobles, Peter asked for Augustus's help if he should try to avenge the insult which he had suffered at Riga almost eighteen months earlier. By itself this did not mean very much. But it was the first distinct sign that the tsar's mind was now beginning to turn to war with Sweden. For such a war there were much more substantial reasons than mere personal pique. The Swedish empire, by its possession of Karelia, Ingria and Livonia, denied Russia direct access to the Baltic; and two earlier tsars, Ivan IV from 1558 to 1582 and Alexis from 1655 to 1661, had carried on long, expensive and eventually unsuccessful struggles against Sweden in an effort to win a Baltic coastline. To Peter the lack of one not merely hampered the justified territorial and economic growth of Russia by helping to isolate her from Europe: it held back every aspect of her development. The Swedes he complained, had 'not only robbed us of our own necessary harbour but in order to deprive us of the desire to see have put a heavy curtain in front of our mental eyes and cut off our connections with the whole world'.[20]

The prospects of success seemed good. Sweden's remarkable military achievements and territorial conquests during the seventeenth century had made it unpopular in varying degrees with all its neighbours. Poland and Brandenburg–Prussia had cause to resent its growth, and Denmark in particular was bitterly hostile. Russia might therefore hope to fight as a member of a powerful anti-Swedish coalition. Moreover the growth of royal absolutism in Sweden during the 1680s had aroused much resentment among the nobility; in particular, the efforts of the Swedish crown in the 1680s to reclaim from the Livonian nobles estates formerly alienated to them as security for loans (when the income from the land in question could be claimed to have repaid the loan with interest) provoked bitter opposition. An able and energetic landowner, Johann

Reinhold von Patkul, had by the late 1690s been struggling for years to construct an anti-Swedish alliance to avenge the wrongs this policy of 'reduction' had allegedly inflicted on his class. Finally, the new king of Sweden, Charles XII, was at his accession in April 1697 a boy of only fourteen.

A Danish–Saxon treaty directed against Sweden had been signed as early as March 1698. This was followed by another in September of the following year. Two months later Peter and Augustus formed an alliance against Charles XII. From the spoils of the Swedish Baltic empire Augustus was to receive Livonia, which he hoped then to offer to the Poles in return for their making his family their hereditary rulers. Russia was to receive Ingria, while Peter in return promised to attack Sweden as soon as news of a peace with the Turks was received. Until his hands were free in the south, it was important for him not to arouse suspicion of his intentions. Therefore only a few days after the agreement with Augustus, in an act of official duplicity notable even in that unscrupulous age, he solemnly confirmed, to a Swedish embassy sent for the purpose, the Russo-Swedish treaty of Kardis of 1661. (The Swedes were not deceived and were fully aware that they might soon have to face active Russian hostility.)

The anti-Swedish alliance was in no sense a Russian creation. It was beginning to take shape well before Peter had seen that he must transfer his hopes of conquest from the Black Sea to the Baltic. Its main architects were two successive kings of Denmark, Christian V and Frederick IV, deeply embroiled with the rulers of Sweden by disputes over the duchy of Holstein-Gottorp. It was Augustus and the Danes who began the war by invading Livonia and Holstein-Gottorp in February and March 1699. Once embarked on his new course, however, Peter pursued it with all his usual headlong energy. At the end of 1699 he began, in preparation for the imminent struggle, the rapid expansion and modernization of the Russian army.[21] On 19 August 1700, the day after news of the treaty with the Porte was received from Ukraintsev, war was declared on Sweden 'for the many wrongful acts of the Swedish King, and especially because during the journey of His Majesty through Riga, much opposition and unpleasantness was caused to him by the inhabitants of Riga'. Peter had embarked on a course which was to raise immeasurably his and his country's standing in Europe. He could not foresee the cost and effort, the sometimes agonizing struggle and the mass suffering, which this great achievement was to demand.

. . .

NOTES

1. Quoted in E. Schuyler, *Peter the Great, Emperor of Russia* (New York, 1884) I, 243–44.
2. M. M. Bogoslovskii, *Pyotr I. Materyaly dlya biografii* (Moscow, 1940–48), I, 290.
3. See the letter from Francesco Guasconi in Moscow to his brother Alessandro in Venice, of 8 January 1696, in A. Theiner, *Mémoires historiques relatifs aux règnes d'Alexis Michaelowitch, Féodor III et Pierre le Grand* (Rome, 1859), p. 364.
4. See *Medals and Coins of the Age of Peter the Great* (Leningrad, 1974), No. 14. This medal cannot have been struck before the opening of the Admiralty Mint in 1701.
5. See the list in N. Ustryalov, *Istoriya tsarstvovaniya Petra Velikogo* (St Petersburg, 1858–63), II, 306, and the documents illustrating the workings of the company system in II, 501–31.
6. K. Nikul'chenkov, 'Sozdanie Azovskogo voennogo flota', *Morskoi Shornik*, 1939, No. 6, p. 72.
7. Bogoslovskii, *Pyotr I*, III, 172.
8. See the discussion of this still rather obscure episode in K. Forstreuter, *Preussen und Russland von den Anfängen des Deutschen Ordens bis zu Peter dem Grossen* (Göttingen-Berlin, 1955), pp. 177–80.
9. Forstreuter, *Preussen und Russland*, p. 177 fn.
10. Quoted in E. Schuyler, *Peter the Great*, I, 285–6.
11. N. Luttrell, *A Brief Historical Relation of State Affairs from September 1678 to April 1714* (Oxford, 1857), IV, 407–8.
12. Quoted in E. Schuyler, *Peter the Great*, I, 307–8.
13. B. B. Kafengauz and N. I. Pavlenko (eds), *Ocherki Istorii SSSR: period feodalizma. Rossiya v pervoi chetverti XVIIIv.; preobrazovaniya Petra I* (Moscow, 1954), pp. 416–18.
14. *Pisma i Bumagi Petra Velikogo* (St Petersburg-Moscow, 1887–   ), I, 266, 268–9.
15. J.-G. Korb, *Diary of an Austrian Secretary of Legation at the Court of Czar Peter the Great* (London, 1863: reprinted London, 1968), p. 251.

16. J.-G. Korb, *Diary*, pp. 274–9.
17. See the despatches quoted in E. Dukmeyer, *Korbs Diarium Itineris in Moscoviam und Quellen die es ergänzen* (Berlin, 1909–10), I, 52–5.
18. See below, p. 118.
19. *Sbornik Imperatorskogo Russkogo Istoricheskogo Obshchestva* (St Petersburg, 1867–1916), LXI, 35. His protest of 8 August 1699 to William III against the Carlowitz terms can be found in Public Record Office, S.P. 104/120.
20. W. Mediger, *Moskaus Weg nach Europa* (Braunschweig, 1952), p. 7.
21. See below, pp. 94–5.

Chapter 4

EMERGENCE INTO EUROPE: THE GREAT NORTHERN WAR

. . .

DISASTER AND TRIUMPH: FROM NARVA TO POLTAVA, 1700–9

Peter entered the war with high hopes and ambitions. He looked forward in the first place to the partition of the Swedish empire and the permanent gain by Russia of a substantial coastline on the Baltic, in Ingria and Karelia. To these, as territories held by former Russian rulers, he was confident that he had a moral claim. He also seems to have envisaged, at least as a possibility, drastic changes in the form of government in Sweden, forced on it by its enemies to make it less able to contemplate the recovery of its lost territories. The Swedish monarchy, so aggressive and expansionist throughout much of its history, might, he hoped, be abolished and replaced by a republic since 'republics were less dangerous to their neighbours'.[1] He had already put forward ideas of this kind in his meeting with Augustus at Rawa; and his attitude foreshadowed the policy of systematically weakening both the Swedish and the Polish monarchies which was to be followed by every ruler of Russia, with considerable success, for half a century from about 1720 onwards.

Even before Russia's declaration of war, however, the whole situation had changed sharply in Sweden's favour. The Saxon forces with which Augustus had attempted to seize Riga had been beaten back. Although he was a belligerent as elector of Saxony, the Polish Republic, of which he was merely the elective ruler, had not entered the war – a fact which was to produce many future complications and difficulties. On the very day that news of Ukraintsev's treaty with the Turks was received in Moscow, Frederick IV of Denmark was forced by a Swedish landing in Zealand and a direct threat to his capital to sign with Charles XII the treaty of Travendal and withdraw from the war. The young Swedish king had already begun to show the military gifts and qualities of leadership which were to make him for the next two decades the most spectacular figure on the European political stage. Already it was becoming clear that Russia's allies were unable or unwilling to give much effective assistance; and the practical limitations of the programme of military development which Peter had begun a few months earlier were soon to be mercilessly exposed.

The first Russian initiative was an attack on the Swedish fortress-city of Narva. Russian territory near-by already reached to within about twenty miles of the Baltic: if the city fell, Swedish land communication between Livonia and Ingria would be cut. Early in October the siege was begun by an army of about 40,000 men, which Peter himself accompanied, ostensibly as an officer of the Preobrazhenskii regiment. (Once more we see his unwillingness to assume publicly any military or naval rank to which he did not feel himself entitled in terms of technical proficiency and experience.) The siege went badly. The garrison of Narva was active and self-confident, and little impression was made on the defences. In the Russian camp morale was shaken. Early in October Charles XII landed at Pernau with a Swedish army, and on 20 November the battle of Narva, fought in a blinding snowstorm, resulted in a crushing and humiliating defeat for Peter's new forces at the hands of a numerically far inferior enemy.

The panic in many of the Russian regiments was striking. The Saxon General von Hallart, an eye-witness, complained that 'they ran about like a herd of cattle, one regiment mixed up with the other, so that hardly twenty men could be got into line';[2] and so many prisoners were taken that all except the officers had to be released, since the Swedes had no means of feeding such numbers. (On the other hand, the Russian left wing continued to fight well until dawn on the 21st, when it was completely surrounded.) All the Russian artillery was lost. Peter himself had left the army two days earlier and gone to Novgorod to organize the despatch of reinforcements. Like the other leaders on the Russian side, he had not expected the sudden Swedish attack. The duc de Croy, the experienced foreign commander to whom he had entrusted the army only a few days before, himself surrendered to the Swedes after seeing several non-Russian officers murdered by soldiers who suspected them of treachery.

Peter was surprised and bitterly disappointed by the defeat. It seemed to open the way for a Swedish advance on Pskov, Novgorod and even Moscow itself. The fortification of the first two, the reorganization of the regiments routed at Narva, the raising of new forces and the production of cannon to replace those lost, were undertaken with desperate energy. It was during these critical months that Peter's single-mindedness and willingness to disregard traditional prejudices were illustrated by a famous incident – the melting-down of church bells to provide metal for the casting of the new artillery.

The Swedish onslaught on Russia, which had seemed so threatening, did not materialize, though detailed planning for it went on at Charles XII's headquarters until October 1701.[3] Instead the king turned south and in July 1701 crossed the Dvina to attack Augustus II, who was now the only one of his enemies who had not suffered crushing defeat at his hands and whose position in Poland was becoming stronger. For the next five years or more Charles was to be enmeshed in the endless complexities and uncertainties of Polish factional politics. A good many Polish nobles, including some very important ones, such as the commander of the Crown army, Jablonowski, disliked any idea of cooperation with the Russians. Still more wished to remain neutral in the struggle as far as possible and to support neither Charles nor Peter, while there was widespread distrust of Augustus's obvious desire to strengthen the position of the monarchy in Poland and the threat this might involve to the traditional privileges of the nobility. All this, allied with the ambitions of leading noble families (notably the great Sapieha family in Lithuania) and the rivalries they generated, made Polish politics a morass in which there was little solid ground. Poland was now weaker, more divided and more at the mercy of outside pressures, than at any time since the disastrous decades of the 1650s and 1660s. 'This unsettled nation like the Sea', complained an English diplomat in 1706, 'tho' it foams and roars only moves as it is agitated by some superior Power.'[4] It was this weakness and instability, along with the sheer geographical size of the Polish Republic, which made it impossible for either Augustus or Charles to control it.

For several years the international situation prevented Charles XII from using the one expedient which would quickly

have driven Augustus out of the war. This was a direct attack
on the electorate of Saxony, the real base of his power. Such
an attack was certain to be bitterly opposed by England and
Holland. Their position in the war of the Spanish Succession,
which broke out in 1701–2 and henceforth dominated the
entire situation in western Europe, would, they felt, be seriously
complicated and even weakened by such a move on Charles's
part. The Swedish king relied on the English and the Dutch to
enforce Danish neutrality and observance in Copenhagen of
the treaty of Travendal, and as a result he did not dare to invade
Saxony until 1706.[5] Up to then he was doomed to struggle with
the depressing complexities of the Polish situation; and Peter
was well aware of the valuable breathing-space which this gave
Russia. In February 1701, in a new meeting with Augustus at
Birsen, he made large concessions to stiffen his ally's will to
continue the struggle. A promise that the tsar would lay no
claim to Livonia or Estonia when the Swedish empire was
partitioned, a Russian auxiliary corps of 15,000–20,000 men,
a subsidy of 100,000 roubles, supplies of gunpowder – all these
inducements were held out to the ambitious but unreliable king
of Poland.

The investment of Russian resources in stiffening resistance
to the Swedes in Poland proved a good one. There were
important Swedish victories there, notably at Kliszow in July
1702 and Fraustadt in February 1706; and Charles set up
a claimant of his own to the Polish throne, the nobleman
Stanislaus Leszczynski, as a rival to Augustus. But the men
and money spent in these Polish struggles meant some corresponding weakening of the Swedish hold on the Baltic
provinces. Here the Russians rapidly won important successes.
In 1702–3 the breakthrough to the Baltic was accomplished.
This time, in contrast to the unsuccessful efforts under Ivan
IV and Alexis, it was to be permanent. The Swedish fortress
of Nöteborg, at the mouth of the Neva, fell in October1702;
Peter characteristically gave it a new, and western, name –
Schlüsselburg, the key fortress. A few months later, early in
1703, he began the building of a new city, St Petersburg, on
a site nearby. This was rapidly to become the most visible and
impressive, and also the most costly, symbol of his desire to
set Russia on a new course. In March 1703 the fortress of
Nyenskans, and in May the old Russian towns of Yam and
Kopor'e, fell into his hands. The upshot was that by the

summer of that year Russian control had been established over a still narrow but very important stretch of coastline on the gulf of Finland. This maritime outlet, so wished for and so dearly won, Peter was determined never to surrender. During the next three years there were further and larger-scale territorial gains. In the summer of 1704 Dorpat and Narva fell to Russian armies. Simultaneously Peter was able to make an alliance, as he had long wished, with the Polish republic (as distinct from Augustus, its elective ruler). In 1705–6 most of Courland was overrun. For the peasantry of the Swedish Baltic provinces these were years of martyrdom. Much of Estonia and Livonia was systematically devastated by the tsar's forces; and the growth of Peter's power in the area made it increasingly unlikely that Livonia would ever be handed over to Augustus as had been promised at Rawa and Birsen.

The Russo–Swedish struggle had from its beginnings more than merely Baltic or Polish significance. It was a part, though for many years a relatively distinct and self-contained part, of the complex web of international diplomacy which now more and more bound together every part of Europe. The English and Dutch governments hoped to be able to hire soldiers from Sweden and the German states for use in western Europe against Louis XIV in the struggle over the Spanish succession. While the war in Poland and the Baltic lasted it was impossible to obtain such help from either Sweden or Saxony. The result was that as early as October 1700 William III offered English mediation in the Russo–Swedish struggle, an offer which Peter accepted in May 1701.[6] But nothing came of this; and though the offer was renewed at the end of 1702 (inspired by the belief that peace would free 12,000 Swedes and 8,000 Saxons to be taken into English service) this new initiative was equally fruitless.[7] From the moment he had gained an outlet to the Baltic, Peter was determined never to surrender it. Charles for his part believed that even a restricted Russian Baltic coastline, and the power it would give the tsar to build up a powerful naval force on that sea, would be very dangerous to Sweden. The result was that, though the Russian government continued until at least the end of 1705 to make vague suggestions of British mediation, there was never a chance of any practical result.

The French also hoped that a Russo–Swedish peace might be turned to their advantage. It might, Louis XIV and his ministers thought, allow the sending of Russian forces across Poland to Transylvania, where Hungarian nationalist feeling and resentment of Habsburg rule were strong and where a serious rebellion broke out in 1703. It might even, it was imagined with supreme lack of realism, allow Peter to make a loan to help Louis in his increasing financial difficulties.[8] Again these hopes proved groundless. The French were unwilling to do anything that might weaken Sweden, a traditional ally; and it soon became clear that Peter desired a French alliance less than had been at first imagined.

The early years of the Great Northern War thus produced no striking change in Russia's relations with the powers of western Europe. Nevertheless the position was slowly altering. Russian embassies to western capitals were ceasing to be the temporary and *ad hoc* affairs of the past. Permanent Russian diplomatic representatives were beginning to be seen at the courts of the great powers; of these A A. Matveev, who was sent as minister to the Dutch Republic in 1700, and Prince P. A. Golitsyn, who became ambassador in Vienna in the following year, were the first examples. There were also signs, though isolated and incomplete ones, of a slowly growing realization in Europe that a significant new power was emerging on the eastern fringes of the continent. In 1701, for example, the Emperor Leopold apparently contemplated, though probably not very seriously, the marriage of one of his sons to a Russian princess. In July of that year he asked for portraits of Peter's favourite sister, Natalia, and of one of his nieces, to be sent to Vienna with this in view; and these in fact arrived in the Austrian capital a year later, though the idea of such a marriage came to nothing.[9]

In spite of territorial gains and some increase in the attention paid to Russia by the powers of western Europe, these years were the most difficult of Peter's reign. In Poland Charles XII, though suffering setbacks, was gaining ascendancy over Augustus. At the end of August 1706 he invaded Saxony and a month later, by the treaty of Altranstädt, forced his opponent to abandon the Polish throne and recognize Stanislaus Leszczynski as king. Peter responded by efforts to find a new ruler for Poland who might be willing to continue the struggle: among others the two outstanding military commanders of western Europe, Prince Eugene of Savoy and the duke of Marlborough, were approached. But this was no more than a desperate clutching at straws. More and more Charles was treating Poland as a Swedish satellite: a treaty he signed with Leszczynski at Warsaw in November 1705 had already shown this. The way for a large-scale Swedish invasion of Russia was now opening. With this end in view, Charles spent much of the next year in strengthening and reorganizing his army. For Russia and its ruler these were years of increasingly burdensome military conscription and forced labour and of acute money shortage. They were also years when Peter's ambitions seemed increasingly menaced by the discontent of his subjects and the threat of internal revolt. A difficult colonial war with the Bashkirs, a warlike non-Russian people in the Ural area, began in 1705 and dragged on until 1711; in Astrakhan there was a considerable military mutiny in 1706, and a rising of the Don Cossacks broke out in the following year. So gloomy did the future seem that in May 1706 the British minister in Moscow reported that Peter's ministers were trying 'to divert him by Shipbuilding and Sailing from the melancholy thoughts of his Country's Ruin'.[10]

Faced by the ever more menacing threat of Swedish invasion, the tsar and his ministers redoubled their efforts to strengthen Russia's defences. Everything possible was done to shake the Swedish hold on Poland. Attempts to strengthen anti-Swedish feeling there and to stimulate the election of a rival to Leszczynski were redoubled. There were prolonged negotiations in 1707–8 between Peter and the Hungarian nationalist leader Francis Rakoczi, whom the tsar hoped to establish as the new ruler of Poland. An agreement by which Rakoczi accepted this unstable throne was in fact signed at Warsaw in September 1707, though it had no practical result.[11] The hostility to the Swedes of most of the Lithuanian gentry (in the main a by-product of their hatred of the potentially overwhelming power of the Sapieha family) was encouraged as far as possible. The payment of Russian money to Polish magnates for the upkeep of forces to be used against Charles XII, which had begun in 1702, was greatly increased. Payments of this kind in 1707–8 totalled as much as in the previous five years. In the spring of 1709 this expenditure was reinforced by the first large-scale Russian military intervention in Poland, with the despatch of an army of 13,000 under Field-Marshal Goltz, the most important foreign commander still in Russian service.[12] A Russian noble, Prince B. I. Kurakin, was sent in the spring of 1707 on a special mission to urge Pope Clement XI not to recognize Leszczynski as king of Poland and thus to make somewhat easier the task of setting up a rival Russian-backed claimant to the throne.[13] In fact the advance of Charles XII from Saxony into Poland in September of that year made any effort to hold another royal election there impracticable; nothing short of a clear-cut and decisive military defeat of the Swedes could really shake their hold on the wretched republic.

Poland, then, was no more than an outwork in the system of Russian defences, and, in spite of the strength of the Russian position in the eastern part of the republic, a rather feeble one. Nor, it was clear, had Peter anything to hope from western Europe; renewed efforts in 1707–8 to obtain English, French, Austrian or even Prussian mediation as a means of warding off the Swedish onslaught were quite fruitless. Russia must seek its own salvation, must rely on its innate strength and the tenacity and resolve of its ruler. The growth of the army and the production of arms became, if anything, even more important after 1705–6 than they had been before. In 1707–8, when all Russian forces were withdrawn from the Swedish Baltic provinces conquered since 1702 (only St Petersburg was retained), Peter showed his ruthlessness and determination by devastating the whole of Ingria, which had already suffered so much, in order to make it as valueless as possible to the reoccupying Swedes. The German population of Dorpat was forcibly deported, in long trains of sledges, to Vologda in the interior of Russia, and in early July 1708 the city was burnt. More far-reaching still was a plan drawn up to make a huge belt of Russian territory, well over a hundred miles deep and running along the entire frontier from Pskov as far south as Cherkassk on the Dnieper, useless to the invader. Peasants in this territory were ordered on pain of death to conceal supplies of grain and forage and to prepare hiding-places in which they might take refuge on the approach of the Swedish army. Finally the seriousness of the situation was underlined by orders for the fortification of Moscow itself. In 1707–8 the Kremlin and Kitai-Gorod, the central parts of the city, were surrounded by earthworks built by 30,000 conscripted labourers.

By the later months of 1707 Charles XII had assembled in Poland an army of some 44,000 men for the attack on Russia. There was also a separate force of 11,000–12,000 in the Baltic provinces under Count Lewenhaupt, whom

Charles intended to join the main body, and about 14,000 men in Finland who might be used for a diversionary attack on St Petersburg.[14] Well trained and disciplined, the heirs of a great military reputation and with a tradition of success on the battlefield, these were formidable forces. Their self-confidence was increased by the fact that they greatly, indeed fatally, underestimated the fighting power of the army which Peter had built up since Narva. Moreover Charles was well aware that it might be possible to construct against Peter a coalition of different enemies which, at least on paper, would be very dangerous. Early in 1708 a Turkish emissary, Mehemet Aga, visited Swedish headquarters; and though this, like so many negotiations of these confused years, led to no practical result, an alliance of Sweden with the Turks and their vassal-state in the Crimea would have faced Peter with an unprecedented threat. There had also been contacts between the Swedes and Ivan Mazepa, the ambitious and untrustworthy old Cossack hetman of the Ukraine, whose potentialities as an ally, inspired by the hope of creating an independent Ukrainian principality, seemed considerable. A revolt of the Don Cossacks under Kondraty Bulavin emphasized the possibility of using domestic discontent also as a weapon against Peter. Though the rebellion lasted less than a year (October 1707–July 1708), it inflicted several defeats on the tsar's forces and involved a serious though unsuccessful attack on Azov. If it had had more success it might well have opened the way to a union, though no doubt a very loose and unstable one, of all Peter's enemies.

In spite of all this the Swedes, as they advanced across Poland and White Russia from September 1707 onwards, faced increasing difficulties. By early July 1708 they had reached the Dnieper at Mogilev, after a victory over the Russians at Holovzin (Golovchino). But shortage of food (now accentuated by Russian scorched earth tactics), disease, appalling roads made worse by a wet summer, and not least the hostility of the population, had kept down their rate of progress on the march through White Russia to an average of only four or five kilometres a day.[15] Moreover the Russian army was offering much stiffer resistance than had been expected. By September 1708 an English observer with the Swedish army had been driven to the conclusion that Peter's soldiers 'equal if not exceed the Saxons both in discipline and valour'.[16] The food situation had become so difficult by then that in the middle of that month the crucial decision was taken to abandon the idea of an advance on Moscow through Smolensk (along the route to be taken a century later by Napoleon) and to turn south towards the Ukraine, where supplies seemed easier to obtain. A fortnight later Lewenhaupt's army, after crossing the Dnieper, was defeated in a hard-fought battle at Lesnaya – the first time the Russian army had beaten the Swedes on a significant scale in the open field and a considerable boost to Russian morale. Though Lewenhaupt was able to join Charles with about 7,000 men, the great supply-train which he had brought from the Baltic coast was completely lost.

It seemed for a moment that the effect of these setbacks might be overcome when, early in November, Mazepa at last threw off the mask and openly joined the Swedes. For long he had hesitated, trying to keep a foot in both camps and latterly even feigning mortal illness to evade Peter's demands that he act against the Swedes. In the end his hand seems to have been forced by the threat that Menshikov, now in command of the Russian forces on the Ukrainian borders, would march on Baturin, Mazepa's capital, and compel him to play his part in the struggle with Charles XII. The hetman's motives will never be known with certainty.[17] But it was immediately clear that the cunning old man had, for the first time in a long and chequered career, backed a disastrously wrong horse. Of the 5,000 Cossacks with whom he left Baturin only 2,000 were still with him when he joined the Swedish king. A week later Menshikov, showing great energy and considerable skill in a critical situation, took Baturin by storm. The fury which the treachery of 'Judas Mazepa' had inspired in Peter was reflected in the savagery of Menshikov's treatment of the hetman's capital – the entire town burnt, Mazepa's bodyguard and many of the civilian inhabitants massacred, the commander of the garrison broken on the wheel. But the moral effect was considerable; and it was reinforced by a series of measures intended to limit still further the effects of Mazepa's action. Wartime taxes and impositions, allegedly introduced in the Ukraine by the old hetman for his own profit, were annulled. Assurances were given that the tsar would observe the existing rights and privileges of the Cossacks. A new and reliably loyal hetman, Skoropadskii, was quickly elected. Within a matter of days it had become clear that Mazepa could muster very little effective support from his erstwhile Ukrainian subjects. By the end of the year, untrustworthy as ever, he was trying to change sides once again and even offering to bring the Russians the head of Charles XII if opportunity offered.

There were still other cards, however, which could be played against Peter. The Crimean Tatars, even the Turks, might be used against him. More immediately another Cossack group, the Zaporozhians of the lower Dnieper, centred on their traditional river stronghold, the Sech, might be roused to revolt against Russian rule. Their hetman, Hordienko, demanded in the first days of 1709 that Russian forts in his territory be destroyed and all Russian and Ukrainian landlords banished. The inevitable refusal led to a serious rebellion; and Hordienko, though his name bulks much less large in the works of historians, proved in fact a more dangerous adversary for the tsar than Mazepa. In April Charles undertook to make no peace with Peter until the independence of the Ukraine and the Zaporozhians had been obtained: he was now committed not merely to the recovery of his own lost territories but to a partial dismemberment of Russia. Yet the Zaporozhian revolt too was defeated. In the Sech there was opposition to Hordienko which led to his replacement by a rival leader, Sorochinskii. In May 1709, a decisive blow was struck by the Russians when Menshikov sent two regiments to seize and destroy the Sech. It was razed even more completely than Baturin. Once more energy and determination had reasserted Peter's authority in the south Russian steppe, so vital and so unruly.

The crisis of the war, the greatest and most dramatic event of Peter's reign, was now at hand. Weakened by the terrible winter of 1708–9, the worst in living memory, and by the harassing tactics pursued with increasing skill by the Russians, the Swedish army laid siege in April 1709 to the fortified town of Poltava. There was fought the battle which decided the outcome of the Great Northern War. Before it, the position of the Swedes, though increasingly difficult, was still far from hopeless. Though they had lost heavily in the campaigning of 1708–9 the Russian losses, both absolutely and as a proportion of the forces involved, had been still heavier (though also, of course, more easily replaced). Almost to the eve of the battle Peter showed himself willing to discuss possible peace terms, though never to abandon his cherished St Petersburg. The Swedes were still confident enough in their qualitative superiority to attack, at dawn on 8 July, an army twice as large as their own in an entrenched position and with a great superiority in artillery. Within a few hours they had been decisively defeated. A day or two later most of the remains of the army capitulated at Perevolochna on the left bank of the Dnieper. Charles XII, with Mazepa and Hordienko, escaped across the river and took refuge in Ottoman territory at Bender in Moldavia.

Peter played an active role in the battle (as he had also done in that at Lesnaya). One bullet passed through his hat and another hit his saddle. After it was over he was courteous and complimentary in his reception of the senior Swedish officers, Marshal Rehnskiöld and others, who had become his prisoners. He could afford to be, for he understood the importance of what had been achieved. Poltava, he wrote, had been 'a very outstanding and unexpected victory' in which 'the whole army of Phaetons has received its deserts'. The spoils of the victory had now to be gathered.

. . .

NEW OPPORTUNITIES AND NEW DIFFICULTIES, 1709–17

Peter was well aware of the importance of his victory and, as far as he could, strengthened the impression it made both within Russia and abroad. In December 1709 it was celebrated in Moscow by a great ceremonial triumph of the kind he loved so well. The sight of captured Swedish officers and officials being marched through the streets, followed by a spectacular firework display, set a public seal on his triumph. A fine commemorative medal was ordered from the workshop of Philipp Heinrich Müller of Nuremberg, the greatest living master of this art. The tsar had ample justification for drawing attention to what he had achieved, for Poltava transformed Russia's position on several different levels.

In Poland the situation changed almost overnight. Even before the battle Augustus, who had never accepted the Altranstädt settlement as final, had signed treaties with Denmark and Prussia and begun to assemble forces in Saxony for an invasion of his former kingdom. As soon as he received news of the Swedish catastrophe, he signed at Dresden a treaty by which Peter promised him help in men and money and support for his efforts to make the Polish throne hereditary in his family. By October Leszczynski had been driven across the frontier and forced to take refuge in the Swedish stronghold of Stettin. Russian power was now dominant in the Polish Republic, however much many Poles might resent this; and though in 1709 and again in 1711 Peter repeated his promise that when victory was won Livonia should be handed over to Augustus it became more and more clear that this was unlikely to happen. During the following years the Poles, burdened by both Russian and Saxon armies of occupation, became increasingly discontented with their ruler. By 1716 the conflicts between Augustus and a confederation of hostile nobles were so acute that Peter intervened to settle them. In November of that year an agreement between the king and his opponents negotiated by the Russian minister to Poland, Prince Dolgorukii, provided among other things for the reduction of the Polish army to a mere 24,000 men, an almost ludicrously small force in view of the length of Poland's exposed frontiers. The military impotence and defencelessness of the country had now been given a more formal and public form than ever before. Furthermore, Dolgorukii himself signed the agreement, which in this way acquired something in the nature of a Russian guarantee and became in practice impossible to alter without Russian consent. Peter thus consolidated in Poland a hegemony which was not to be seriously shaken until the First Partition, if then. Further north, in the Swedish possessions on the eastern shore of the Baltic, the situation also changed with striking suddenness. Ingria was rapidly reoccupied. Riga, Reval and Viborg fell to Russian forces (the first after a stout defence and a long siege) in the summer of 1710.

The victories of 1709–10 meant for Russia not merely security in Poland and territorial gains on the Baltic but a new international position, a revolutionary change in its standing in the outside world. Peter could no longer be regarded as a picturesque but fundamentally unimportant ruler on the fringes of Europe with little power to influence events in the western or even the central parts of the continent. In France, for example, initial astonishment at the defeat of the apparently invincible Charles XII was followed by a rapid rise in the estimate of Peter's standing and abilities, as presented by the writers of the period.[18] The change is also illustrated by the negotiations for the marriage of the Tsarevich Alexis to Princess Charlotte of Brunswick-Wolfenbüttel. When these began in 1707 her father, Duke Anton-Ulrich, was advised against agreeing to the match on the grounds that Peter, as a European ruler, was almost insignificant: yet after Poltava it was swiftly concluded. The tsar's eligibility as an ally, whether by marriage or otherwise, had leapt upwards spectacularly.[19]

Nowhere was this truer than in the German world. The news of Poltava led to the despatch from Vienna of an imperial representative, Count Weltzeck, empowered to suggest an alliance against the Turks. Simultaneously the Prussian court began to consider ways of using Russian strength for its own purposes: when King Frederick I met Peter at Marienwerder in East Prussia in October 1709 the idea of a partition of Poland in which both might share was aired. In November 1710 there was even a Russian suggestion that Livonia might be added to the territories of the Holy Roman Empire if in return Peter, as its new ruler, were given a seat and a vote in the imperial Reichstag.[20] The idea was never followed up; but that it could be put forward seriously was a striking indication of how rapidly the situation was changing. Soon there were to be signs in the German states of a growing fear of the overmighty neighbour who now seemed a potential threat in the east. By the autumn of 1711 a Prussian diplomat, alarmed by Russian expansion, could be found urging an alliance with Denmark and Augustus to hold Peter's growing power in check.[21]

Almost at once after Poltava Russia began to be treated with a new seriousness in western Europe as well. Might not Peter with his new-found strength be able, at least once peace with Sweden had been made, to mediate between hard-pressed France and her opponents? As early as August 1709 the British minister to Russia had conjectured that 'perhaps the Czar may have a fancy to be moderator in your quarrel [i.e., the war of the Spanish Succession], for, if these people have success and ease, you may expect to find them troublesome and capable of going into the most wild projects.'[22] To Louis XIV, in desperate straits in 1709–10 after a series of great defeats followed by one of the worst famines in French history, Russian intervention of this kind seemed to offer escape from a most ominous situation. In the peace negotiations with his enemies which took place in the Netherlands in 1709 Louis' minister Torcy, seriously though unsuccessfully, proposed the tsar as a mediator (other suggestions were Frederick IV of Denmark and Augustus of Poland). About the same time the British government tried to explore the possibility of inducing Peter to join the Grand Alliance against France.[23] In the following year Louis and his ministers still hoped for help from Peter: might he not be brought to demand the acceptance of his mediation by the anti-French powers, using to back this demand the threat of attack on British and Dutch trade in the Baltic and help for Rakoczi and the Hungarian nationalists against the Emperor? Or would he support with men and money an effort by the elector of Bavaria (France's only significant ally in the German world) to make himself king of Hungary? It was even suggested that the tsarevich might become ruler of an independent Hungarian state.[24] 'Cardinal Richelieu', wrote Torcy, 'drew Gustavus Adolphus from the conquest of Livonia in order to bring down the power of the House of Austria. It would be a happy stroke, in the present state of things, to draw the Czar away from the conquest of the same provinces to make use of him in the same way'.[25]

Again nothing came of these advances. Peter was too cautious and realistic to allow himself to become the tool of France. In any case he was confronted by too many problems nearer home – instability in Poland and an increasingly difficult relationship with Augustus; continuing Swedish resistance; the rumblings of discontent still all too audible within Russia – to have much inclination towards grandiose political adventurers further afield. Yet the mere fact that such proposals were made to him is striking proof of how much the international status of Russia had risen. The contrast with the complete indifference to Russian interests shown in the negotiations at Carlowitz illustrates the almost revolutionary changes which had taken place within a decade.

Poltava and its results had dealt a crushing blow to Swedish power. In the south, however, the Ottoman empire, a greater and more solidly based opponent, remained intact and threatening. One of Peter's main preoccupations between 1700 and 1709 was to remain on good, or at least peaceful, terms with the Turks. This was not always easy. The growth of Russian power, and particularly the presence of an enlarged Russian fleet on the Sea of Azov, was now arousing much uneasiness in Constantinople and stimulating a series of attempts to strengthen the Turkish position. In December 1702, for example, the Porte demanded the razing of the Russian fortress of Kamennyi Zaton on the Dnieper, the burning of the warships at Azov and Taganrog, the restriction of the shipbuilding at

Voronezh and a delimitation of the Russo–Turkish frontiers. In the following year a new Ottoman fortress, Yenikalé, was built on the Straits of Kerch to bar more effectively any movement of Russian warships through them into the Black Sea. In the spring of 1704 there was a demand for the building of another fort on the Dnieper above Ochakov which, if carried out, would have been a breach of the treaty of 1700. Faced with a desperate struggle in Poland and the Baltic provinces, Peter had to temporize. In December 1704 P. A. Tolstoy, his very able representative at the Porte, was empowered to promise, if need be, the evacuation of one of the Russian fortresses on the Dnieper and in the last resort even the withdrawal of the ships at Taganrog 'to a suitable place'.[26] In 1704–5, extensive frontier delimitation was carried out by mutual agreement both in the Dnieper area and in the Kuban east of Azov, much to the tsar's relief. Yet throughout the critical years 1706–9 Peter was deeply worried by the activity of Leszczynski's agents in Constantinople and by the apparent threat of a Swedish–Turkish alliance. In the early months of 1709 this threat was a real one. The remarkable slowness with which the siege of Poltava was carried on (which puzzled many of the besiegers) was probably caused by the fact that Charles XII was waiting for his negotiations with the Turks and Tatars to bear fruit; and he finally risked a battle partly because victory would increase his chances of obtaining help from them. The spectacular military events of the Russo-Swedish struggle should not blind us to the critical importance for Russia of the diplomacy which maintained peace on its southern frontiers until the turning point of that struggle had been passed.

The flight of Charles XII to Bender after his defeat created new frictions. He began at once to press the sultan, Ahmed III, to pursue an actively anti-Russian policy. Peter, he warned in a letter written almost immediately after his arrival on Turkish soil, would now attack the Turks as he had the Swedes in 1700, 'in the midst of peace, without the slightest declaration of war'. The tsar's building of frontier fortresses and a powerful fleet showed what he intended. Against this threat the only protection for Turkey was alliance with Sweden. 'Accompanied by your valiant cavalry I will return to Poland, strengthen my remaining forces there and again carry my arms into the heart of Muscovy to set bounds to the ambition and love of power of the tsar'.[27]

On his side Peter (who was deeply disappointed by the failure to capture Charles and Mazepa after Poltava) pressed Ahmed to prevent the king from leaving Turkish territory and to hand over the hetman as a traitor. Although Mazepa died early in the autumn of 1709 the Crimean khan, Devlet-Girei, who was deeply anti-Russian, soon joined Charles in pressing the Porte to make war on Russia. In February 1710 relations seemed for a moment to improve, when news was received in Moscow that Tolstoy had succeeded in obtaining from the Turks a confirmation of the peace of 1700. Yet by July Peter was writing personally to Ahmed III to warn him against any attempt to send Charles XII with a large Turkish and Tatar escort through Poland to join the Swedish army in Pomerania. Three weeks later the new Russian commander in Poland, M. M. Golitsyn, was given instructions to meet a possible Turkish invasion of the republic.[28] Turkish policy, as so often, was tightly bound up with factional and personal conflicts in Constantinople and already, in July, the decisive step towards war had been taken with the fall of the pacific grand vizier, Chorlulu Ali-Pasha. The anti-Russian party led by Devlet-Girei was now in control. In November the Porte declared war, justifying its action by pointing to the building of forts by the Russians in breach of the treaty of 1700, the strengthening of the Azov fleet, the infringement of Turkish territory by Russian forces pursuing Charles XII and the Russian occupation of the Polish Ukraine.

At first Peter did all he could to limit the effects of this unwelcome complication. In January 1711 he tried, in a letter to the Sultan, to avoid the outbreak of a full-scale war,[29] while approaches were made both to the powers of the Grand Alliance and to France for possible mediation. When, however, it became clear by the spring that a war with Turkey would have to be fought (the Russian declaration of war, a response to the Turkish one several months earlier, was issued only on 11 March) he began to form far-reaching plans. For a decade or more it had been clear that in such a war Russia might hope for some active support from the Orthodox Christian population of the Balkans. In 1698 an agent of the hospodar of Wallachia, the Danubian principality which had been under Turkish suzerainty since the fifteenth century, had visited Moscow and proposed an alliance.[30] In 1706–7 Rakoczi's agents in Constantinople had reported that

the Wallachians, Moldavians, Greeks and Bulgarians were ready
to support Peter against the sultan because of their religious
ties with Russia. Now in the spring of 1711 a Russian ruler
attempted for the first time to play this potentially powerful
religious card in a struggle with the Ottoman empire. In
March a 'Proclamation to the Montenegrin People' and a
'Proclamation to the Christian Peoples under Turkish Rule'
were issued.[31] Both were explicit calls to revolt; and they
were followed by a series of other appeals of the same
kind. Agents were sent to the Balkans to organize risings
there, while through the newly appointed Russian consuls in
Venice and Vienna, Caretta and Botsis, money was channelled
for the same purpose. By August Botsis was assuring the tsar
that, if his forces crossed the Danube, there would be armed
rebellion throughout Rumelia, Macedonia and Greece. Already
in April the newly appointed hospodar of Moldavia, Demetrius
Kantemir, had signed an agreement which in effect made the
principality part of the Russian empire, though an autonomous
one with full internal self-government.

All this seemed to promise brilliant success; and in May Peter
told his military commanders that he meant to advance across
the Danube in the expectation of help from both Wallachia
and Moldavia and perhaps of armed risings all over the
Balkans. But a bitter disappointment followed. From the
start the Russian army was hampered by supply difficulties
which slowed its movements. Advancing through the Polish
Ukraine accompanied by the tsar, it crossed the Dniester only
in June. The Turks, on the other hand, moved north across the
Danube with unexpected speed. The result was that by 19 July
the Russians had reached Stanelishte on the Pruth, where they
found themselves surrounded by a numerically much superior
Turkish force and very short of supplies (the lack of forage for
the cavalry-horses was the greatest difficulty). Two days of stiff
fighting left the Russian army in a desperate position: all of it,
and the tsar himself, seemed about to become prisoners of the
sultan. As Peter himself later admitted, its position was in some
ways similar to that of the Swedes after the battle of Poltava.
When Baron P. P. Shafirov, Peter's most able subordinate
in foreign policy matters, was sent to the Turkish camp to
negotiate for peace terms the tsar had to instruct him to
'agree to all they demand, apart from slavery'.[32] In fact the
terms imposed by the grand vizier, Baltadji Mehmed Pasha,

who commanded the Turkish army, were much less disastrous than Peter had feared. He had been willing, if necessary, not merely to surrender Azov but to abandon Livonia, to recognize Leszczynski as king of Poland, perhaps even to give up Pskov to the Swedes. In the event only Azov, Taganrog and the forts on the Dnieper had to be surrendered. But this meant the loss of the fleet built up at such cost from 1696, the fleet which embodied Peter's first bid to make Russia a naval power. This was the bitterest pill he had to swallow throughout his reign. As he put it, 'The Lord God drove me out of this place, like Adam out of Paradise.'[33] He also had to undertake to end Russian intervention in Poland, to give up the embassy in Constantinople and to allow Charles XII free passage to Sweden.

A number of factors averted the complete disaster which had seemed imminent. There was considerable friction between the Turks, who wanted a short war and no more than the recovery of territory lost in 1700, and Charles XII and Devlet-Girei, who hoped for a far-reaching war of revenge and a large-scale invasion of the south Russian steppe. The grand vizier was almost certainly anxious for a quick peace settlement before the bellicose king of Sweden could arrive from Bender and throw his weight behind the demand for more severe terms. When Charles reached the Pruth he at once quarrelled with Baltadji, asserting that given 20,000–30,000 of the best Turkish soldiers he would himself capture Peter and hold him prisoner until tough terms had been exacted from the Russians. There is also evidence to indicate that many of the Turkish commanders had entered upon the war with misgivings and that they personally disliked the Crimean khan. The disunity of Peter's opponents, in other words, was an immense asset to him at this critical moment.[34] In addition the Russians, for all their difficulties, had fought well and inflicted considerable losses on their opponents, so that the request for an armistice surprised the Turks and was at first taken for a trick. For all these reasons Peter emerged at relatively little cost from the most critical position in which he ever found himself. Though the grand vizier received presents from the Russians in the way normal in such negotiations, there is no convincing evidence that he was bribed to show leniency. The peace terms gave the Turks all they really wanted; and it was not until September that allegations of bribery began to circulate both in Moscow and in Constantinople.[35]

Nevertheless, Peter had suffered a serious and humiliating setback. On the military level he had been defeated by overconfidence and supply problems. On the political level, the Moldavian hospodar Kantemir, once he had committed himself to the Russians, proved unable to give them any effective help, while in the wealthier principality of Wallachia neither the hospodar nor the majority of the nobles were willing to take any clear line until it became obvious which was the winning side. The result was that the high hopes which had been placed in the Orthodox Christians of the Balkans proved almost completely deceptive. Miloradovich, one of Peter's agents, was able to help raise substantial forces in Montenegro and Herzegovina for use against the Turks; but these were too far away from the main area of conflict to influence the outcome.

Peter consoled himself with the thought that he was now free to concentrate his efforts against the Swedes in Pomerania. He also did his best to limit the blow which had been dealt to Russian prestige by modifying the version of the peace terms which his agents circulated in western Europe. (The wording of some of the clauses was altered, and the humiliating one which provided that Shafirov and General Sheremetiev must go to Constantinople as hostages for the carrying-out of the treaty was omitted altogether.)[36] But Peter was far from having seen the end of Turkish complications. He applied the terms agreed on the Pruth only with extreme reluctance. It was not until the turn of the year that Apraksin, as governor of Azov, was ordered to hand the city over to the Turks and to destroy Taganrog; and a few days before this was done the Turks once again declared war. This was no more than a paper declaration: in April 1712 Shafirov was able to sign another peace settlement. Yet the situation remained unstable, partly because of continual Turkish suspicion of Russian activity in Poland (from which in fact Peter temporarily withdrew most of his forces in 1711 and the first half of 1712) and also because Turkish foreign policy was largely at the mercy of incessant personal and factional struggles at the Porte. Another Turkish declaration of war came in November 1712, and yet another in May of the following year. Shafirov did not much exaggerate when he complained to Peter that 'this inconstant and false government changes its policy every hour'.[37] Not until June 1713, after complicated negotiations, were Russia's relations with the Ottoman empire put on a reasonably firm footing. The treaty signed in that month was not especially favourable to Peter; in particular he had to promise a complete Russian withdrawal from Poland within two months. Nevertheless it continued to govern his relations with his great southern neighbour for the rest of his reign. In November 1720 one important result of the disastrous Pruth campaign was reversed, when Russia recovered the right to maintain a diplomatic representative in Constantinople. But Peter never regained Azov, the scene of his first military victory. Nor was he able to rebuild the fleet lost in 1711. The effort at southwards expansion in which so many resources and energies had been swallowed up had been, in the final event, a failure.

Distractions and uncertainties on the southern frontiers and promises to give up interference in Poland did not prevent a continuing advance of Russian power on the eastern shores of the Baltic and the continuing collapse of the Swedish empire. Finland was overrun by Russian forces with little resistance in 1713–14, while in the autumn of the latter year the first direct attack on Sweden itself was launched: a Russian force occupied Umeå on the gulf of Bothnia and remained there for a month. Peter was also acquiring new allies, though difficult and unreliable ones. In June 1714 a Russo–Prussian treaty provided for the division of much of the Swedish empire between the two powers (Russia to have Estonia, Ingria, Karelia and Viborg, Prussia the much-desired port of Stettin) and on 1 May 1715, after long hesitation, the Prussians declared war on Charles XII. In October 1715, a treaty signed with the Electorate of Hanover at Greifswald in north Germany agreed once more that when peace was made Peter should retain Ingria, Karelia and Estonia and, by implication, that Hanover would give him diplomatic support in retaining Livonia (the text was later modified to reduce its obligation in this respect). In return the Swedish possessions of Bremen and Verden were to go to Hanover, whose troops had been in occupation of Verden since 1712. As the Elector George of Hanover had since 1714 also been king of England it seemed for a moment that a *de facto* Anglo–Russian alliance based on the territorial ambitions of the two rulers might come into existence. A commercial treaty was being seriously discussed in London; and Peter repeatedly held out the possibility of an agreement of this kind as bait to attract British support.[38]

The larger and more heterogeneous the anti-Swedish alliance became, however, the more difficult it was to hold it together and the more certain was conflict between the interests and ambitions of the different members. The Danes were seriously worried by the support for the duke of Holstein-Gottorp which seemed to be implied by the Russo–Prussian negotiations of 1713–14. The Prussians were intent merely on gaining Stettin with the minimum of effort and risk on their own part. British opinion tended to resent the weakening of the position of the German Protestants which seemed inevitable if Sweden were totally defeated, while uneasiness over the growth of Russian power and its possible results was steadily gaining ground over much of central and western Europe. By making Russia a great power, or at least putting it well on the way to becoming one, Peter had inevitably involved it as never before in the conflicts and rivalries of Europe as a whole and had roused fears which no previous tsar had been able to inspire.

The 'Northern Crisis' of 1716–17 made this unmistakably clear. The geographical focus of this complex series of events was the north-German duchy of Mecklenburg-Schwerin. Its ruler, Charles-Leopold, who was engaged in a bitter dispute with the nobility of the duchy, married in April 1716 Catherine, Peter's niece. The marriage was disliked in both London and Vienna; and on the very day when it was celebrated Peter roused further anxieties by a treaty which made dangerously explicit his support for the duke. Charles-Leopold was promised Russian backing, if necessary with armed force, against all internal and external enemies. He was also, against the wishes of George I, promised the port of Wismar when it had been taken from the Swedes. In return Peter was to be allowed to use Mecklenburg as a base of operations against Sweden, while Russians were to have the right to trade there on the same footing as the Mecklenburgers themselves. The commercial aspects of the treaty were of real importance to Peter. He envisaged Mecklenburg becoming a centre for Russian trade with the west, and even had hopes of fostering this by cutting a canal from Wismar to the Elbe and thus giving Russia an outlet to the North Sea which would bypass the Sound. This grandiose project, which no doubt owed something to the large-scale canal-building which he had set on foot in Russia,[39] is typical of the mixture of ambition, imagination and disregard of practical difficulties which marks so much of his thinking.

The more obvious the growth of the tsar's ambitions, however, the greater the uneasiness of his ostensible allies. Russian forces were prevented by them from taking part in the siege of Wismar, which surrendered in April 1716. This sign of distrust deeply angered Peter; and even more patent evidence of deep disunity was to follow. By a convention of 3 June, the Danes agreed to supply 24,000 men who, with 30,000 Russians, would undertake a combined invasion of southern Sweden from the Danish island of Zealand. By September, in spite of a good deal of Russo–Danish friction, there were about 50,000 men, with British naval support, ready for action. In the middle of that month, however, Peter gave up the idea of invasion. For this there were very respectable military reasons. The best months of the campaigning season had been lost. The Swedish defences were strong. General Weyde, the commander of the Russian infantry, himself urged the tsar to abandon the enterprise. But there is little doubt that the factor which weighed heaviest in Peter's decision was his distrust of his allies. He was understandably unwilling to leave Russian soldiers, once they had landed in Sweden, dependent on transport and supply facilities provided or safeguarded by the Danes and the British. As soon as the abandonment of the invasion of Sweden became known there were widespread rumours that Peter now meant to overrun Denmark. The Danish government hastened to demand the immediate departure of all Russian troops from its territory. They were evacuated to Mecklenburg; and it is significant of the tsar's relations with his allies that Baron Bernstorff, George I's chief Hanoverian minister, now proposed a British attack on the Russian ships involved and the seizure of Peter himself as a prisoner.

The establishment of a Russian army in one of the German states gave new impetus to the hostility with which Peter was now widely regarded. In the summer of 1716 there had already been almost a mass flight of the Mecklenburg nobility caused by the oppression and arrogance of Prince Repnin, the Russian commander there. Their complaints in Vienna became increasingly loud and Habsburg dislike of this foreign occupation of part of the Holy Roman Empire increasingly marked. The Hanoverians were alarmed by the presence of a powerful and potentially hostile force so near their own frontiers; and in December Bernstorff proposed to an Imperial representative that the Russians be driven out of the Empire and an agreement made with Poland to bar their return. In Britain there were several reasons for apprehension.

Peter might support the Jacobites, who in the immediate aftermath of the 1715 rebellion seemed a real danger to George I's régime. Russia might come to control so much of the Baltic coastline that it would acquire a near-monopoly of the 'indispensable needful' of naval stores, the supplies of tar, hemp and above all tall pine trees suitable for masts and yards, upon which the British navy depended so heavily. 'A due distribution of Livonia', urged George Mackenzie, the new British minister in St Petersburg, in August 1715, 'is of the utmost importance to Us not only for Trade but other Motives to which We can't be indifferent.' To allow Peter to retain St Petersburg as well as Archangel would be 'to lay our Nation and Navy at his discretion'.[40] One important result of this attention to commercial considerations was a marked British insistence on preserving the independence of the great trading city of Danzig, which seemed more and more threatened by Russian bullying. The new Russian Baltic fleet also alarmed some British observers. In 1714 it had won its first significant victory by defeating the Swedes at Gangut (Hangö Odde) off the coast of Finland. Might it not soon outnumber the fleets of Sweden and Denmark combined and allow the tsar to become master of the Baltic? These were more or less unreal fears. But the hostility of George I and his ministers to Russia was genuine. In the summer of 1717 Peter, anxious not to arouse too much enmity in western Europe, and particularly in France which had joined Britain and the Dutch in a triple alliance in January of that year, withdrew his forces from Mecklenburg.

. . .

PEACE AT LAST, 1717–21

The fears and resentments which had flared up in 1716–17 were not to be completely assuaged while Peter lived. His power to threaten much of north Germany, coupled with his position in Poland and his relations with Prussia, continued to alarm the emperor. His contacts with the Jacobites and the growth of his navy remained sources of uneasiness in Whitehall. His ambitions in northern Europe now seemed as great a threat to European stability as those of Spain in the Mediterranean. The most important result of these feelings was a defensive alliance signed at Vienna in January 1719 between the Emperor Charles VI, George I as Elector of Hanover and Augustus II as Elector of Saxony. Its central objective was to drive Russian forces from

Poland and to prevent their return. During February, deeply angered but unwilling to risk a conflict with the emperor and his allies, Peter began slowly to withdraw his regiments from the republic, though the movement took months to complete. His enemies hoped to push their advantage further; and a Hanoverian–Swedish peace treaty in November 1719, which ceded Bremen and Verden to George I, seemed to open the way to further pressure on Russia. James Stanhope, one of the two British Secretaries of State and now the most active of all Peter's opponents, hoped to construct a wide-ranging anti-Russian coalition of Hanover (tacitly supported by Britain), Sweden, Saxony, Prussia and Poland. The return to Sweden of all the territory lost to Russia, even the possible restoration of Kiev and Smolensk to Poland, were talked of should the tsar refuse the terms offered him. Admiral Norris, the commander of the British fleet in the Baltic, was told near the end of the year that there was 'so powerfull an Allyance now forming in the North as will be Sufficient to keep him [Peter] within bounds' and perhaps force the tsar to accept British mediation and make peace with Sweden.⁴¹

These were only dreams. The anti-Russian alliance never came into existence. The Polish Republic (as distinct from its ruler, Augustus II) was not a signatory of the treaty of Vienna. Without its adherence it was difficult for the anti-Russian powers to achieve much; but in February 1720 Peter and Frederick William I of Prussia agreed to preserve its neutrality as well as its existing political structure. This is the first appearance in history of a factor which was to unite these two powers for the next two centuries – a shared desire to keep Poland weak and disunited. In July the king of Prussia, who had himself made peace with the Swedes in February, declared that he would do nothing to help Sweden or oppose Russia while the war continued. Without Poland and Prussia no anti-Russian league could have real effect. Hopes of driving Peter from his Baltic conquests were now mere fantasy, particularly as Charles VI, once the Russians had left Mecklenburg and Poland, became much less interested in taking any kind of effective action against them.⁴²

If Charles XII had lived only a little longer (he was killed in December 1718 while besieging the Norwegian fortress of Frederiksten) it is possible that he would have agreed to a Russo–Swedish peace, even to one involving heavy territorial

losses on the eastern shores of the Baltic. In October–
November 1714 the Swedish king, after five years of self-
imposed exile in Turkey, had made a remarkable coach and
horseback journey, much of it with only a single companion,
from Demotika in Thrace to Stralsund, one of the few relics of
the Baltic empire still left in Swedish hands. In the remaining
years of his life he made great efforts, with considerable success,
to rebuild Swedish military power. In these years too, there was
an active argument over the political line which Sweden should
follow in coping with the enemies now arrayed against it. On
the one hand it was argued that what had made Sweden for
three generations at least a kind of great power was its position
in Germany. To recover its German possessions, Bremen,
Verden and Pomerania, in face of the greed of Hanover,
Denmark and Prussia, it was worthwhile to make concessions to
Peter in return for peace and perhaps even Russian help against
Sweden's other foes. Against this it could be contended that
the tsar was the most dangerous of all its enemies. Peace with
Denmark and Hanover would free resources for use against
him. It would have the important advantage of moving the
seat of the fighting to the Baltic provinces, away from Sweden
itself, thus easing the strain of the war. It might also bring in
its train British naval support which would be very useful in any
new campaigns, in Livonia or Estonia. The shaky anti-Swedish
coalition must be broken. But in which direction should the
peace offensive be launched? The decision was difficult and
complex, particularly since it was closely bound up with dynastic
and factional struggles in Sweden centred on the succession to
the childless Charles XII. The king's nephew, the young Duke
Charles Frederick of Holstein-Gottorp, whose own lands had
been overrun by the Danes and who hoped to recover them,
stood for the reassertion of Swedish power in north Germany
and was backed by a strong party in Sweden. Against him Prince
Frederick of Hesse, who had in 1715 married Charles's sister
Ulrika Eleonora (and who in 1720 became King Frederick I of
Sweden), had no such personal interest in the German position
and was more sympathetic to the idea of continued resistance
to Russia.

It is difficult to fathom Charles's intentions. Certainly he
seriously considered a settlement with Peter. As early as July
1716 he told Georg Heinrich von Görtz, the Holsteiner who
was now his main adviser on foreign policy, that he was willing

to allow the tsar to retain Karelia and Ingria if in return Peter promised help against Sweden's other enemies. In May 1718 prolonged Russo–Swedish peace talks opened at Lövö in the Åland islands. By August Görtz and Ostermann, the Hanoverian in Russian service who was the head of the Russian delegation, had reached at least ostensible agreement. In return for the Baltic provinces Peter would provide a Russian auxiliary corps of 20,000 to act under Swedish command against George I. He would also allow Charles XII to take Norwegian territory from Denmark, cooperate with him in Poland in support of Leszczynski and mediate a peace between Sweden and the republic. But there was still powerful resistance in Sweden to peace with Russia. Görtz was personally very unpopular. More important, there were widespread hopes that Peter might soon die and that his death would be followed by great internal disorder in Russia and an abandonment of foreign ambitions: the tragic and spectacular fate during this year of the Tsarevich Alexis did much to strengthen such feelings. The opportunity of a settlement was therefore missed. By October Prince B. I. Kurakin, the Russian minister in The Hague, was urging strongly that a peace with Sweden which meant a breach with several west-European states was not in Russia's interests, while Ostermann himself thought the discussions at Lövö should be ended. Even before Charles XII was killed (whether shot by an enemy soldier or by one of his own followers has never been conclusively decided), Peter had withdrawn his agreement to the August terms.

Upon the king's disappearance the whole situation changed. The party which favoured concessions in Germany and a fight to the finish for Livonia and Estonia was now in the saddle in Sweden. Görtz was executed in March 1719. British influence over Swedish policy markedly increased. A mission by Ostermann to Stockholm in July–August of that year had no result and the Åland islands negotiations at last came to an end. Peace with Hanover in November 1719 and with Prussia in February 1720 freed Swedish resources for continued struggles against Russia. Peter remained nonetheless determined in face of these new difficulties and his own increasing isolation. 'I assure Your Majesty from my earlier experiences', he wrote to Frederick William I of Prussia, 'that I see no other way of securing a reasonable peace with Sweden ... than through firmness; and if I had given way and allowed myself to be frightened by the many dangers which threatened me then I should not have attained what I now clearly have through the help of God.'[43] He had substantial reasons for confidence. In 1719 Russian forces made large-scale landings in Sweden and ravaged the countryside to within a few miles of Stockholm itself. The presence in the Baltic of a strong British squadron intended to protect the Swedes and even if possible to destroy the Russian fleet did nothing to prevent this: the powerful British ships of the line were hopelessly ill-adapted for coping, among reefs and islands, with the quick-moving shallow-draught Russian galleys. (These now proved far more useful to Peter than the larger sailing vessels upon which he had lavished such love and energy.)

The Swedes did not give in easily. An alliance signed with George I in February 1720 gave them a formal promise of British support. There was no repetition in this year of the destruction which the Russians had inflicted during the previous summer: though Peter's forces made a small landing in northern Sweden the British squadron was able to prevent any large-scale attack from the Åland islands. But the Swedish position was rapidly becoming hopeless. In Britain there was widespread dislike of Baltic entanglements and the resulting risk of damage to the valuable Russian trade (though Peter, in spite of Anglo–Russian hostility, carefully refrained from any interference with British trade relations). Furthermore the South Sea Bubble crisis, which reached its height in the summer of 1720, shook severely, if temporarily, Britain's ability to carry on any strong foreign policy. The result was that in November George I had to urge the Swedish government to make peace with Russia as soon as possible. In Stockholm hope of any effective outside help had already been abandoned. It was clear that the war was lost: as early as April 1720 Baron Sparre, the Swedish ambassador in Paris, had discussed peace terms with Schleinitz, the Russian minister there.

In February 1721 representatives of the two powers arrived at the little town of Nystad in Finland, which had been agreed on as the site of the peace conference. Even at this stage the Swedes placed some hopes in French mediation as a means of softening the terms they would have to accept. Preliminary discussions showed, however, that the Russian diplomats were unwilling even to discuss the possibility of giving up Livonia or Estonia. Peter, reported the French ambassador to Stockholm in March, had 115,000 regular soldiers available for use, his infantry 'the best imaginable', as well as 48 ships of the line and 300 galleys. He already had 25,000 men in Finland and was about to send 11,000 more, as well as embarking 40,000 on his galleys to devastate Sweden itself.[44] In such a situation diplomacy had only limited scope; the brutal realities of the situation were driven home by destructive raids on northern Sweden which continued for weeks after the conference had officially opened on 22 May. By the end of July all the main questions at issue had been settled, though argument over a number of secondary ones went on for two months more. The treaty was signed on the night of 10–11 September. Livonia, Estonia, Ingria and Karelia became Russian, though for Livonia Peter agreed to pay Sweden two million reichstaler (the way in which this payment should be mentioned in the text had been one of the last sticking-points). Sweden was also to retain the right to buy duty-free a limited annual quantity of Livonian grain. In the ceded provinces the existing privileges of the towns, guilds, etc., and the position of the Lutheran church, were not to be interfered with. The king and republic of Poland were to be admitted to the treaty as the allies of Russia, and Britain as that of Sweden.

Peter also promised not to intervene in domestic struggles over the form of government in Sweden or in the succession to the Swedish throne. Yet the victory of the Hessian party in the dynastic conflict which followed the death of Charles XII had already driven the rival candidate, Charles Frederick of Holstein-Gottorp, to take refuge in Russia. This meant that whatever paper promises might be made, the tsar now had available, whenever he chose to use it, a powerful tool with which to interfere in Swedish domestic politics. In the last years of his reign he showed that it might well be used. After 1721 Russian influence in Stockholm was thrown in favour of the Holstein party; and when in November 1724 the tsar agreed to the marriage of his eldest daughter, Anna, to Charles Frederick, the marriage contract included Peter's promise to uphold 'if necessary' the duke's claim to the Swedish throne. Sweden's new status was symbolized by its new constitution of 1720. This ended absolutism, cut at the roots of monarchical power and made the government a kind of parliamentary oligarchy. The Swedes were never to plumb the depths of weakness and humiliation experienced by the 'crowned republic' of Poland. But the new régime marked the end of any pretence that Sweden was still a great power. The wheel of fortune had turned indeed, as moralizing contemporaries were not slow to point out. While its rival, apparently invincible in the first stages of the long struggle, had contracted and declined, Russia had leapt to a startling new level of strength and power. And this seemed to contemporaries the almost unaided achievement of its ruler, the fruit of Peter's own vision, determination and persistence. The triumphal procession in Moscow with which the tsar celebrated the coming of peace was for him the ceremonial seal placed on a work, often hard and frustrating, sometimes even desperate, which had dominated his reign and occupied almost half his lifetime.

.   .   .

RUSSIA AS A GREAT POWER

The widespread uneasiness and hostility which Russian achievements had aroused took time to disappear. 'We know very well', said Shafirov to a French diplomat in November 1721, 'that the greater part of our neighbours view very unfavourably the good position in which it has pleased God to place us; that they would be delighted should an occasion present itself to imprison us once more in our earlier obscurity and that if they seek our alliance it is rather through fear and hate than through feelings of friendship.'[45] Nevertheless, Russia's status as an important part of the European political system was now a fact that could not be denied.

One of the most striking and provocative symbols of the new position was the title of Emperor (*Imperator*) which Peter assumed in 1721 at the end of the war with Sweden. Many of the states of northern Europe – Prussia, Sweden, Denmark, the Dutch Republic – made little or no difficulty about giving it formal recognition. Britain and Austria, however, did not recognize it until 1742; and France and Spain not until three years after that. For two decades after 1721 the Habsburgs in particular were bitterly opposed to a title which seemed by implication to devalue that of Holy Roman Emperor which members of their family had held continuously since the 1430s. If Peter's assumption of it were not resisted, it was argued in Vienna, other rulers might be tempted to follow his example. This would threaten not merely the amour-propre of the Habsburg family but the unity of Christendom which the Holy Roman Emperor and his hitherto unique imperial title symbolized.

The result was a long and sometimes acrimonious controversy which dragged on for decades. Hesitation or refusal to accept Peter's new title were, however, themselves an indirect but unmistakable recognition of Russia's new international position. In the sixteenth and seventeenth centuries, when Russia was not regarded as part of Europe in any significant sense, few European monarchs had objected seriously to granting the tsars whatever complicated and outlandish designations they chose to claim. 'Emperor' or 'Imperial Majesty', applied to the ruler of an exotic country apparently outside Europe, were not titles which raised serious issues. If the Romanovs in Moscow were more or less on a par with the Safavids in Isfahan or the Moguls in Delhi, exactly what they called themselves or were called by others was a secondary issue. The first two decades of the eighteenth century, however, had ended this position for ever. Peter was now a European ruler: his titles must now be weighed in a European scale. When, during his second visit to western Europe in 1717, he negotiated with British plenipotentiaries at Amsterdam and complained that their credentials did not refer to him as 'Emperor', he was told that such 'fine flourished letters' were sent only to Turkey, Morocco, China 'and other nations shut out of the pale of Christianity and the common course of correspondence': if he wished 'to be treated as the other Princes of Europe' he must conform to European standards.[46]

Another unmistakable sign of Russia's new standing was the presence in every significant European capital of permanent Russian diplomatic missions. By 1721 Peter had twenty-one of these if consuls are included: this number was not to be exceeded during the rest of the eighteenth century.[47] Russia was for the first time an integral part of the network of European diplomacy. 'Formerly', said Shafirov in 1720, 'the Russians did not maintain ministers or emissaries at foreign courts; today they have so many that they are ignorant of nothing that happens there.'[48] An equally convincing index of change, on a rather different level, was the beginnings of intermarriage, later to become so frequent and important, between the Russian ruling dynasty and foreign houses. Peter was never able to negotiate such marriages with members of any of the most prestigious European dynasties. Frederick William, duke of Courland, who in 1710 became the husband of Peter's niece, Anna Ivanovna; the Princess Charlotte of Brunswick-Wolfenbüttel to whom the Tsarevich Alexis was married in the following year; Charles-Leopold, duke of Mecklenburg-Schwerin, to whom another niece, Ekaterina Ivanovna, was given in 1716 – these were at best of second-rate importance. All, moreover, were Protestants – a reflection of the fear and hatred of Catholicism which, a legacy of generations of struggle with Poland, was still so powerful in Russia. The Courland and Mecklenburg marriages considerably strengthened Russian influence in the Baltic and north Germany; but it was not until Peter's last years that he could seriously hope to unite the Romanovs with a European ruling family of indisputably first-class importance.

A marriage alliance with the Bourbons in France then seemed for several years a real possibility. When in 1717 he paid his second visit to western Europe it was to France and the Dutch Republic that he went. Significantly, France was now the centre of his interest and attention and not, as two decades earlier, England. As in the 'Great Embassy' of 1697–98, one of his objects was to engage foreign specialists and skilled technicians for work in Russia. Over sixty of these were recruited in Paris; and they included artists and architects as well as practitioners of more utilitarian trades. But this aspect of the journey was much less significant than on the more famous earlier pilgrimage to the west. France, in spite of setbacks in the war of the Spanish Succession, seemed to Peter, with justice, the greatest European power. It now had for him a prestige and attraction which seem to have been curiously lacking two decades earlier. Louis XIV, whatever his mistakes and failings, was in Peter's eyes the greatest monarch of the age, the model which more than any other he wished to equal. A French alliance would wean the duc d'Orleans, regent for the infant Louis XV, away from cooperation with George I while stamping Russia as the equal of any state in Europe and crowning its achievement of great-power status. Such an alliance he tried, in a typically headlong and impetuous way, to obtain when he visited Paris in May–June 1717. 'France', he told the Maréchal de Tessé, the spokesman of the French government, 'has lost its allies in Germany; Sweden, almost destroyed, cannot be of any help to it; the power of the Emperor [Charles VI] has grown infinitely; and I, the Czar, come to offer myself to France to replace Sweden for her. . . . I wish to guarantee your treaties; I offer you my alliance, with that of Poland. . . . I see that in the future the formidable power of Austria must alarm you; put me in place of Sweden.'[49] This frank appeal had no effect. The French ministers were well aware that this new power in eastern Europe might become a valuable check to the growing strength of the Habsburgs. But Peter, when it came to the point, was unwilling to commit himself to any effective action against Charles VI; while the government in Paris, out of consideration for Britain and the Dutch (its allies by the Triple Alliance of January 1717) refused to make the commercial treaty with Russia which the tsar suggested. The sole political fruit of Peter's visit was the treaty of friendship signed with France and Prussia at Amsterdam in August. This, though skilfully drafted to give each of the signatories the illusion of having made some genuine gain, had little practical significance.

Nevertheless the idea of a French alliance and of an accompanying dynastic marriage continued to be bruited until Peter's death. In particular the possible establishment of the duc de Chartres, a junior member of the house of Bourbon, as king of Poland, and his marriage to the younger daughter of the tsar, were actively considered from the end of 1721 onwards. Like so many of the projects of this complex period of European diplomacy, this one bore no fruit. In France the regent was determined to make no agreement with Russia which threatened his alliance with Britain. Discussions continued none the less to the very end of Peter's reign, while in 1722 Philip V of Spain (himself of the house of Bourbon) made tentative approaches for the marriage of one of his sons to a daughter of the tsar.[50] Marriage proposals of this kind, in a Europe still dominated by absolute monarchs with a strong sense of dynastic prestige and dignity, are highly revealing. They are in many ways a more convincing proof than military victories or territorial gains of the fact that Peter had now successfully asserted his position as the equal of any of his fellow-rulers and that of his country as a true great power. 'Russia', wrote the French ambassador in St Petersburg to Louix XV in March 1723, 'formerly scarcely known by name, has today become the object of the attention of most of the European powers, who seek its friendship, either through fear of seeing it take the side opposed to them or through the advantage which they hope for from its alliance'.[51] This remarkable change was not the single-handed work of Peter. It was perhaps implicit in the 'logic of history', which though a vague and difficult concept is not a meaningless one. Foreshadowings of it can be seen in Golitsyn's policies in the

1680s. It was made possible by physical factors – Russia's size, resources and relative invulnerability to invasion – which the tsar did not create and could do little to affect. But without him its form would have been different, less abrupt, less spectacular. More than anything it was the suddenness of the change which impressed contemporaries and led them to attribute to Peter in his last years a degree of wisdom and heroism to which he was not fully entitled.

. . .

NOTES

1. E. Hassinger, *Brandenburg-Preussen, Schweden und Russland, 1700–1713* (Munich, 1953), p. 51, fn. 16.
2. Quoted in E. Schuyler, *Peter the Great, Emperor of Russia* (New York, 1884), I, 398.
3. R. M. Hatton, *Charles XII of Sweden* (London, 1968), p. 161.
4. Whitworth (minister to Russia) to Harley (Secretary of State), 3 February 1706, Public Record Office, S.P. 91/4.
5. Hatton, *Charles XII*, pp. 156–7.
6. William III to Peter I, 2 November, 1700; Peter I to William III, 23 May 1701, Public Record Office, S.P. 104/20.
7. Instructions for John Robinson (minister to Sweden), 22 December 1702, S.P. 104/153.
8. Instructions to Baluze (minister to Russia), 28 September 1702, *Sbornik Imperatorskogo Russkogo Istoricheskogo Obshchestva* (St Petersburg, 1867–1916), XXXIV, 408–14.
9. N. N. Bantysh-Kamenskii, *Obzor vneshnykh snoshenii Rossii (do 1800 god)* (Moscow, 1894–1902), I, 40–1.
10 Whitworth to Harley, 19 May 1706, S.P. 91/4.
11. Ya. A. Shternberg, 'Russko-vengerskie otnosheniya perioda poltavskoi pobedy', *Poltavskaya Pobeda* (Moscow, 1959), pp. 72–80.
12. Yu. A. Gerovskii, 'Pol'sha i pobeda pod Poltavoi', *Poltavskaya Pobeda*, p. 41.
13. J. Staszewski, 'Die Mission des Fürsten Boris Kurakin in Rom im Jahre 1707', in W. Steinits and others (eds), *Ost und West in der Geschichte des Denkens und der kulturellen Beziehungen* (Berlin, 1966), pp. 200–14; P. Pierling, *La Russie et le Saint-Siège*, IV (Paris, 1907), 205–19.
14. Hatton, *Charles XII*, p. 233.

15. Z. Yu. Kopysskii and V. I. Meleshko, 'Pomoshch belorusskogo naroda russkoi armii v gody severnoi voiny', *Poltavskaya Pobeda*, pp. 219–20. The authors claim that Swedish demands meant that in Mogilev the price of bread and other foodstuffs rose 10–15 times (p. 224).

16. Hatton, *Charles XII*, p. 266.

17. He may well have hoped to become ruler with Swedish help of some form of independent Ukrainian state, especially as the annexation of the Ukraine to Russia was scarcely as yet felt to be permanent. He may also have feared that if he did not support Charles the latter would hand over the Ukraine to Stanislaus Leszczynski, who wished to regain much of it for Poland (it was with this argument that he tried to persuade his Cossack subjects to follow him into the Swedish camp). He probably also believed, especially after the Swedish victory at Holovzin, that Charles was certain to defeat Peter. The argument of some Soviet historians that he wished to intensify, with the help of Swedish generals and Polish nobles, the subjection and exploitation of the Ukrainian peasantry (*e.g.*, in V. E. Shutoi, 'Izmena Mazepy', *Istoricheskie Zapiski*, **31** (1950), 154–90), is unconvincing. The position of the landowners and the church in the Ukraine had for many years been becoming stronger while that of the ordinary Cossacks and peasants deteriorated; and Mazepa had notably contributed to this process (see *e.g.*, V. A. Golobutskii, *Zaporozhskoe Kazachestvo* (Kiev, 1957), p. 323). But his motives in 1708 were certainly more personal and more defensive than those attributed to him by theories of this kind.

18. A. Lortholary, *Le mirage russe en France au XVIII siècle* (Paris, n.d.), p. 17.

19. S. A. Feigina, 'Poltava i zarubezhnaya obshchestvenno-politicheskaya mysl', *Poltavskaya pobeda* (Moscow, 1959), p. 177.

20. R. Wittram, *Peter I, Czar und Kaiser* (Göttingen, 1964), II, 226–7.

21. Hassinger, *Brandenburg-Preussen, Schweden und Russland*, p. 259.

22. Whitworth to Boyle (Secretary of State), 21 August 1709, *Sbornik* L, 231.

23. Sunderland (Secretary of State) to Whitworth, 1 November 1709, S.P. 104/120.

24. Instructions for Baluze, 24 July 1710, *Sbornik*, XXXIV, 425–33. Rakoczi made strenuous efforts after Poltava to arrange a Franco–Russian agreement (Shternberg, 'Russko-vengerskie otnosheniya', pp. 93ff.).

25. *Receuil des Instructions données aux ambassadeurs et ministres de France depuis les traités de Westphalie, Russie*, I (Paris, 1890), 116.

26. *Pisma i Bumagi Petra Velikogo* (St Petersburg-Moscow, 1887–   ) III, 716–22.

27. Quoted in V. E. Shutoi, 'Pozitsiya Turtsii v gody severnoi voiny, 1700–1709gg.', *Poltavskaya Pobeda*, pp. 148–9.

28. *Pisma i Bumagi*, X, 233–6, 263–9.

29. *Pisma i Bumagi*, XI(I), 24–5.

30. A. V. Florovsky, 'Russo-Austrian Conflicts in the early 18th Century', *Slavonic and East European Review*, XLVII (1969), 107.

31. *Pisma i Bumagi*, XI(I), 117–19, 151–3.

32. *Pisma i Bumagi*, XI(I), 317.

33. Quoted in B. H. Sumner, *Peter the Great and the Ottoman Empire* (Oxford, 1949), p. 40.

34. On this disunity see S. F. Oreshkova, *Russko-turetskie otnosheniya v nachale XVIIIv.* (Moscow, 1971), pp. 118–19, 131–2.

35. For discussion of this question see Oreshkova, *Russko-turetskie otnosheniya*, pp. 132–4; Sumner, *Peter the Great and the Ottoman Empire*, pp. 40–1.

36. Oreshkova, *Russko-turetskie otnosheniya*, pp. 183–9.

37. Oreshkova, *Russko-turetskie otnosheniya*, p. 183.

38. Various projects for such a treaty can be found in S.P. 103/61. A Russian draft (drawn up in 1716) of a proposed defensive alliance is in *Arkhiv Knyazya F. A. Kurakina* (St Petersburg, 1890–1902), III, 325–9.

39. The joining of tributaries of the Neva and Volga by a canal in 1708; the Ladoga canal, meant to allow shipping to avoid the severe storms on that lake, begun in 1718 and not completed until after his death; and the unsuccessful effort to build a Volga-Don canal.

40. Memorandum on the Baltic provinces conquered by Russia, 31 August 1715, in S.P. 91/107.

41. Craggs (Secretary of State) to Norris, 3 November 1719, S.P. 104/155.

42. There is a good discussion of the attempts to form an

anti-Russian alliance and their failure in L. R. Lewitter, 'Poland, Russia and the Treaty of Vienna of 5 January, 1719', *Historical Journal*, XIII (1970), 3–30.

43. S.A. Feigina, 'Missiya A. I. Ostermana v Shvetsiyu v 1719g.', *Voprosy voennoi istorii Rossii XVIII i pervaya polovina XIX vekov* (Moscow, 1969), p. 294.
44. *Sbornik*, LX, 208–10.
45. *Sbornik*, LX, 341
46. Norris and Whitworth to Sunderland (Secretary of State), 5 August 1717, S.P. 84/257; see in general K.-H. Ruffmann, 'England und der Russische Zaren- und Kaisertitel', *Jahrbücher für Geschichte Osteuropas*, 3 (1955), 217–24.
47. *Ocherk Istorii Ministerstva Inostrannykh Del'*, *1802–1902* (St Petersburg, 1902), p. 38.
48. *Sbornik*, LX, 129–30.
49. *Receuil des Instructions, Russie*, I, 186; see also *Sbornik*, XXXIV, 196–201, 532–6.
50. Bantysh-Kamenskii, *Obzor vneshnykh snoshenii Rossii*, I, 165–6.
51. *Sbornik*, XLIX, 313–14.

Chapter 5

A NEW STATE AND SOCIETY?

. . .

THE ARMY AND NAVY

Any discussion of the new Petrine institutions and methods, any attempt to understand the whole drift and nature of Peter's achievement, must start with the armed forces. It was the demands of the army and navy for men, for equipment, for money and not least for organization and leadership, which inspired many of the most important changes and the most striking innovations of the reign. These demands were, at least for the first twelve years or more of the eighteenth century, crushingly heavy. The life and death struggle with Sweden faced the creaking traditional machinery of government with tasks which it was ill-equipped to fulfil. It imposed upon the Russian people unprecedented burdens. At times, during the crisis of the Great Northern War in 1708–9 and the struggle with the Ottoman empire in 1711–13, it seemed that these tasks might become unmanageable, these burdens unbearable.

The protracted war with Sweden meant the provision of men for the army not merely in great numbers but in a regular and sustained fashion over a period of many years. Russia had made great military efforts in the past: in 1654–67, for example, over 100,000 men had been recruited for the war with Poland. But never before had so great an effort been kept up for so long. This involved the creation of a system of recruiting more effective and enduring, in other words more efficiently ·coercive, than anything hitherto seen in Russia, or for that matter in almost any other European state. Moreover, to challenge successfully the naval power of Sweden in the Baltic meant not only the creation, entirely from scratch, of a large and expensive fleet but also the equipment and fortification of completely new bases from

91

which it might operate. To equip these unprecedentedly large and demanding armed forces meant a great extension of existing industries (iron- and copper-smelting, the manufacture of small arms) and even the development of quite new ones (the manufacture of sailcloth). The demands of the army and navy, in other words, were the driving force behind much of the effort, often unsuccessful, to foster Russia's industrial strength which marked Peter's reign. To pay and maintain the army and navy the government needed money in unprecedented quantities. The demands of the armed forces explain Russia's sometimes desperate financial position, particularly in the first decade of the eighteenth century. These demands were the reason for a resort to a wide variety of sometimes bizarre financial expedients which culminated in the introduction, from 1718–19, of the new poll-tax, with all its far-reaching social implications. The need for trained officers and for experts of many kinds – artillerymen, engineers, shipwrights, teachers of navigation and even of elementary mathematics – explains the rapidly growing importation of such men from western Europe in the later 1690s and the early years of the eighteenth century (an import which, in the case of the navy, continued to the end of the reign) and also the sending of unprecedented numbers of young Russians to study abroad. This need also produced a number of specialized schools for army and navy officers: these were much the most successful aspect of the unsystematic efforts of the tsar to educate at least a small proportion of his subjects. Finally the problems of organizing and maintaining forces of hitherto unknown size and complexity led to the establishment of new organs of central government. This process, for long essentially *ad hoc*, a hand-to-mouth response to immediate necessities and short-term demands, culminated in the establishment after 1718 of the new War and Admiralty Colleges, institutions which were to rank for the rest of the eighteenth century among the most important parts of the machinery of central government.

In other words, war and the demands it generated were the mainspring of much of Peter's innovating and creative activity in Russia. This fact was in many ways unfortunate. It was the main reason for the hurried and unplanned character of so much of the tsar's work. Preoccupied by day-to-day necessities, forced for years on end to scratch together men, money, equipment, arms and forage wherever and however they could be obtained, he had little opportunity (and, it is fair to add, for long also little taste) for real planning, for the careful elaboration of new methods or construction of new institutions. Only after the war with Charles XII was clearly won does a spirit of mature reflection and careful weighing of alternatives become discernible in his hitherto headlong and largely unplanned activities. The way in which the war for so long overshadowed everything else probably strengthened Peter's tendency to rely for the execution of his policies on straightforward and often brutal coercion. Increasingly, as his reign went on, he imposed on Russia a power-structure, a hierarchy of authorities, which were essentially military in spirit and inspiration. The explicit militarization of much of the machinery of government in his last years is the final and most striking illustration of this tendency. The harshness, the rigidity, the mechanical insensibility which came to characterize much of the Petrine governmental machine was largely due to the strains generated by a long period of difficult and intensely exacting military struggle.

The new armed forces and their demands had thus both constructive and destructive effects. In a variety of ways they stimulated innovation and helped to complete the transformation of Muscovy into Russia. At the same time they imposed upon the ordinary man obligations much heavier than any he had previously borne and did much to give the new official Russia a tone and ethos different from any known in the past. Different historians have struck, and no doubt will continue to strike, differing balances between these credit and debit factors. But war and its effects are central not merely to Peter's foreign policies but also to his achievements and failures within Russia. Without a grasp of this fact no real understanding of his reign is possible.

The army which Peter inherited was a complex and somewhat heterogeneous force composed (apart from Cossack, Bashkir and other irregular levies) of three distinct elements. The oldest and now the least useful of these was the feudal cavalry recruited through the obligation of landowners (*pomeshchiki*), as a condition of holding their lands, to serve in case of war with a specified number of followers. Well before the beginning of the seventeenth century this service, rendered by men at best no more than partially trained and normally limited in duration to a single campaign, was a quite inadequate basis for an effective fighting force. From the 1550s, therefore, it had been supplemented by the creation of the streltsy; but these, as has been seen, had become of only limited military value well before the end of the seventeenth century, as well as being a symbol of many aspects of the old Muscovite Russia from which Peter wished to break free. Finally, as the most modern and efficient element in this complex military mixture, there were the regiments 'of the new formation' (*novogo stroya*), organized on something like west-European lines and led by European, predominantly German, officers. In the second half of the seventeenth century these were, in numbers and fighting power, the major element in Russia's armed strength. The first two regiments of this type were created in 1631; by 1682 there were twenty-five of cavalry and thirty-eight of infantry and the new forces made up at least two-thirds of the Russian army. They represented, particularly in the infantry regiments, a massive irruption of foreign influences into Russian military life, indeed into Russian life in general. The extent to which Germany provided the model and the leadership for the new forces can be seen in the prevalence of German loan-words used to describe different types of soldier – *reitar, dragun, soldat* – or different military ranks and titles – *kapitan, rotmistr, kvartirmistr.* Peter seems to have prepared for the creation of his new army partly by study of the formation and organization of these regiments;[1] and it is important to remember that in military affairs, as in so many other areas, he accelerated and intensified a process of change which had begun long before he was born.

The first major step in the making of Russia into a great military power was taken at the end of 1699, in preparation for the imminent struggle with Sweden. In November of that year Peter gave orders for the enlistment on a large scale of both volunteers and peasant conscripts and the formation from them of new regiments. Commissions for this purpose were set up in Moscow, Novgorod, Pskov and Smolensk. Volunteers were to have the surprisingly high pay of 11 roubles a year together with an allowance for food equal to that given to members of the Semenovskii and Preobrazhenskii regiments. Landowners performing military service had to provide from their estates a conscript footsoldier for each fifty peasant households and a cavalryman for each hundred such households. If they served merely in the civil administration, or had retired from all forms of government service, they must provide an infantryman for each thirty peasant households they owned, while monasteries and church servants had to raise men at the still higher rate of one for every twenty-five households. By these means some 32,000–33,000 men, about 70 per cent of the total planned, were obtained. From them twenty-seven new infantry regiments and two of dragoons were formed. By July it was possible to group these into two divisions, under F. A. Golovin and the German General Weyde, for the war against Sweden. The tsar had forced Russia onto a path of military expansion which it was to follow for the rest of his reign.

The disaster of Narva showed how far there was still to go before the Russian army could face those of western Europe on equal terms. Nevertheless, Peter's efforts to increase his country's military power continued with energy and persistence. The battle was followed by a decision to create no fewer than forty-seven infantry and five grenadier regiments. The critical situation created by the loss of almost all the Russian field artillery at Narva was met by the seizure of church bells and the rapid casting from them of large numbers of new guns – 300 by November 1701. Simultaneously a large-scale effort was made to increase the cavalry strength of the army. Twenty-five thousand potential recruits, former members of cavalry units and suitable landowners, were summoned to Moscow in 1701: from these, nine new cavalry regiments were formed in the next year. In 1704 a decree ordered the recruitment of former streltsy and their incorporation into new field and garrison regiments.[2]

These were heroic efforts; but as yet the Russian army had no unified and systematic recruiting mechanism. The obstacles in the way of creating one were formidable. In particular the information at the government's disposal was so fragmentary and unreliable that it was impossible to form any accurate idea of the number of men available for service. (In 1704 an effort was begun to collect information of this kind for the Moscow region; but it progressed too slowly to be of much use.) Nevertheless, early in 1705 a decree, in which the word 'recruit' appears for the first time, established the system upon which Peter was in the main to rely for the rest of his reign. A young man between fifteen and twenty years old, healthy and fit for service, was to be provided by each twenty peasant households. This levy, together with another at the same rate in December 1705, produced in that year close to 45,000 men, while there was also a special levy for the cavalry at the rate of one man for each eighty peasant households. Recruiting on this scale imposed unprecedentedly heavy burdens on the Russian people. It continued, however, with little or no respite until after the turning-point of Poltava. In 1706, for example, there were again two levies for the infantry regiments and no fewer than three for the cavalry, as well as a special one of 1,000 men for the navy. Drafts of peasant conscripts to the armed forces remained a dominant feature of Peter's régime until his death,[3] though many of them were confined to distinct social groups such as townsmen or monastery servants, or to specific geographical areas.

Poltava made possible some reduction in the scale of this call-up of recruits. Yet the military establishment laid down in 1711 showed how far Russia had come as a military power in little more than a decade. It provided for forty-two field infantry regiments with a total strength of 62,000 men; garrison forces of two dragoon and thirty infantry regiments totalling 58,000; thirty-three cavalry regiments numbering in all nearly 44,000 men, and also an artillery regiment. The war with Turkey led to the formation in 1712–13 of considerable militia forces, recruited from former soldiers, in the Ukraine and the Baltic provinces, and the intensity of recruiting reached a new peak in these very difficult years. It should be noted that these figures take no account of Cossack and other irregular forces which on occasion reached, at least on paper, a strength of something like 100,000 men. The war also gave a great impetus to artillery production. In 1713 eighteen major Russian fortresses mustered between them well over 4,000 cannon of different types.

Russia thus provided the manpower for a really formidable army. To produce well-trained officers was much more difficult. The rapid raising of new forces in 1699–1700 showed up a crippling shortage of middle-ranking officers and subalterns and to a lesser extent of N.C.O.s. In July 1700 eight of the new regiments, which had a paper complement of 264 officers of the rank of captain and below, had in fact only seventy-eight serving (forty-five Russians and thirty-three foreigners). One traditional method of overcoming shortages of this kind, at least as far as the higher ranks were concerned, was recruitment from abroad. But this had serious limitations. Foreign officers were often unpopular with the men they commanded and sometimes afraid of them. They were also often of mediocre quality; few of them, after all, would have come to Russia in the first place had they been able to make satisfactory careers for themselves in their own countries or at least somewhere in western or central Europe. F. A. Golovin, the commissioner mainly responsible for the raising of the new regiments in 1699–1700, complained bitterly of their shortcomings; and in 1702 Peter, in a proclamation encouraging foreigners to enter Russian service, stressed that he wanted only skilled and competent officers from abroad. This did not imply any denial of the superiority of western technical and professional knowledge. The tsar on occasion sent young Russians to serve in and learn from foreign armies (for example, a group of thirty was sent for this purpose to France in 1712) while a number of nobles sent their sons to study the art of war under the great Prince Eugene. But it was clear that what could be hoped from the foreigners willing to serve in Russia was limited in both quality and quantity.

From the beginning, therefore, only a small minority of the officers in Peter's new army were foreign – only about a tenth, for example, of those in the new regiments of 1699–1700. The overwhelming majority were members of the landholding 'serving-man' class, to which the tsar inevitably turned as the only available source of supply. A decree of May 1700, by which the more substantial landlords of the Moscow area (those holding more than forty peasant households) were forced to provide nearly a thousand recruits for officer-training, began a process of systematic recruitment which was to last for the rest of the reign and far beyond it. Young men recruited in this way were often trained by service in one of the guards regiments, which in practice became the most important military institutions in Russia. The Preobrazhenskii regiment had a training school, the first military school ever established in Russia, from 1698 onwards. Peter himself attached great importance to this method of producing regimental officers: edicts of 1711, 1719 and 1724 attempted to prevent the promotion to officer rank of anyone who had not gained adequate practical experience by service in the ranks of one of the guards regiments. These, however, could not provide the specialized training needed by officers in the technical branches of the service, for which other provision had to be made. The result was the creation of an artillery school (the first of several) in 1701 and of engineer schools in Moscow in 1709 and St Petersburg in 1719.

Throughout Peter's reign, indeed until the fall of the tsarist régime in 1917, the quality of its officers was a weak point of the Russian army. Nevertheless much was achieved. This is most obvious in the rapidly declining importance of foreigners. In 1706 foreign officers entering Russian service ceased to be promoted automatically to a higher rank than they already held, while there was a growing readiness to get rid of those proved incompetent. The near-disaster of the Pruth campaign of 1711 was followed by the dismissal of five foreign generals, six colonels and forty-five staff officers.[4] It was inevitably in the more technical aspects of warfare, the artillery and engineers, that foreign skills remained longest in demand. Even in these, however, foreign influence was declining. By 1721 the War College could order that henceforth in the artillery only Russians should be promoted to officer rank: this is an illustration of how much Peter had achieved in making Russia not merely a great but a self-sufficient military power.

The effort of recruitment, training and equipment involved in the creation of the new forces demanded a supporting structure of administration and regulations. In 1716 the *Ustav Voinskii* (Military Regulation), a comprehensive code which attempted systematic regulation of the whole organization of the army, was issued. This elaborate document, which replaced and completed a series of more fragmentary regulations drawn up at intervals from 1699 onwards, was carefully prepared with the direct participation of Peter himself and under his strict personal control. Its issue was one of the first signs that improvisation and *ad hoc* expedients were now being replaced, in all aspects of policy-making, by calmer and more systematic methods.[5] Military administration at the highest level did not, until the establishment of the War College in 1718–19, achieve a coherent or lasting form. The *Prikaz Voennykh Del* (Department of Military Affairs), set up in 1701, lasted only until 1706, when it was replaced by the *Voennaya Kantselyariya* (War Chancery) which endured until 1719. The old seventeenth-century *Pushkarskii Prikaz* (literally Gun Department) was succeeded in 1701 by the *Prikaz Artillerii* and this in 1714 by the *Artilleriiskaya Kantselyariya*. To recruit soldiers and even to train and officer them proved easier in many ways than to provide stable and efficient administrative backing for the new army.

Russia's increased military strength was one of the most far-reaching achievements of Peter's reign. Upon it depended the country's survival and eventual victory in the war with Sweden. From it stemmed the spectacular rise in Russia's international standing. It was, moreover, an achievement which easily attracted the attention and admiration of foreigners. In 1709 the Italian General Belleardi, after some time in Peter's service, was impressed by the excellence of his artillery and thought his infantry better than any to be found in Austria, the United Provinces or Great Britain 'by the great order which it observes in combat'. A decade later the Hanoverian minister in St Petersburg concluded that the tsar 'has put the State of War upon an admirable foot, and brought his Soldiery, particularly the Infantry, to that Reputation that they yield to none in the World.'[6] Peter's contemporaries were well aware of the importance of what he had accomplished in this field and perhaps overestimated its originality.

The sudden emergence of a powerful Russian navy, though in practical terms much less significant, was a far more abrupt and self-conscious break with the past than any of the tsar's military successes. For no aspect of Peter's activities was there less precedent in Russian history. None was so directly and unmistakably the work of the tsar himself. Throughout his adult life the fleet was his greatest passion, the greatest single focus of his hopes. The practical details associated with it, the building, navigation, even the names, of its ships, its organization, the system of signals it used, never ceased to attract his loving care.[7] In one sense it was little more than a gigantic, complex and expensive toy built and operated for his personal gratification. On this toy he joyfully worked, as a young man, with his own hands. It was noticed by the Prussian diplomat Vockerodt, one of the most acute observers of the later years of the reign, that 'no victory could bring him so much pleasure as the slightest success which his ships and galleys gained', while 'on the other hand nothing afflicted him so keenly as when his ships met with the slightest misfortune', and that 'in sum, the passion for the navy triumphed in him over all other desires and preferences'.

A clear view of the use to which a powerful fleet might be put evolved only gradually in Peter. Indeed it is debatable whether it ever completely developed at all. His shipbuilding with Kordt and Brandt in the later 1680s and early 1690s had been an adolescent enthusiasm. His first view of the open sea at Archangel in 1693 had confirmed and rooted still more deeply his passionate interest in everything maritime; but this remained a matter of personal taste. Even the building of the galley-fleet on the Don in 1696 was ancillary to a military operation. Nevertheless, his appetite for naval power grew with feeding. By the last years of the seventeenth century it was clear that the young tsar would move further, and rapidly, down this road. In 1698 a school of navigation was opened at Azov. At the end of the same year the *Voennyi Morskoi Prikaz* (Navy Department) was set up as the main controlling organ of the new fleet: in 1701 the Admiralty Prikaz came into existence to supervise shipbuilding for it. The achievement of a territorial outlet to the Baltic in 1703 opened new possibilities which were at once grasped. Naval shipbuilding on an unprecedented scale, first on the river Svir and then, from 1705 onwards, in the great new Admiralty yard in St Petersburg, rapidly gave Russia a powerful Baltic squadron for use against the Swedes. Whereas the two departments mainly concerned had spent less than 81,000 roubles on the navy in 1701, they expended almost 204,000 in 1706.[8] By 1715 over 700,000 roubles were being spent in this way, and by 1724 1,200,000. When Peter died, the Baltic squadron mustered, apart from smaller vessels and those under construction, thirty-four ships of the line and fifteen frigates, manned by 28,000 men. This made Russia a decisively greater naval power than either Sweden or Denmark.[9]

Like the army, the navy suffered from a shortage of competent officers; and in its case the fact that specialized knowledge of navigation, gunnery and seamanship was indispensable made the problem particularly hard to solve. The setting-up of a naval academy in St Petersburg (which by 1718 had 500 pupils) and a school of navigation in Moscow were serious efforts to cope with it; but throughout Peter's reign the navy continued to be far more dependent than the army on foreigners. Both the sending of young Russians for training in foreign navies and the import of foreign officers, teachers and technicians had begun in the later 1690s. In 1697 fifty-eight young men were sent abroad to prepare to become naval officers, while of the thousand foreigners brought to Russia by the 'Great Embassy' of 1697–8 the majority were concerned, directly or indirectly, with the development of the navy. Both processes continued until Peter's death. In 1716, for example, twenty embryo naval officers were sent to serve in the French navy, another twenty to Amsterdam and thirty to Venice. Foreign officers, particularly in the higher ranks, and foreign shipbuilders, continued to be indispensable to Russian naval power; Dutchmen were to the fore in the first years of the century, though Englishmen and Scots soon became more important. Of the fifty-four ships of the line built for the Baltic fleet between 1708 and 1725 twenty were the work of British builders.[10] The *Morskoi Ustav* (Maritime Regulation) of 1720, which systematized the organization of the navy, was based on foreign codes of discipline and was considerably more dependent on west-European influence than the corresponding military regulations issued four years earlier.[11] It is significant that when Konon Zotov, one of the tsar's closest associates, was sent to Spain in 1715 one of his main tasks was to collect information about naval affairs and organization there.

The interest which attaches to the growth of the navy as a reflection of the interests and personality of Peter himself should not blind us to the fact that the energies and resources used for this purpose were largely wasted. The galleys built in 1696 helped substantially in the capture of Azov. The Baltic galley-fleet aided operations in Finland and did great damage to Sweden in 1719–20. The much larger and more expensive ships of the line, and even the frigates, were a different matter. The squadron based on Azov, whose construction had been begun in 1697, never achieved anything and had to be destroyed after the Pruth campaign. The Baltic fleet, in spite of the victory at Gangut in 1714 which gave Peter so much pleasure, and its growing numerical predominance, did little real damage to the Swedes. During the entire war it took only one Swedish ship of the line, while in 1715 alone the Danish navy captured four. Since it responded to no deep national need, it went into a rapid decline after the death of its creator.

The impressive growth of Russia's army and navy had, apart from its role in altering the country's international position, some constructive results. It stimulated a certain amount of administrative improvement. It provided, through the encouragement it gave to the translation of foreign works on military and naval affairs, some stimulus to intellectual life, though a very limited one. Undoubtedly it gave an impetus to certain kinds of economic growth. It helps to explain the rise in Russia's production of iron from some 120,000–150,000 poods (a pood weighed thirty-six English pounds) in the first years of the eighteenth century to 1,165,000 poods by 1725. It brought about the establishment of the first state-owned textile factories in Russia, in 1704 near Voronezh and in the following year in Moscow, to provide cloth for army uniforms. The unprecedented demand for small arms which it generated (the army establishment of 1711 called for 122,600 muskets for the infantry and 49,800 for the cavalry) led to the creation of a number of arms factories.[12] Yet as far as the Russian people were concerned, all these limited and indirect benefits were far outweighed by the direct and brutally heavy burdens which the new military and naval power involved.

These burdens took a number of forms. The most obvious was the military service which has already been briefly discussed. Between 1705 and 1715 there were twelve general levies of men for the army, generally at the rate of one from each twenty peasant households, as well as many local and partial conscriptions from specific social groups and for special purposes.[13] There were also a series of levies for the new navy from 1702 onwards, though normally on a much smaller scale than for the army. From 1699 to 1714, the years when the demands of the government were at their highest, about 331,000 recruits were raised for both services, an average of 22,000 a year. Peter's régime became more demanding as the harsh necessities of the struggles with Sweden and the Turks weighed more heavily. At first only bachelors in the 15–20 age-group were taken; but soon married men were held liable, and those of thirty or even forty years of age. At the time of the Turkish war men of up to fifty were not spared if they seemed fit for service, so pressing did the need for manpower become during those hard years. It is also indicative of the difficulties the government was facing that levies increasingly had to be enforced by menaces as time went on. The recalcitrant and uncooperative were threatened with having to provide recruits at double the normal rate, with the seizure of the estates of landlords unwilling to surrender peasants to the army, even with death for obstructive or inefficient officials or village headmen. The picture, at least until the last decade of the tsar's life, is one of heavier demands made good with growing difficulty by the use of more and more brutal methods.

This raising of men for the army was accompanied by an equally ruthless and determined drafting of others for forced labour on Peter's great building projects, all of which had some relevance, direct or indirect, to the war effort. New fortresses and harbours (those at Azov, Taganrog and Narva, for example); new canals; most demanding of all, the raising on swamp and marshland of the new capital – all these ambitious schemes could be made realities only by the toil and sweat of tens of thousands of conscripted labourers. It has been calculated that between 1699 and 1714 Peter managed to raise forced labour for such purposes at an average rate of some 17,000 men each year. Between 1699 and 1701 about 20,000 men were drafted each year for work at the Voronezh shipyards, while in 1701 there were almost 9,000 labouring on the harbour-works at Taganrog (though this number fell somewhat in the following years). In 1698 20,000 peasants were assembled for work on the Volga-Don canal; while 15,000 army recruits were despatched to canal-building in 1721 and 20,000 soldiers used for the same purpose in 1724. From the end of 1709 efforts were made to conscript as many as 40,000 men a year for work on the building of St Petersburg, besides the large numbers used in other parts of Russia; while in March 1713, the war with Turkey resulted in orders for the raising of 12,000 in the southern provinces for fortification-building. In this sphere also threats were freely employed to raise the required numbers. Thus in October 1711 recalcitrant towns which failed to supply the specified quota of workers were threatened with 'terrible and merciless punishment'. There was nonetheless great and continual difficulty in assembling the workers whom the tsar incessantly demanded. Though there were in 1709 well over 10,000 conscript labourers engaged in the building of St Petersburg this was much fewer than Peter had called for. In the following year the Moscow *guberniya* (province) sent only a quarter of the specified number for work on the capital. In 1714 and 1715 the numbers sent by other *gubernii* reached only about a third of what had been demanded. It is also clear that many of the workers destined for St Petersburg often had to be sent elsewhere. In 1706, for example, half of those originally destined for St Petersburg went in fact to Narva.[14]

The Admiralty in St Petersburg was by far the largest productive enterprise in Russia, probably the largest in Europe. Apart from the shipyards which were its real *raison d'être* it included a large group of factories to meet the needs of the fleet. At the height of its activity it employed up to 10,000 men. Most of its skilled workers were recruited by compulsion, by the forced settlement for life in the new capital of artisans and technicians of many kinds. This process began in the summer of 1705 with the forcible removal to St Petersburg of men from the Olonets shipyard and continued in the following years. Thus as a result of an edict of 1710 the Admiralty received during the next two years 1,626 skilled workers who were compelled to settle for life in the new capital, while in 1713 another decree demanded (rather unsuccessfully: more than half of them had run away within a year) the settlement there of 1,000 carpenters. Free wage-labour was also used for skilled work, especially in Peter's later years; but the cost set fairly narrow limits to the extent to which workers of this kind could be recruited. For its unskilled workers, however, who made up two-thirds of its whole labour-force, the Admiralty always relied on compulsion. In 1714, for example, Peter 'ascribed' to it 24,000 peasant households in the St Petersburg and Archangel *gubernii*. These were forced to send men to work in the capital, as a rule about 3,300 at a time, who remained for a four-month period.

This forced labour was a heavy burden on those subject to it. The Admiralty regulations drawn up in 1722 specify a working day (not including meal-breaks) of 13 hours in summer and 11½ in the other months. It is true that in addition to Sundays there were forty-four other days, church festivals and saint's-days, when no work was done; but on the other hand the living conditions of conscripted labourers were very bad. Normally no provision at all was made for housing them in summer, when they lived in huts and dug-outs. It is not surprising that of the 32,000 men engaged in forced labour on the new capital in 1716 1,000 died and another 1,000 were seriously ill.[15]

There were other important ways in which the growth of the armed forces impinged on the life of the ordinary Russian through new or intensified government demands. An obvious one was the increasing tax burden. In the first decade of the eighteenth century, when the difficulties of the struggle with Sweden were at their most acute, 75–80 per cent of all government expenditure was on war needs; and even in 1725 74 per cent of all the money spent by the state went to the army and navy. The growing weight of taxation was thus very much a result of the inexorable demands of the war with Sweden. Indeed many of the new taxes of the early years of the struggle clearly show this by their names – *dragunskie dengi* (dragoon money), *korabel'nie dengi* (ship money), *rekrutskie dengi* (recruit money). Another type of war-generated demand which leaps perhaps less easily to the eye was the need to transport on an unprecedented scale and over long distances equipment and supplies for the army and to a lesser extent the navy. This type of service fell in the main on the peasants of parts of northern and central Russia, notably on those owned by monasteries. In 1702, 4,428 cartloads of bread and 8,593 of other war supplies went from Moscow to the north-west for the use of the army. In the following year the corresponding figures were 5,290 and 11,318: the increase reflects more intense military activity and the beginnings of the building of St Petersburg.[16] Whereas carrying-services of this kind had been demanded in 1702 from only twenty districts (*uezds*), in 1703 fifty were forced to provide them. The same point can be made on a smaller and more intimate geographical scale. In 1701 only six households in the Vorotynsk district (about 200 miles south-west of Moscow) were forced to work in this way, whereas by 1706 the number had risen to fifty.[17]

The payment of taxes in kind, normally in rye or oats, sometimes in meal or flour, had a long history in Russia. There was now added to it, however, the need to provide great amounts of food and forage for the army and navy. In 1711, for example, it was ordered that supplies of this kind for military use were to be collected in all the *gubernii* except that of St Petersburg. In 1712 the Moscow *guberniya* was commanded to provide a six-months' supply of forage for four regiments and in August 1714 Peter commanded the levying of large supplies of food for the fleet. Demands of this kind could provoke serious protest even from the government's own agents. Thus the vice-governor of the St Petersburg *guberniya* complained in December 1712 that if three new regiments were stationed in the towns of the area and had to be supplied by them 'these towns and the *uezds* will be reduced to complete ruin'; and there is plenty of evidence of similar difficulties elsewhere in Russia. More than a decade after Peter's death the Prussian secretary of legation, after a quarter-century's experience of the country, noted that the ordinary Russian still saw the army the tsar had created as 'new chains' by which he was subjected more completely than ever before to the arbitrary will of the ruler.[18]

The Russian peasant reacted against all these demands most frequently by flight. Sometimes he went to frontier regions, such as the Cossack areas on the Don, where Peter's writ inevitably ran less effectively than in central Russia. A decree of 1704 speaks of frequent complaints to the tsar by landowners whose peasants were fleeing to the Cossacks, while another a decade later complains of those who 'having fled, live under the rule of the hetman in the towns of Little Russia and in various places in the lands of Slobodskaya Ukraine'. Sometimes escape was to the non-Russian peoples, Bashkirs or Mordvinians, of the middle Volga and Urals. Thus in 1712 the Troitsa-Sergeev monastery, the greatest and wealthiest landowner in Russia, complained to the Senate of fugitive peasants who 'live in the Alatyr *uezd* in the desolate lands of the Mordvinians'; while in 1715 the governor of Kazan bewailed the loss of those who 'have fled and still flee from the towns of the Kazan *guberniya* to the Ufa *uezd*, and the Ufa Bashkirs . . . and Tatars receive these fugitives and do not give them up'. Sometimes Russian peasants might take refuge in Poland (often with the active encouragement of Polish landowners anxious for their labour) or even in the Tatar khanate of the Crimea.[19] Very often, however, a fugitive peasant simply moved in the hope of better conditions to some nearby estate or village. It was not until the 'revision' (census) of 1722, which showed up more clearly than in the past the presence of fugitives in many areas, that landlords began to be unwilling to shelter them.[20] This new-found reluctance may have owed something also to legislation of the previous year which provided for severe penalties against anyone who harboured such runaways; and in 1722–5, Peter's last years, a large number were in fact handed over to the authorities or gave themselves up (though flight to Poland also seems to have increased sharply at the same time). In 1724 the Senate ordered the War College to reinforce the frontier guards on the Polish frontier in an effort to prevent such escapes; and on one occasion it even discussed deploying the entire army in the western border areas to guard against this. Simultaneously peasants were forbidden to travel more than thirty versts (about twenty miles) from home without a pass signed by their lord, or failing him his steward and the parish priest; while printed passports were introduced to counteract the forged ones which at once began to appear. There could hardly be a more telling illustration than all this of the indispensable role of coercion in much of Peter's work.

Flight as a means of escaping unbearable demands and pressures was by no means confined to the peasant. Army recruits deserted in large numbers, at least after the first years of the war with Sweden. Conscripted workers were often brought to St Petersburg like convicts, in chains to guard against their running away on the road to the new capital. In one case a group of 539 carpenters and smiths from Voronezh was despatched under the surveillance of fifty soldiers and an officer; on the road they were joined by thirteen marines and another officer. This meant that an armed guard was considered necessary to control each eight or nine of these conscripts.[21] The ratio reveals once more how heavily the strengthening of Russia, and Peter's whole accomplishment, depended upon force and coercion.

. . .

ECONOMIC LIFE AND SOCIAL STRESS

The war with Sweden and Peter's ambitious plans for the strengthening of Russia produced intensified demands not merely for labour and services of many kinds but also for money and industrial products, in other words for economic growth. From the 1690s this was one of Peter's major objectives. His efforts to achieve it, in spite of great obstacles, continued to the end of his life.

The struggle to raise money for the war with Charles XII runs through the early years of the eighteenth century as a continually recurring motif. It produced a heterogeneous and bizarre assembly of taxes; duties on inns, on baths, on beards (graded by the social rank of the wearer), on weddings, on native Russian dress, on horse-collars, on ferries. It is indicative of the effects produced by this torrent of new impositions that the Bashkirs of the Volga basin and the Urals could believe that duties were now to become payable on their eyes, at different rates for black and grey ones. The salt-gabelle of 1705, which doubled the price of an essential commodity, and the making of tobacco a state monopoly in the same year, were other examples of this desperate search for resources wherever they could be found. Those difficult years also saw the raising of money, more effectively, by the best-tried method of all – debasement of the currency. The silver content of the coinage began to be lowered from 1698 onwards; and between 1704 and 1717 the government regularly struck twenty roubles worth of copper currency from a pood of the metal which had cost it six to eight roubles. In 1723 this process was pushed still further when orders were given for the minting of 500,000 roubles in five-kopeck coins at a rate of forty roubles to the pood. During the years 1701–9 alone about 4,400,000 roubles were procured by currency manipulation, the biggest source of revenue in the first decade of the war with Sweden. Nor were the government's demands much reduced in the later years of the reign: in real terms its income by 1725 was two or three times as great as it had been in 1680. During these forty-five years the yield of direct taxes in real terms grew almost fivefold, while the cost of administering Russia increased if anything even more rapidly.[22]

The paramount importance to Peter of increasing state income and making sure that it was spent wisely and productively shines through many of his policies. In 1701 every government department was ordered to provide accounts of its revenue and expenditure, together with much other detailed financial information: this foreshadowed serious efforts in 1710–11 to produce a genuine budget (then scarcely known even in western Europe) though these had little practical effect. Throughout the reign, moreover, there was a continual struggle to accumulate stocks of precious metals. The country had hardly any domestic sources of these; for though the lead-mines at Nerchinsk, on the Chinese frontier, began to produce a little silver in the first years of the eighteenth century this was never of much importance. The export of bullion was therefore strictly prohibited and merchants were forced to surrender, in return for Russian coinage at a fixed rate, gold and silver they acquired in dealings with foreigners.

Of all the new taxes introduced under Peter one far transcended all the others in its lasting social effects. This was the poll tax or 'soul tax' (*podushnaya podat'*) decreed in

1718. This immensely important innovation had already been suggested to Peter more than once (notably by the *Oberfiskal* Nesterov in 1714). Its introduction was clearly inspired by a desire to provide for the needs of the army, now being increasingly quartered on the Russian provinces as the war with Sweden slowly drew to an end. In February 1720 it was reckoned to need each year four million roubles to maintain it; and the new tax was adjusted to produce precisely this sum. It was also intended to make taxation more equal and more centralized, to reduce the inequalities between social groups and geographical regions which had characterized the old system of basing direct taxation on the plough or the household rather than on the individual. An elaborate new census was called for. Lists of privately-owned peasants were to be drawn up by their landlords, of state peasants by clerks, village headmen or in some cases elected representatives, of townsmen by urban magistrates. These returns were then to be collated in St Petersburg. Such ambitious plans were slow to bear fruit, in spite of the frequent use of guards officers as census-takers in an effort to speed up the work. The first returns were also very inaccurate; the scrutiny and revision of them which began in 1721 showed that many taxable 'souls' had been concealed from the predatory eye of the government. Not until 1724 did the new tax begin to be levied, with peasants paying seventy kopecks each and townsmen and merchants eighty. The census did not reach its final form until 1727, after Peter's death.

How far the poll-tax in fact increased the real burden of taxation is not altogether clear. Prices in Russia approximately doubled in the first thirty years of the eighteenth century; and this must have done something to limit the impact of a tax defined in money terms. But neither these doubts nor the administrative difficulties of collecting it can conceal the vast implications of the new tax. It meant in the first place a further extension of government control over the landowning class and through it over the population generally. In 1724 it was ordered that alphabetical lists of landlords should be compiled with details of the male peasants owned by each; from these the Senate was to compile a central register. Such methods illustrate the centralizing and rationalizing authoritarianism which was a leading characteristic of Peter's rule. More important, however, was the effect which the new tax had on the peasantry. It tended to blur existing distinctions between hitherto fairly well-marked social groups and increasingly to unify them, at least in terms of their common liability to the 'soul tax'. On the one hand the bondsmen (*kholopy*), virtual slaves, now disappeared by being raised to the status of enserfed peasants, since both groups were subject to the new tax. On the other the *odnodvortsy*, a category of small independent landholders, originally military colonists, who had hitherto been sometimes regarded as the lowest rank of the nobility, now found themselves classed as peasants for tax purposes; though they struggled throughout the remainder of the century, with little success, to retain privileged status. Peter's need for revenue was thus tending, in a rough-and-ready way, to simplify what had hitherto been a complex traditional society, to divide it more and more between a great peasant majority, largely unfree, which paid the new impost and a privileged ruling minority of landowners who did not. Such a simplification was to have, at least in the long run, serious and dangerous effects.

Furthermore, the mechanics of the 'soul tax' did much to tighten the grip of the lord on his peasants. He was responsible for the collection from them of the new tax and for its payment to the representatives of the central government in his locality. This helped to strengthen his already dominant position in the Russian countryside and to increase his ability to abuse his powers. Coupled with the system of passports introduced in 1724 in an effort to check flight and evasion of military service (this also struck at the free movement of townsmen) it meant that when Peter died the peasant throughout much of Russia was more helpless, more vulnerable and exploited, than ever before.

It is essential to realize, however, that Peter's economic policies, and certainly his economic ambitions, went far beyond any mere increase in government receipts and expenditures. Throughout his reign he aimed at making Russia richer and its economic life more productive and efficient. As early as his visit to Archangel in 1693 he had been impressed by the need to develop production, particularly in industry, and to foster trade. Economic growth, in other words, was forced on him from the beginning of his active reign by Russian conditions. The need for it was not, so far as he was concerned, something created by his introduction in 1697–98 to the relative wealth of western Europe or even by the demands of the war with Sweden (though the latter made the need more imperative). His reign saw in Russian economic life both the introduction of foreign influences and techniques on a greater scale than ever before and extensive and pervasive government control and encouragement, above all in the development of industry. Yet it would be a mistake to see him either as an uncritical borrower of expedients from western Europe or as a believer in the superiority of state over private initiative in economic life. He never hesitated to adapt foreign institutions or methods to fit Russian conditions; thus, for example, he insisted in a decree of 1722, against normal European practice, that entry to guilds in Russia should not be restricted.[23]

It is doubtful whether he can be considered a mercantilist in any real sense of that vague term. He had only a general and indirect acquaintance with the body of mercantilist and cameralist writing which now existed in western and central Europe and was little influenced by it. To him it was first and foremost the demands and opportunities of Russia's position which mattered. He was convinced of the imperative need to foster the growth of trade and industry, and was a thoroughgoing protectionist in commercial policy as the highly protective tariff of 1724, the most systematic of his reign, clearly shows. This imposed duties of up to 75 per cent on a wide range of imported goods, while at the same time greatly raising the existing export duties on such raw materials as linen yarn and hides. But policies of this kind were rooted in his own temperament and experience. They were not a slavish or mechanical imitation of west-European models. At bottom his economic policies were directed to calling forth in Russia a new spirit of work, enterprise and efficiency, by direction and if necessary compulsion from above. Only through the creation of this new spirit could a vast thinly-populated country, full of untapped wealth, take advantage of the opportunities which now presented themselves. Just as the great war with Sweden seemed to Peter a hard school from whose trials Russia must emerge strengthened and purified, so in his attitude to economic development there is clearly a moralistic element, a stress on duty, work and achievement.

The state, in Peter's eyes, must play in economic affairs as in others a creative and educative role. When it ordered that henceforth leather must be cured with train oil and not with pitch, or that grain must be harvested with the scythe and not the traditional sickle, or that linen cloth must be woven on wider looms (which turned out to be too big to fit into the cottages of peasant handicraft workers), or that the boats used to transport goods on the Russian rivers should be made of sawn planks rather than with those shaped with the traditional axe, it was acting as the teacher and guardian of a backward and ignorant people, leading and if necessary driving them to a new level of wealth and efficiency. Constant and detailed instructions, continual chivvying and propaganda, were unavoidable. The image of the schoolmaster or the parent was frequently used in the preambles to his edicts on economic matters. 'Our people are like children about their learning', said one of 1723, 'they will not learn the alphabet until they are forced by their master. At first they complain, but when they learn, then they are thankful. . . . In factories we apply not only proposals, but we also force and instruct and use machines and other measures to teach you how to be a good economist.'

In spite of all this, Peter never doubted that private initiative and enterprise were the mainspring of national wealth. His most fundamental ambition was to create a class of entrepreneurs with the knowledge, the innovative capacity and the capital which fitted them to take the lead in making Russia richer and more productive. Much government control and direction might be needed. But this was to be a means to an end, an expedient to meet needs which would in the long run best be satisfied by other means. Decrees of 1711 provided that 'people of all ranks may trade in any commodity anywhere'; and in the last decade of the reign, with external pressures and constraints relaxing, there was an unmistakable movement towards liberalization of Russian economic life. Of the many commodities which had been government monopolies in the first years of the eighteenth century – salt, tobacco, tar, bristles, potash and others – only two (potash and resin) were still in this situation after 1719. From about 1714 all the tsar's advisers on commercial affairs – Baron Ludwig Luberas, Count Savva Raguzinskii, A. A. Kurbatov, P. S. Saltykov – were in favour of more liberal attitudes; and the virtual state monopoly of foreign trade which had existed until 1716 was relaxed after that date. Demands that industry supply the government with large quantities of goods – cloth, leather, iron, copper – at artificial and often very low prices (in effect a heavy tax on the factory-owners concerned) were slowly relaxed. From about 1719, especially as far as metals were concerned, there was an increasing tendency for the prices paid by the government to approximate to market ones. From the same year all the tsar's subjects were granted the right to 'seek, smelt, melt and refine all metals'. In his last years, there was also a tendency for state-owned industrial enterprises to be transferred to individuals or companies, though the government retained the right to resume possession if they were badly or unsuccessfully conducted, and to control the quality of the goods they produced.

Few aspects of his activities display better than his economic policies Peter's view of himself as responsible for the strengthening of Russia and the improvement of his people's lot. The mere fact that some of the most important decrees of the reign on trade and industrial questions were written originally in the tsar's own hand illustrates this. His attention to economic life also displays his willingness to experiment and innovate. Employing English and Dutch brewers to make beer for his own household, summoning shepherds from Silesia to Kazan to improve sheep-shearing and the preparation of wool, experimenting with the planting of vines in the Astrakhan area, even in 1721 making tempting offers to the French financier, John Law, to induce him to settle in Russia,[24] Peter shows in this field throughout his reign the outpouring of energy, the often chaotic striving towards improvement, which distinguished all his activities.

The difficulties were enormous. Poor communications, shortage of capital, scarcity of suitable labour, technological backwardness, the weakness and low social status of the merchant class and the lack of a tradition of enterprise and innovation, made the sort of economic growth to which Peter aspired very hard to achieve. Whatever his preferences, government control and direction were still widespread even in the last years of his reign. Achievement was often substantial, even great; but it was also often patchy and short-lived. The reign saw the creation in Russia of perhaps 178 establishments which can be described as factories;[25] but the mortality among them was high and the proportion which took root and became permanently viable relatively small. Of the new enterprises, moreover, about half were government creations. Of the thirty-one metal-works built in the Ural area in the first quarter of the eighteenth century, the most successful new industrial growth of the period, fifteen were state establishments; and these produced over half the iron output of the area and nine-tenths of its copper. Normally about 8–10 per cent of the government's revenues seems to have been spent on industry: sometimes this proportion went as high as 20 per cent.[26]

The state not only produced on its own account, but also tried in many different ways to tempt private individuals into industrial development. A whole armoury of aids and inducements came to be held out to anyone, Russian or foreign, who was willing to set up a factory; but their effect, though not negligible, was limited. Interest-free loans were sometimes made to merchants and manufacturers to encourage new production. Subsidies, occasionally large ones, might be paid to individuals and companies. Manufacturers might be granted exemption from taxes on the sale of their products or given the right to import materials or tools duty-free. Monopolies were sometimes granted; for example to a company formed by close associates of Peter in 1717 for silk production and to another set up two years later to manufacture chemicals. In 1722 the tsar supported, against the protests of many merchants, the claim of manufacturers to sell their products retail directly to the consumer.[27] The tariff of 1724 was an elaborate and systematic effort to stimulate domestic production. In general these expedients, many of them disjointed and *ad hoc*, achieved little. Peter's decrees on economic affairs, like so much of his legislation, were full of demands which could not be met, of orders which could not be enforced, and of exhortations which produced no practical result. An *ukaz* of 1712, to take one example, ordered the creation of companies of merchants to establish textile factories and thus make Russia independent of cloth imports; but the merchants concerned were hostile to such ideas and the companies which were formed soon broke up, having achieved nothing.

There was, however, one form of government help to industry which had wider implications than any other and which added appreciably to the burdens which Peter imposed on the Russian people. This was the provision of large supplies of forced labour. Sometimes soldiers were used for this purpose, as when in 1723 a regiment from Tobolsk, in western Siberia, was detailed to build a factory at Ekaterinburg. Criminals, vagrants and beggars were regularly pressed into service in industry. Both these methods were well known throughout western and central Europe. A more distinctively Russian practice was the 'ascribing' of groups of peasant villages to the service of particular factories, a method which had been known since the mid-seventeenth century but which Peter greatly extended. Such methods were admittedly a second-best. Peter and his advisers, and Russian factory-owners, were unanimous in the justified conviction that free hired labour was much more efficient than unfree: in his decrees the tsar frequently recommended the use of free workers whenever possible. Landowners objected strongly to peasants (for example, runaway serfs) being recruited for work in factories and thus permanently lost to their former masters; and Peter was clearly unwilling to antagonize a group on which he depended so heavily, by appearing in any way to attack their position in the countryside. The result was that during the whole of his reign only four private factory-owners had peasants ascribed to them, though all four were important. In 1721 the need for a plentiful supply of labour in privately-owned factories forced the tsar to decree that factory-owners could henceforth buy serfs, indeed whole villages. But these were to be attached to the factory, not to the person of the owner; and in the last years of the reign factories which used workers bought in this way were not numerous.

State factories, however, were another matter. Here the ascription of peasants was common, its scale increasing and the burdens it imposed heavy. In the last years of Peter's life there seems to have been a growing tendency to regard state peasants as a standing reserve of labour, at the disposal of the government for all purposes, so that at the time of his death there were about 54,000 ascribed to metallurgical works alone, the great majority of them to state-owned ones. Often these peasant conscripts had to build the factories in the first place; and besides working in them once they were built, they supplied timber for fuel, burnt charcoal, performed a wide variety of carrying services and even provided apprentices to be trained for skilled work. In the development of industry in Russia, coercion could not predominate quite as it did in the growth of the armed forces; yet it was resorted to on a large scale. Within the factories and workshops, moreover, there was severe discipline. Lazy, drunken or merely careless workers were punished not only by fines but by beatings and being put in chains or in prison. In the development of industry, as in everything Peter did, growth and progress, not consideration for the feelings of his subjects, state power not individual welfare, was the keynote.

In spite of many failures and false starts, Peter's reign was a time of great achievements in the development of industry in Russia. It has been calculated that by 1726, the year after his death, 52 per cent by value of all Russia's exports consisted of simple manufactured goods (mainly linen, canvas and iron).[28] Some of the factories set up during these years were among the largest in Europe – for example, a sailcloth factory in Moscow which at the end of the reign employed 1,162 workers. Most important of all, a great new metal industry, producing iron and copper in large quantities, took root in the Urals. Though iron ore had been discovered there in the 1620s and the first small foundry established in 1631, Tula, Olonets and some other areas continued until the end of the seventeenth century to be far more important as producers of metals. From the late 1690s, however, large government foundries made their appearance in the Urals, a process in which A. A. Vinius, head of the *Sibirskii Prikaz* for several years after 1694 and for some time a close associate of the tsar, played a large role. Rich veins of ore, plentiful fuel supplies, the movement (often forced) of skilled workers from central Russia and the use of ascribed peasants to supply unskilled labour, combined to produce a rapid expansion in output in 1699–1703.[29] At the same time the first copper-foundry in the area was established, again on government initiative; and the growing demand for this metal by the mints of Moscow and St Petersburg soon gave a great fillip to production. Nor were the mineral riches of the Urals exploited only by government factories. They laid the foundation of the vast fortune of Nikita Demidov, an illiterate artisan from Tula, who began a burst of foundry-building from 1716 onwards and became the greatest and most successful industrialist in Russia. He was ennobled in 1720 and his family received hereditary noble status five years later. His meteoric rise is the outstanding illustration of the opportunities which the Petrine age could offer to the few who were enterprising and lucky enough to be able to seize them. By the time of Peter's death the Urals were the greatest iron-producing area in Russia and almost its only source of copper. There were then perhaps 30,000 ascribed peasants at work in the area –

almost equal to its entire population less than two decades earlier.

Of all aspects of Russia's economic life, it was the development of industry which most aroused Peter's interest and in which he achieved most success. In agriculture the picture was different. The area under cultivation grew and there was settlement of unoccupied land, notably in border areas and parts of south-central Russia. Landlords fairly often transferred peasants to these areas from the more populous but less productive ones of the north and centre. The internal trade in grain was increasing, with markets in Moscow, St Petersburg, Archangel, Vyatka, Nizhnyi-Novgorod and other towns. The market for flax and hemp was also developing. But none of this owed anything to the tsar and his activities. There were indeed a series of rather fragmentary and disconnected government efforts to improve agricultural methods and productivity. Peter, after seeing in the conquered Baltic provinces the superiority of the scythe to the sickle in reaping, adopted the typically direct method of buying several thousand scythes and sending them to various Russian provinces in an attempt to spread their use. Efforts were made to encourage sheep-rearing (the need for woollen cloth for army uniforms was important here) and to improve stock-breeding. Sheep from Silesia, horses from Persia, were imported for this purpose and government stud-farms set up. Initiatives were taken to stimulate the production of silk; and experts from Italy were imported for this purpose just before Peter's death. But none of this had any great or lasting effect. The improvement of agriculture ranked lower in the order of official priorities than the growth of industry. It also presented problems, both material and psychological, of far greater magnitude. An illiterate and intensely traditional peasantry, deeply suspicious of all innovations, was an obstacle to change beyond the power of any ruler or government to overcome, a fact clear to many contemporaries. Weber, the Hanoverian minister, for example, felt of the Russian peasants that 'their Minds seem so darkned [sic], and their Senses so stupefied by Slavery, that though they are taught the most obvious Improvements in Husbandry, yet they do not care to depart from the old Way, thinking that no body can understand it better than their Ancestors did.'[30]

The creation of a merchant marine and the ending, or at least the reduction, of Russia's dependence on foreigners for the conduct of its growing trade with the outside world was an ambition close to Peter's heart. It arose naturally from his intense interest in all things maritime and fitted with the growth of a powerful navy and the building of the new capital and its rapid evolution as an important seaport. England and the Dutch had become rich through the possession of great merchant fleets and a vastly profitable overseas trade: could not Russia benefit in the same way? This ambition was doomed to disappointment. Within Russia, however, something could be done to encourage the merchant class, still weak and lacking in status and self-confidence, and to develop internal trade. The growth of the army and navy and their demands for supplies of many different kinds had in itself a significant effect. Administrative changes might also contribute to the same end. In 1699 the *Burmistrskaya Palata* or *Ratusha* (from the German *Rathaus*) was established as a central organism for the collection of taxation from the Russian towns. The most important motive for this was a desire to increase government revenue; but another significant one was to strengthen the urban merchant class by freeing it from control by the *voevod* and other provincial officials. In fact the innovation had slight success in this latter respect. Peter demanded increased tax payments from the towns in return for the limited degree of autonomy he offered them; and they were unwilling to accept such a bargain. The *Ratusha* remained, nonetheless, an important financial institution for most of the reign. It marked a notable step towards a more rational and centralized system of tax-collection, since the work it took over had previously been divided between no fewer than thirteen different *prikazy*.

A substantial group of rich and self-confident merchants was only beginning to develop in Russia and would be slow to grow in a society still so predominantly agrarian and military. Russian traders, whether importing or exporting, were at a great disadvantage compared with those of western Europe. They had to pay higher rates of interest on borrowed capital, and higher shipping and insurance rates; nor did they have at their disposal the relatively accurate and up-to-date information about markets and prices from which their foreign rivals benefited. All this intensified their natural conservatism and timidity. The result was that they traded with the west merely 'passively', in their own ports (though in trade with Poland, Hungary, the Ottoman empire, China and Persia, where they were not confronted by such obstacles, their attitude was much more enterprising and aggressive).[31] This meant that the overseas trade conducted by Russian merchants in Russian ships of which Peter dreamed was beyond reach. Efforts in 1699 and 1723 to form Russian trading companies modelled on those which had proved successful in England and Holland had little result. Favourable rates of customs duty on goods carried to or from Russia in Russian ships were just as ineffective.

The few active new trading ventures of the reign were usually completely dependent on government initiative and support. Thus in 1717 two Russian frigates arrived in Leghorn, one of the greatest Mediterranean ports, from Archangel with Russian products, while another ship was sent from St Petersburg. In 1724 a decree ordered the establishment of a company to develop trade with Spain (always attractive as a possible indirect source of bullion from Spanish America) and three government-provided ships were sent to Spanish ports with Russian goods. But these limited efforts were not followed up: not until the 1750s did a Russian trade with the Mediterranean begin to appear a practical proposition. Lack of capital, the opposition of foreign merchants and governments, and the persisting shortage of entrepreneurial skills, made ambitious schemes of foreign commerce as yet impossible to realize.

Peter's achievements in Russian economic life were thus extremely uneven. There was substantial industrial development. In the metal-producing and metal-working industries, stimulated by the new demands of the armed forces, there was rapid and striking progress. The smelting of iron and copper, the casting of artillery and anchors, the manufacture of small arms, grew as never before in Russia's history. In other industries connected with the army and navy, such as the production of sailcloth, and in one or two of the luxury ones, there was appreciable progress. Yet little of this made much difference to the life of most ordinary Russians; and when it did make a difference it was often for the worse, as in the growth in the number of peasant households 'ascribed' for factory labour or even bought by factory-owners. The government's growing demands were met by a more rigorous exploitation of the existing economy, dominated by traditional peasant agriculture, at least as much as by the creation of new resources and the generation of new wealth. To reproach Peter for this would be quite unfair. His economic policies were as intelligent, as consistent and as successful as those of any ruler of the age in western Europe. Indeed both in his aims and in many of his methods he often closely resembled his fellow-monarchs in the west. But in economic life, more than in almost any other aspect of his many-sided activity, he was limited by the sheer inability of a poor and thinly-spread agrarian society to satisfy all his demands and give substance to all his hopes.

. . .

RELIGION AND THE CHURCH

In a limited way Peter was a religious man. His formal education, with all its shortcomings, had inevitably included a considerable element of traditional piety. From it he derived an extensive knowledge of the Bible; and he was a regular churchgoer who took an active part in services. He believed in the divine origin of the power he wielded and in his duty to protect the Orthodox faith and those who professed it. He seems to have been buoyed up on a number of occasions during his reign by a genuine feeling that he was the agent of God's will – for example, during the struggle for Azov in 1695–96. During his reign there was a significant increase in the number of churches in virtually every Russian diocese, from a total of 11,000–12,000 in 1702 to over 14,000 two decades later.[32] Yet his faith lacked both psychological depth and intellectual subtlety. None of his associates in his formative years was well informed about or qualified to discuss the more intellectual aspects of religious belief; and in these Peter displayed little interest throughout his life. More important, he had little feeling for Russian religious tradition: indeed he was actively hostile to many of its manifestations. Ritual, conventional observances, the externals of religion in general, were always likely to arouse his suspicion or even contempt. His personal faith was real. But it was also narrow and above all practical, a 'simple soldier's faith' of duty and constructive worldly activity. To him religion meant morality, education, positive action. To its liturgical and sacramental aspects, which to the great majority of his subjects were the only ones which carried true emotional weight, he was insensitive. From early in life a wide acquaintance with foreigners of differing creeds (Gordon, a pious Catholic; Lefort, at least formally a Calvinist), coupled with constant travelling and changes of scene, bred in him a markedly more tolerant attitude in religious matters than any taken by his predecessors. This tolerance was merely comparative. Peter supported the forcible or semi-forcible conversion to Orthodoxy of the non-Christian peoples of east and south Russia, partly at least because this transformed relatively free tribesmen into tax-paying Russian subjects. Though from 1716 onwards he relaxed the severe punishment to which, in law, Old Believers were still subject, he replaced this with an obligation to pay taxes at double the normal rate. His attitude to Jews seems to have been uniformly hostile; and in 1719 he ordered the expulsion from Russia of the Jesuits, always suspect as the spearhead of Catholic political influence. Nevertheless, even a very limited degree of openmindedness in religious matters was enough to raise a barrier between him and the mass of his subjects.

Peter's personal faith did not prevent him from indulging throughout his reign in parodies of religious rites which were at best gross and at worst deliberately blasphemous. The most famous example of this is the 'Most Drunken Synod', a body of the tsar's cronies and supporters which came into existence early in 1692. Its leading members adopted titles taken from those of the church hierarchy and clearly intended to mock it. Its first 'patriarch' was Matvei Filimonovich, an elderly drunkard related to the family of the tsar's mother. He was soon succeeded by N. M. Zotov, one of Peter's closest associates, who in turn gave way at the beginning of 1718 to P. I. Buturlin. The activities of the 'Synod' were in brutal contrast to the behaviour traditionally expected of an Orthodox tsar. On Palm Sunday, for example, the entry of Christ into Jerusalem was parodied by Zotov riding on a camel to an inn where riotous drinking took place. These antics of the 'Synod' outraged many contemporaries. 'Now, who would believe', wrote the secretary of the Imperial minister in 1699, after seeing in its ceremonies two tobacco-pipes placed at right angles used to mimic a cross, 'that the sign of the cross – that most precious pledge of our redemption – was held up to mockery?'[33] The purpose of these childishly provocative ceremonies remains obscure. There is no doubt that Peter himself attached importance to the 'Synod': he wrote out its relatively complex rules with his own hand and revised them several times. A generation later one of the last acts of his life was to attend one of its meetings. Certainly, therefore, it was not the casual outcome of youthful high spirits.

Nor is it likely, as used to be thought, that it resulted from the tsar's failure in 1690 to secure the appointment as patriarch of the candidate he himself favoured. It has sometimes been argued that the 'Synod' reflects nothing more serious than the tsar's odd taste in amusements and his dislike of the deeply felt conventional pieties of his subjects. But it may also have embodied a half-conscious attempt, by satirizing the formal and traditional aspects of religion, to devalue them and to assert that it was by daily conduct, not ritual observances, that the sincerity and value of belief must be measured. More probably, however, the brutal grossness of its activities reflects a dark side of Peter's character which it is difficult for the historian to explore, pathological distortions of feeling whose nature he himself did not really understand.

There was much in the Russian church of the later seventeenth century to satirize and attack. In spite of the efforts of the Patriarch Adrian (1690–1700) laxity and corruption were increasing. There were too many priests: while the fact that they could marry allowed the priesthood to become a hereditary caste. Usually drunken and servile, often wandering from place to place over large areas of Russia, its members were often hardly distinguishable from any ordinary peasant. A tendency for men to enter monasteries to escape military service and the other growing demands of the secular world had swollen the number of monks; and the personal quality even of the bishops, drawn from their ranks, was depressingly low. Clerical wealth, as far as the regular clergy were concerned, was as marked as clerical weaknesses. There were by 1700 some 557 monasteries and convents, which between them owned about 130,000 peasant households (the greatest of all, the Troitsa-Sergeev monastery, had over 20,000) while some great church dignitaries were very rich. The patriarch possessed almost 9,000 peasant households and the Metropolitan of Rostov about 4,400.[34]

What Peter demanded of the church was that it should be useful to the state and society. It must use its resources, once its own immediate needs had been satisfied, to support education, to care for the poor and sick, and if necessary to meet the general needs of the state. He proceeded, from the beginning of the war with Sweden, to put his ideas into practice with increasing thoroughness and effect. In October 1700, when the Patriarch Adrian died, no successor was appointed and the choice of a new patriarch was postponed. Stefan Yavorskii, Metropolitan of Ryazan, was nominated acting patriarch. He remained a figure of importance for a number of years; but he was never in complete agreement with the tsar and relations between them were more than once under considerable strain. Early in 1701 a new government department, the *Monastyrskii Prikaz* (Monastery Department), was set up to control the finances of the church. The next twenty years were to be dominated by two trends – an increasing subjection of the church to state control and the resulting loss of its independence, and a diversion of clerical revenues on a large scale to secular and state purposes.

Neither of these tendencies was completely new. From 1696–97 a series of decrees had sought to restrict clerical expenditures and divert surplus church revenues into the government's coffers. The founding of new monasteries and the payment of salaries to priests, abbots or archimandrites with estates of their own had been forbidden, while in 1699–1700 the tax privileges of the church had been abolished. With the creation of the *Monastyrskii Prikaz* policies of this kind were pushed further and faster. At the end of 1701 it was decreed that henceforth every monk was to have an annual stipend of only ten roubles, together with fixed quantities of grain and firewood. Any monastic revenues surplus to these requirements were to be used for charitable purposes.

During the next decade this ruling put about a million roubles into the government's hands, and much of it was used to finance the war with Sweden. About 90 per cent of this new revenue was so diverted in 1703, but that high proportion was exceptional. Between 1709 and 1716 a similar policy forced a number of bishops to hand over much of their revenues to the *Monastyrskii Prikaz* or to local officials, and retain only a proportion (on average rather less than half) for the upkeep of their households. The church was also under heavy pressure to use its resources for the general good (for example, the setting-up of almshouses or the maintenance of old and disabled soldiers) and above all for education. In an interview with the dying Adrian in October 1700 Peter had stressed the need to foster education in Russia for the sake of both church and state;[35] and in the following years the church was forced to use an increasing proportion of its resources in this way. By 1706 perhaps as much as a quarter of its income was being devoted to education of all kinds. It must be emphasized, however, that none of this involved outright confiscation of church property. Peter might appropriate the surplus revenue from monastic estates, but the estates themselves were not touched: in 1722 it was officially calculated that about a fifth of all the peasants in Russia had clerical landlords.

Side by side with this diversion of clerical wealth to secular purposes went an increasing insistence that the church must acknowledge, as never before, its subjection to the state and its duty to act as the agent and subordinate of the ruler. The solemn clerical anathematization of Mazepa in November 1708, on Peter's express orders, is an illustration of this. So is the oath which, from 1716, new bishops were obliged to take, and which tied their hands in several important respects. They could not increase the number of clergy in their dioceses or build 'unnecessary' churches. They must ensure that monks did not travel without their written permission, which was to be given only in exceptional cases. They were not to interfere in secular affairs and legal proceedings unless injustice were plainly being done; and then only after reporting the matter to the tsar.[36] The exaltation of the ruler's rights and power implicit in demands of this kind was made explicit in the writings of the man who was to become, from 1718 if not before, the dominant influence in Peter's church policies and later the first and perhaps the greatest propagator of the Petrine legend. This was Feofan Prokopovich, Archbishop of Novgorod, a highly cultivated Ukrainian well acquainted with western Europe and its ideas (notably certain forms of Protestantism, with which he had a good deal of sympathy). The width of his intellectual horizons and his grasp of the main currents of thought at work in the west are shown by the contents of his library of over 3,000 books, which entitle him to the description of 'the first authentic voice in Russia of the Early Enlightenment'.[37] His most important work, the *Pravda voli monarshei* (Right of the Monarchical Will) (1722), was written to justify Peter's claim, embodied in a decree issued in the previous year, to nominate his own successor. This claim Prokopovich strove to justify in terms of historical precedent and, more interestingly, of natural law, a west-European idea of profound significance which now made its first important appearance in Russian intellectual life. Like many western writers, he presupposed a fundamental and irrevocable contract between ruler and people by which the latter gave the former control over them. The monarch's powers were unlimited and his subjects' obligation to obey him absolute. Though he might and indeed should obey the law this was only to set a good example: there were no legal rights enforceable against him. This was a systematic statement of absolutist ideas of a kind hitherto unknown in Russia. Apart from the Bible, the main source of its arguments was the seventeenth-century English writer Thomas Hobbes, who had stated seventy years earlier, with a clarity shocking to his contemporaries, absolutist doctrines of a logical and secularist kind. It is highly significant that Prokopovich refers hardly at all to the patristic writers traditionally so important in Orthodox thought and consistently plays down any idea of an Orthodox ruler as in any essential way different from those of western Europe. His arguments are based on what he claims as the rights of 'every autocratic sovereign' and of 'sovereigns' in general. The book underlines the fact that by his later years Peter had laid the intellectual as well as the administrative foundations of a new kind of monarchy and state, and that this had been made possible largely by the weakening and subjection of the church.

Yet thoroughgoing change, as distinct from the mere exploitation of the church and its resources, came only in the very last years of the reign. In January 1721 a decree of fundamental importance, the *Dukhovnyi Reglament* (Spiritual Regulation) was issued: it placed the direction and control of the church in Russia on a basis which was not to alter in essentials for the next two centuries. This long document of some three hundred paragraphs was based on proposals elaborated by Prokopovich from 1718 onwards and adopted and altered in matters of detail by the tsar. Its central achievement was to create for the church a directing body similar to the administrative colleges with jurisdiction over various aspects of secular affairs which had begun to take shape in 1718–19. Like them it was composed of a president, a vice-president and eight other members. The similarity was underlined by the title first proposed for it, *Dukhovnaya Kollegiya* (Spiritual College), though this was soon changed to that of *Svyateishii Pravitel'-stvuyushchii Sinod* (Most Holy Directing Synod), a concession to traditional sensitivities aimed at disguising the fact that the new church leadership was an organ of the secular government. The Synod was to replace the patriarch and the church councils which had met in the past and to have jurisdiction in all spiritual matters and control of church property. (The *Monastyrskii Prikaz*, after a brief disappearance, was revived as a body subordinate to the Synod and charged with the control of monastic lands.)

Efforts were made to heighten the religious and spiritual status of the Synod. Its name was to replace that of the patriarch in the litany, an innovation which Prokopovich defended in a pamphlet, while Peter took the precaution of forcing all the major ecclesiastical dignitaries of Russia (except the Bishop of Tobolsk, in Siberia, who was too distant and inaccessible) to sign the Spiritual Regulation on issuance, as a sign of their acceptance and approval. None of this, however, could obscure the fact that the new machinery subjected the church to the control of the state and the ruler. In theory the Synod wielded all the powers of the patriarch. But it did not act as an independent authority, as the patriarchs of the seventeenth century had done, but as the agent of Peter. This subordination was for the tsar the essence of the new state of affairs. Indeed he explicitly justified the abolition of the patriarchate on the grounds that 'the ignorant Vulgar People do not consider how far the Spiritual Power is removed from, and inferior to, the Regal, but in Admiration of the Splendor and Dignity of an High-Priest consider such a Ruler as a second Sovereign, equal in power to the King himself, or above him.'[38] The new régime had been produced by Peter's decision, acting in virtue of the supreme and uncontrolled power which he now claimed. No church council was called to discuss the changes introduced in 1721. Nor were the Orthodox patriarchs outside Russia consulted, though in September 1723 they were brought to recognize the new Synod as their 'holy brother in Christ'. And, although a proposal that the Synod should include lay members was dropped and its membership was left entirely clerical, secular and governmental influences dominated it from the beginning. In 1722 the new and important office of its *Ober-Prokuror* was filled not by a churchman but by an army officer, I. V. Boltin. He was to supervise its work in general, see that its decisions were carried out and inform Peter of any wrong actions or disobedience committed by it. The practical effectiveness of the new body was thus monitored by a layman loyal to and completely dependent on the tsar. Peter had initially meant the Synod to be an equivalent in spiritual affairs of the Senate in secular ones; but this soon proved to be little more than an empty theory. Efforts to assert such an equality and to claim that the state was divided between a secular sphere over which the Senate presided and an equally important ecclesiastical one controlled by the Synod were unsuccessful. The tsar had apparently intended, in 1721, to pay a weekly, or at least monthly, visit to the Synod to supervise its work, but in fact he appears to have come to no more than half-a-dozen of its meetings in all before his death.[39] This is perhaps the surest of all indications of the feebleness of its grip on real power.

In Peter's last years there were intensified efforts to use the church and its resources as an arm of the government. A supplement to the Ecclesiastical Regulation, also issued in 1721, gave detailed instructions about the conduct of priests and shows the extent to which Peter intended to exploit them as his agents. They were to reveal any information given in confession which indicated an intention to commit a crime, especially those of treason or sedition. They were to administer in church an oath of loyalty to the tsar to all classes except the peasants. They were to keep registers of births, marriages and deaths in their parishes, forwarding the information every four months to their bishop, who would send it on to the Synod (this remained largely a dead letter). Superfluous clergy were to be eliminated by basing the permissible number on the census then in progress for the collection of the poll-tax. The assumption of clerical status to avoid taxation and state service would thus be repressed, but at the cost of asserting the principle that the size of the church was to be determined by secular and utilitarian considerations. The government-imposed tasks placed upon the clergy would make them increasingly part of the state machinery. This would cut them off from their flocks in a way hardly possible in Catholic or Protestant Europe: it was in this change that the significance of Peter's church reform lay so far as the ordinary Russian was concerned.

By the time of his death the tsar had welded the ecclesiastical administration firmly into the structure of centralized bureaucracy which he had, largely without any overall plan, created in Russia. This had some constructive results, notably a marked growth in the use of clerical resources for education. But these were achieved at the cost of draining the church of much of its remaining spiritual vitality and limiting drastically the contribution it might make to Russian life in the future. Henceforth the living forces of religious feeling, largely denied expression through the state-dominated mechanism of the official church, would find outlets increasingly in various forms of mysticism, many of them highly sectarian, inward-looking and even anarchical. Peter had won a victory, but in church affairs as elsewhere at the cost of the psychological price which has to be paid when a highly traditional society breaks radically with its past.

. . .

INTELLECTUAL AND CULTURAL LIFE

As has been seen, a far-reaching transformation of the intellectual and cultural aspects of Russian life was well under way long before Peter was born. By the second half of the seventeenth century the forces of change were too powerful to be withstood; and the way in which they could strengthen Russia had become too obvious for any ruler to wish to oppose them. Peter did little, at least until his later years, to strengthen, at its deepest levels, the new movement. What he did was to favour some aspects of it at the expense of others and to attempt, during much of his reign, to develop certain sides of it for his own purposes.

He deeply desired, however confused and tentative he sometimes was about how this might be achieved, to make Russia more powerful, more modern and more respected by its neighbours. This meant intellectual change and growth. Ignorance and obscurantism had to be fought, knowledge diffused on a far greater scale than before, a new outlook inculcated in, and if necessary forced upon, his subjects. He wished for a kind of intellectual revolution in Russia, of which education, in the broadest sense of the term, would be the mainspring. But for most of his reign the intellectual progress Peter hoped for was severely limited and utilitarian. His own tastes and inclinations were in part responsible for this: his passion for action, for concrete physical achievement of the most obvious kind, his impatient demand for quick and clearly visible results, had a negative as well as positive effect even in the 1680s and 1690s. After 1700 this practicality and utilitarianism seemed to him essential. The sort of knowledge

Russia needed, for victory in the war with Sweden and for the economic growth which was to be one of the foundations of that victory, was technical, often narrowly so. A mastery of shipbuilding, engineering, military and manufacturing techniques, and of enough mathematics and foreign languages to enable this to be acquired, was the immediate need. Everything else – the arts, philosophy, scientific ideas in a deeper and more general sense – could wait. Russia must be taught. But the teaching, for the time being at least, must be predominantly utilitarian, geared to satisfying immediate goals and meeting the insistent pressures of the war. The country must be urged, indeed coerced, from above into a new path; and in the process the printing press, hitherto so little developed, was an indispensable weapon. The flow of printed matter increased rapidly: in the later seventeenth century an average of a mere six titles were printed in Russia each year, while by the early 1720s this had grown to almost fifty. But throughout Peter's reign official pronouncements – laws, manifestos and regulations – made up well over half of all those which appeared.

Peter's tastes and values, and the situation in which he found himself, were also reflected in the west-European books translated into Russian during the early eighteenth century. An unprecedented number of translations was made; and Peter attached great importance to them and organized and encouraged their production. One of the most interesting fruits of his 'Great Embassy' to Europe was the establishment in Amsterdam, in 1698, of a printing-works under Jan Tessing which was to produce Russian versions of foreign works. Tessing and the translator who provided most of his material, I. F. Kopievskii, a Protestant Ukrainian, played for a time a role of real significance in Russian intellectual life.[40] Of the young Russians educated in western Europe during Peter's reign, some sixty were employed as translators on their return home, though not all of these translated books. But the foreign works made available in Russian were markedly, even predominantly, concerned with military and naval affairs, artillery, fortifications and engineering.[41] Books such as this gave some stimulus to intellectual change, but one of a rather specialized kind. Foreign textbooks in Russian translation, or Russian ones based on foreign originals, also played a significant role in Peter's educational plans. Moreover it is important to remember that religious, and particularly devotional, literature such as Books of Hours or psalters, were, under Peter, produced in much greater numbers than ever before. They remained, as in the past, the only form of printed work which most Russians, even if literate, wished to read.

The same demand for down-to-earthness and avoidance of unnecessary flourishes is seen in Peter's instruction that the Russian used in translation of foreign books should be one which avoided 'high Slavonic words' and used 'not high words but simple Russian speech'. The simplified 'civic alphabet' (as distinct from the Old Church Slavonic one) introduced in 1700 is yet another reflection of this attitude: Peter explicitly ordered that books which dealt with historical, commercial or military subjects should be printed in it. The order was not completely obeyed; but such an attitude had real significance. It helped to lay the foundations of a literacy which, however limited, would be wider than in the past. More important, it was to be a literacy no longer focused on religious purposes and the reading of sacred texts. During his own lifetime, however, Peter could do little to improve or stabilize the Russian language. The great influx of foreign words which was a result of his policies did much to confuse the linguistic picture. Until well after his death Russian had only a somewhat arbitrary grammatical structure; and the new elements which were entering its vocabulary took time to digest. His own letters, a bizarre amalgam of often ungrammatical Russian and foreign (usually German or Dutch) words, are in their own way as hard to read as the Baroque rhetoric, full of pseudo-classical allusions and borrowings from Polish, which had been admired in late seventeenth-century Russia. Besides, the 'simple Russian speech' which he demanded of his translators owed more to the style used in the bureaucracy, the army and diplomacy than to the language of ordinary Russians. Nevertheless, even in questions of literary style, we can discern the quest for usefulness which coloured every aspect of Peter's thinking.

The same practicality, the effort to make knowledge the vehicle of concrete achievement, can be seen as an element in Peter's pioneering efforts to assemble reliable information about Russia and its resources. Satisfactory maps, hitherto almost entirely lacking, were one of the most essential aspects of such information. A reasonably accurate map of the Ukraine and the Black Sea area was published by Tessing in 1699, while Peter seems as early as 1710 to have conceived the idea of a geographical survey of the entire country. In the last years of his reign there was a systematic effort to realize this plan. In 1715 and 1720 orders were given for the sending of pupils from the new Naval Academy to the provinces for the accurate mapping of Russia; when Peter died maps of about 12 per cent of all the land area of the empire had been drawn and sent to the Senate.[42] Between 1716 and 1720 part of the shores of the Caspian was surveyed. Siberia, less known than any other part of the empire and with greater long-term potentialities, particularly attracted Peter's attention. From 1710, on several occasions he ordered officials in Siberia to gather geographical information. These orders paved the way for the long series of Siberian journeys begun in 1720 by Daniel Messerschmidt, a German in Russian service (the first travels purely for scholarly research purposes ever undertaken in Russia). From 1719 onwards Peter made efforts to solve one of the greatest remaining puzzles of geographers, the question of whether or not eastern Siberia was joined to North America: orders for the decisive voyage of exploration, that of the Dane Titus Bering, were given at the end of 1724, only a few weeks before the tsar's death.

This practicality and emphasis on immediate benefits and concrete achievement were also reflected in the advice Peter received from some of his associates and from would-be reformers. In their down-to-earth character and their occasional mingling of the far-reaching and the trivial these are typical of the 'literature of projects' so widespread in much of western Europe at this time. Thus the proposals made by F. S. Saltykov in 1713–14 included, as well as large-scale educational developments, the establishment of factories, the creation of trading companies, the sending abroad of the sons of merchants for commercial training, the discovery of a north-east passage and the establishment of a ferry across the Neva. I. T. Pososhkov, the other leading representative of this type of thinking, was a factory-owner and merchant and the son of a peasant craftsman, a background which almost certainly influenced his ideas. He was clearly a genuine entrepreneur, the first such in Russia of whom we have reasonably adequate knowledge: he was at various times a distiller, and concerned with the minting of money, while he acquired a good deal of land and finally tried to become a linen manufacturer.

In his *Kniga o skudosti i bogatstve* (Book concerning Poverty and Wealth), written in 1724, he suggested the union of all Russian merchants in a single company for the carrying on of foreign trade, a mercantilist commercial policy, the regulation of serfdom in the interests of the peasants and a wide-ranging educational programme. Very daringly, he envisaged even peasants being taught to read and write.[43] In their willingness to disregard tradition and readiness to borrow foreign ideas and techniques, but selectively and for purely Russian purposes, these projects are very much in the spirit of the tsar's own thinking. They show how, at least by the second half of his reign, Peter had recruited followers, enthusiastic and often vocal, who looked to him as the regenerator of his country and indeed the creator of a new Russia. A Petrine school of thought on Russia's problems and potentialities had now come into existence. The foundations of a Petrine tradition were being laid.

Any significant and lasting change in Russian intellectual life had to depend upon a growth of education. Peter made efforts to attain this; but their success was very limited. At one level, that of technical training directed largely to the needs of the armed forces, a good deal was achieved. A school of mathematics and navigation (whose pupils were used not merely as navigators but as architects, engineers and hydrographers) was set up in Moscow in 1701. Peter hoped that it would eventually have five hundred pupils; and in fact it had two hundred within a couple of years of its foundation. A naval academy established in St Petersburg in 1715 was meant largely to complete the work of the Moscow school by providing practical training in seamanship: it too had considerable success though its severe discipline drove many of its pupils to truancy and flight. An artillery school founded in 1701 had three hundred pupils by 1704, though the numbers fell considerably after that date. An engineering school established in Moscow in 1712 was at first less successful. Indirectly, moreover, the demands of the army and navy, and of the war effort in general, stimulated other educational efforts of a less obviously war-oriented character: a series of language schools which by 1715 had produced about 250 young Russians with some knowledge of foreign tongues; a school of medicine in Moscow, opened in 1707, which five years later had fifty students; a school of mining set up in 1716.

These were considerable achievements. Nevertheless, they did little more than skim the surface of the problem. Few of the new schools were large and many of them (the Naval Academy, for example) catered almost entirely for the sons of the military and official class. Further down the social and intellectual scale it was very difficult to achieve much of lasting value. It was decreed in 1714 that two graduates of the Moscow navigation school should be sent to each province to teach 'ciphers' (arithmetic) and a little geometry to the sons of landlords and officials. This was the cornerstone of an ambitious plan to force the ruling class to provide its sons with at least an elementary education. It was backed up by one of the most notorious and typical of Peter's decrees – without a certificate that he had satisfactorily completed the course no young member of a noble or gentry family could marry. The fact, however, that the 'ciphering' schools were open also to members of other classes led to strong opposition from the landlords, which did much to reduce their effectiveness. At the end of the reign there were over forty of these schools with some 2,000 pupils. Two years later, however, with the removal of the great tsar and his threatening presence, the number of pupils had been reduced to five hundred. 'Garrison schools' for the sons of soldiers made some contribution to educational progress: in 1717, for example, that in St Petersburg had 159 pupils. But these too were inadequate, in both numbers and quality of teaching, to do more than touch the fringes of the problem. No really extensive system of education, even at a relatively low level, was possible in Petrine Russia. Lack of money, of trained teachers, most important of all of any demand for such an innovation, all set narrow limits to what could be achieved; and Peter's own impetuosity and lack of sustained attention to the subject made any lasting advance difficult.

This educational effort, whatever its shortcomings, had nonetheless the advantage of stimulating a considerable output of textbooks of various kinds. Tessing, for example, produced introductions to history, arithmetic and astronomy around the turn of the century. Increasingly, moreover, these were Russian productions and not translations or adaptations of foreign works. Thus the first important Russian primer for the teaching of reading appeared in 1701 and a Russian grammar in 1706. A textbook of arithmetic, which dealt also with algebra, geometry and trigonometry, made its appearance in 1703 and the first Russian work on dynamics in 1722. In 1710 the first Russian textbook of geography, apparently based on a Dutch original, appeared in Moscow. All this, coupled with such changes as the general use of Arabic numerals after 1700 (they had been known in Russia much earlier but little used) and the publication in 1702 of the first Russian calendar (by Kopievskii in Amsterdam) meant real, though uneven, progress.

To the picture of technical schools supplemented by a very limited structure of elementary education some additions must be made. Not every successful educational institution in Petrine Russia was purely or even mainly vocational. The Moscow Academy, which had flourished for several years after its establishment in 1685, suffered a severe blow in 1693 when the Likhud brothers were denounced by the Patriarch of Jerusalem and confined to a monastery because of the Latin and Catholic elements in their teaching. In 1701, however, the Academy was revived by Stefan Yavorskii and rapidly became the most important centre in Russia of Catholic thought and ideas. Staffed by Ukrainians (nearly all its teachers came from Kiev) and with a student body which was at first mainly Ukrainian, Polish or White Russian, it illustrates the degree to which any intellectual innovation in Russia beyond the technical kind still depended on influences from the Ukraine. By the 1720s the strength of these influences meant that a type of school normal over much of Europe, largely Jesuit in inspiration and providing a classical education based on Latin, rhetoric and philosophy, could be found in many parts of Russia. These schools, though staffed by clergy, freely admitted laymen as pupils, and were to be of real and lasting importance. The fact that a high proportion of the Russian episcopate was still of Ukrainian origin did much to encourage their development; and in the half-century which followed Peter's death they made a large contribution to the development of Russian life and culture.[44]

Their growth, however, though powerfully encouraged by Feofan Prokopovich (a product of this type of school who had himself taught in the Kiev Academy), owed nothing to the tsar. On the other hand Peter personally planned with great care the establishment of the Academy of Sciences which began to function a few months after his death and was the most significant intellectual achievement of his reign. As early as 1720 he approached Christian Wolff, Professor of Philosophy and Physics at Halle and the dominant figure in German academic life, for help in setting up such an institution; and in 1721–22 his librarian, J. D. Schumacher, toured much of western Europe in an effort to establish contacts with eminent foreign scholars. The Academy, which from the first was designed as a teaching institution as well as a centre of research, soon acquired a European reputation. This would have greatly pleased Peter had he lived longer; for one important motive behind the creation of the Academy was a desire to show western Europe that Russia was now capable of maintaining an institution of learning of the highest quality. It was set up partly, as Peter himself admitted, 'to gain for us trust and honour in Europe, to show . . . that in our country also we work for science and that it is time to stop regarding us as barbarians who hold all learning in contempt'.[45] For a long time, however, its reputation owed little or nothing to Russian scholarship. It had no Russian member until the mathematician Adadurov became an 'adjunct' in 1733; and not until 1742 did a Russian (the poet, scientist and polymath Lomonosov) become a full member.

The foundation of the Academy and the intensified efforts to stimulate geographical research are only two of a number of symptoms of a change in Peter's attitudes to intellectual life during the last decade or more of his reign. As the pressures of the war with Sweden relaxed, his interests gained in both depth and width. The need to strengthen Russia by borrowing foreign methods and techniques was now supplemented by an increasing desire fully to understand what was borrowed. On the great journey of 1697–98, he had admired the skills of western Europe: on his journey to France and the Netherlands in 1717 he studied and analyzed what he saw in greater depth. At about the same time he began to buy books on a much larger scale than before; and some of them – for example the thirty-six volume work on the history of the Byzantine empire bought in Amsterdam in February 1717 – were of more than technical or vocational interest. Schumacher, on his return to Russia in 1722, brought almost six hundred books bought abroad for the tsar.

Peter also began for the first time to pay serious attention to the fine arts. By 1716 he was avidly buying pictures through an agent in Amsterdam. In the same year he asked the Grand Duke Cosimo III of Tuscany to allow young Russians to study painting at the Academy in Florence. Two years later another agent

135

was buying pictures and statues for him in Rome and trying to recruit sculptors and painters for work in Russia, where the building of St Petersburg was providing opportunities for such skills. Peter's interest in the past also grew in his later years. As early as 1708 he had set in train the writing of a history of Russia during the seventeenth and eighteenth centuries; though neither this nor the more important *Yadro rossiiskoi istorii* (Kernel of Russian History) which A. I. Mankiev completed in 1715 were ever published. In 1716 the tsar had a copy made for himself of the Königsberg manuscript of the Nestorian Chronicle (the fundamental source for the early history of Russia); and in several decrees in the early 1720s he ordered provincial governors and vice-governors to search out manuscripts of historical interest and send them to Moscow so that copies could be made and preserved in the library of the Synod. The brash young man of the 1690s, with his narrow enthusiasms and limited interests, had by the time of his death broadened intellectually in a most impressive way.

The new intellectual and cultural forces at work in Russia found both a symbol and a geographical focus in St Petersburg. By the autumn of 1704, not much more than a year after the fortress of Sanktpiterburg on the island of Lust-Eland had been built for defence against the Swedes, Peter was beginning to think of the city now emerging around it as his new capital, though it was not formally proclaimed as such until 1712. The desires to launch a Russian fleet on the Baltic and to have a port there for trade with western Europe were probably the main motives behind the transfer of the seat of power. It would also be easier to carry on an active foreign policy and to exert influence in Europe from the new city than from distant Moscow. Moreover, conservative opposition to change would be greatly weakened in a new capital built on conquered territory and with no history of its own. For some years the danger of a successful Swedish counter-attack which might deprive Peter of his creation persisted; but this vanished in 1708 when a last effort by the forces of Charles XII to recover the lost lands at the mouth of the Neva was repulsed. By 1710, following the capture by the Russians of Viborg, the new capital was secure.

Its growth, helped by incessant government direction and compulsion, was rapid. The establishment of an extensive apparatus of government offices in St Petersburg (the great

Admiralty fortress and shipyard dates from 1705) was one aspect of this. Another was the forced settlement in the new city of workers of many kinds: from the summer of 1705 this became a settled policy embodied in a long sequence of decrees. In particular large numbers of skilled men such as carpenters and smiths, together with their wives and children, were drafted to St Petersburg and compelled to settle there. In August 1710, for example, the despatch of almost 5,000 such craftsmen was ordered. Later, in 1719, all landowners possessing more than forty serf households were commanded to build a house on Vassilievskii Island, which Peter now wished to make the centre of the city, and to live there themselves. Measures of this kind inevitably proved hard to enforce. Russian nobles and gentry resented bitterly removal from their estates, hundreds or even thousands of miles away, to the fogs and floods of the Neva and to a city where life was so much more expensive and demanding than anywhere else. The description of the new city by one of Peter's jesters, 'On one side the sea, on the other sorrow, on the third moss, on the fourth a sigh', must have struck a responsive chord in many hearts. Yet at whatever cost in tears and curses, in suffering and death, the new city rapidly took shape. By 1710 it had a permanent population of at least 8,000; and by the time of the tsar's death in 1725 this had grown to 40,000.

Its trade, like every other aspect of its existence, was the outcome of direction from above. From 1713 there were sustained though not completely successful efforts to encourage commercial growth by giving the new city a monopoly of the export of many Russian products – tar, potash, caviar, certain types of leather. From 1720 it was favoured over Archangel, now declining but still its main rival in trade with western Europe, by differential customs duties. Foreign merchants in Russia were encouraged or forced to settle in St Petersburg: the British factory was obliged to move there from Moscow in 1723. Every step in its growth, moreover, was watched with a jealous and paternal eye by the tsar himself. When in 1713 the first Dutch ship arrived in the new capital it was greeted with joy by Peter, who acted in person as its pilot and had a special medal struck to commemorate the occasion. Well before his death his new creation, arisen at his command like a phoenix from the dreary marshes of the Gulf of Finland, had begun to arouse the admiration of foreign observers. 'At present', wrote Weber, the

Hanoverian minister in the early 1720s, 'Petersbourg may with Reason be looked upon as a Wonder of the World, considering its magnificent Palaces, sixty odd thousand houses [the true number was much less] and the short time that was employed in the building of it.'[46]

Even Peter could not totally disregard tradition in the creation of his new city. It had to be linked, as Moscow and Kiev had been for centuries, with a great religious foundation. Thus the Alexander Nevskii monastery was founded there in 1710 (though it is significant that the saint to whom it was dedicated had been in life a warrior-prince, not a monk). But the spirit and tone of life in St Petersburg was different from that in any other Russian city. Distinct groups soon came to predominate in different parts of it – Admiralty workers on Admiralty Island; skilled workers and soldiers on Gorodskii Island; landowners and peasants on Vassilievskii Island – but society, because of the sheer newness and rawness of the environment, tended to be more open and to involve more mixture of classes than was normal in Russia. Foreigners were more in evidence than anywhere else in the country and foreign influences more powerful and pervasive. Active supporters and collaborators of Peter were much thicker on the ground than in Moscow; and the presence in the new capital of a larger concentration of powerful men favourable to the tsar's ideas and ambitions and receptive to foreign influences gave St Petersburg a unique atmosphere.

This was reflected in the physical appearance of the city. It was the first in Russia to be planned. Peter demanded that the streets be broad, straight and paved with stone. Houses were to be built flush with the street and not to stand back from it in courtyards as was traditional in other Russian cities. In this way a continuous façade would be achieved and a greater effect produced on the onlooker. Stone and brick were to be used, at least for the more important buildings, to reduce the ever-present fire risk. A decree of October 1714 forbade new building in masonry anywhere in Russia except in St Petersburg, and this seems to have been strictly enforced, for such building in Moscow, where hitherto Peter had encouraged it, came to an immediate stop. Yet there were limits to what could be achieved. Even at the tsar's death the new capital was still predominantly one of wooden houses and fires were frequent. Nonetheless his passionate desire to beautify his new creation in every possible way is clear. In 1711 Peter had a model cottage built and commanded the inhabitants to copy it when erecting their own houses. In 1714 it was ordered that houses should conform to standard patterns drawn up by official architects, one for members of each social class, while in the following year all building was forbidden unless it followed plans approved by the government. Efforts of this kind at uniformity soon broke down: houses throughout much of the city became as varied in appearance as in other Russian towns. However in one notable respect, its regular street-plan, St Petersburg betrayed the extent to which it was a deliberate creation and not an organic growth. The highly ambitious scheme drawn up in 1716 by the French architect Leblond, which would have given the city a neat but unrealistic oval shape, was not carried out; but it is symptomatic of the conscious planning which bulked so large in its early history.

In the building and adornment of the new city foreigners played a leading role. It has been estimated that at least 1,000 experts and craftsmen from western Europe worked in various capacities to create St Petersburg: their presence is reflected in the fact that by 1717 the city already had three Lutheran churches and a Catholic one. Its position as a gateway through which west-European influences could enter Russia is self-evident. Architects such as the Swiss Nikolaus Friedrich Härbel, the Germans Gottfried Schädel and Georg Johann Mattarnovy, or the Italian Domenico Trezzini; sculptors, painters, gardeners and other skilled artists and craftsmen from many countries (most notably perhaps from France), coupled with the labour of conscripted Russians and latterly Swedish prisoners of war, had by Peter's death made St Petersburg in its own way one of the wonders of Europe. There was, however, another respect, perhaps the most striking of all, in which the city led the way in the adoption by the upper ranks of Russian society of west-European manners and values. It was the new capital which saw the first serious effort to improve the status of Russian women, to bring them out of the seclusion in which, at least among the landowning and well-to-do classes, they had so long been kept. As early as March 1699 women had appeared publicly at a dinner given by Peter in Moscow for the representative of the Elector of Brandenburg and had taken part in the dancing afterwards. This, however, was regarded as 'a great departure from Russian manners' and not for another twenty years did Peter move much further in this direction. Then, in a decree of December 1718, he ordered the establishment of 'assemblies' in his new capital. These gatherings of officials, officers and even merchants met as a rule three times a week during the winter months and offered a variety of different entertainments – dancing, chess, draughts and smoking. The tsar decreed that they must be attended by the womenfolk of the men invited; this compulsory presence of women was a total break with Muscovite tradition, one of the sharpest Peter ever made. Outside a narrow circle in St Petersburg and later in Moscow, to which the 'assemblies' spread, the position of women, however, remained unchanged: to alter it by decree was beyond the power of any government, even had there been real desire to do this. Even in the official society of St Petersburg, it was one thing to put women in west-European dress and expose them to a coarsened form of west-European manners, but quite another to give them the self-confidence needed to allow them to take advantage of the new situation. Foreign observers remarked on this. Weber pointed out that they 'appear indeed perfectly well dressed after the foreign Fashion; but in Conversation with Strangers, they cannot yet conquer their in-born Bashfulness and Awkwardness.'[47] The Holstein representative, Bergholtz, complained in his diary that 'the ladies always sit separately from the men, so that not only can one not converse with them, but it is almost impossible to say a word to them; when they are not dancing they all sit as though they were dumb and do nothing but look at each other.'[48] In a sense, then, Peter's assemblies had little more than curiosity value; but they show yet again the extent to which he was prepared to break with Muscovite tradition.

His efforts to develop and improve the intellectual and cultural climate of Russia had thus only limited success. They reached only a tiny segment of the population. Insofar as they were successful at all, they widened the gap between a small educated and westernized minority and the mass of the population which was quite untouched by these new forces. Snobbery widened this gap still further. By the later years of the reign can be seen in the upper ranks of society a tendency, which became more marked in the decades which followed, to use to an excessive degree foreign terms and phrases as a sign of enlightenment and up-to-dateness. Russian by comparison seemed the language of peasants and artisans. Thus a guide to good behaviour for young gentlemen published in 1717 urged them, as a sign of education and breeding, to converse if possible in a foreign language, especially in the presence of servants.[49] This reflected a division which went much deeper. Increasingly the officer or official who had been trained in one of the new schools and had some contact with new and foreign ideas had access to a mental universe closed to the peasant or craftsman whose horizons remained what they had been for centuries. This intellectual dichotomy was probably less complete than many historians have claimed. For a long time after Peter's reign most members of the Russian ruling class, brought up largely by peasant nurses, sharing popular pieties and superstitions and during their formative years in close contact with peasant life, continued to know and understand the culture of the masses. Nevertheless the intellectual world typified by St Petersburg was one very distant from that in which the vast majority of Russians still lived. Orthodox piety and the immense weight of religious tradition, quite apart from the material difficulties of lack of money and trained teachers, put any thorough transformation of Russian intellectual life out of the question at this time. Side by side with a new élite with largely technical or vocational training there still lived the masses whose imaginations were nourished and views of the world formed by the ceremonies and liturgy of the Church and by a rich repertory of traditional folk-tales. Even among the educated it was still too soon to hope for much creativity of an imaginative kind. A significant modern Russian literature began to evolve only in the middle of the century, under Peter's daughter, the Empress Elizabeth.

The foreign and imported character of much of the educational effort of these years is especially striking. Every one of the technical and vocational schools set up in Russia during Peter's reign had a foreigner as its first head: in this sphere influences from Protestant northern Europe, from the Netherlands, Germany and Great Britain, were predominant. The Moscow Academy and the diocesan schools which it inspired owed almost everything to Ukrainian and Polish influences. The new Academy of Sciences was for long made up completely of foreigners. Throughout his life Peter hoped and worked for the creation of a new intellectual atmosphere, at least at the top of Russian society. He hoped, indeed, for nothing less than the creation of a new type of Russian man, enterprising, public-spirited, open to new ideas, free from inherited prejudices. In this striving he was not wholly unsuccessful. Men of this type, passionate admirers of the tsar, guardians of his heritage and creators of a legend of his achievements, did emerge. But for all their importance they were a tiny minority conscious of fighting an uphill struggle for change and modernization. Eighteenth-century society everywhere in Europe was marked by a cleavage between an educated minority at the top and a dead weight of ignorance and conservatism at the bottom. In no major state was the gulf between the two so wide as in Russia: but Peter cannot be fairly blamed for having widened it. Russia's development, perhaps even its survival, demanded the rapid production of an educated élite with some knowledge of modern techniques and ideas for which he strove.

. . .

THE ADMINISTRATION AND THE ADMINISTERED

The machinery of government which Peter inherited had many defects. It was both primitive and complex. In terms of the area and even the population of Russia it was not large: at the end of the seventeenth century the entire central administration, exclusive of scribes, probably employed only about 2,000 men. It was none the less often cumbersome and slow-moving. The distinctions between legislation, administrative instructions and judicial decisions were still blurred. The administrative machine remained, in the last analysis, merely a hierarchy of officials collecting taxes and tribute, a structure with its roots in the Mongol era of medieval Russia.

Central administration was carried on in the main by the *prikazy*, departments each of which was responsible for a particular aspect of policy (e.g., the *Posolskii Prikaz* for foreign affairs) or for a wide range of functions in particular geographical areas (e.g., the *Sibirskii Prikaz* for Siberia). This system was confusing and irrational. The powers and responsibilities of the various departments often overlapped and conflicted in a bewildering way, while they could be created and suppressed with an ease which made the entire structure remarkably fluid and unstable. Much of the machinery of government could thus be adapted to the wishes or caprices of the ruler more rapidly and with less resistance than elsewhere in Europe. Powerful and deeply rooted institutions with real independent vitality, capable of resisting, at least to some extent, the demands of the monarch, were notably lacking in Russia. Such was the variety of central departments and the variation of their titles and functions that it is hard to say with certainty how many *prikazy* there were at any given moment: in 1699 there may have been forty-four.

The need for rationalization was vaguely recognized. In the 1690s there was a tendency for the headship of a number of different departments to become concentrated in the hands of a single man, so that for a number of years F. A. Golovin, for example, was in charge of as many as six simultaneously. But this did little to modify an archaic system which was the product of unplanned growth over a long period. The boyar council (*Boyarskaya Duma*), the group of great nobles which had traditionally advised the tsars, was now in decay and quite unable to provide central direction of the administration. Even its membership was rapidly declining: in 1691–92 it had had, at least on paper, 182 members, while a decade later this had shrunk to 86. The number who in fact attended meetings in the 1690s seems to have been no more than 30–40, and by then it had little to do with really important affairs of state. Though it was never formally abolished it had in effect ceased to exist by about 1704. Its powers had been taken over by a small and fluctuating group of advisers, with no corporate organization or status, whose importance depended entirely upon their personal influence with the tsar.

In the provinces, administration was in the hands of the *voevody*, governors stationed in provincial towns. These were often not effectively controlled by the central government and could easily develop into local tyrants against whom it was hard to secure protection or redress. Most of them were old 'serving men' with military experience; and their resources, in terms of subordinates, money, or even accurate information about their areas and the people they ruled, were too slight to make effective provincial government possible in a huge, underpopulated country with very poor communications. To the Russian peasant his village community, the church and the local landlords were the forces which regulated his daily life. By comparison the central government and its agents were remote and often almost incomprehensible, merely the source of demands to be evaded if possible. Where the grip of the government was effective it could be severe, even crushing. But the sheer impossibility of administering Russia with the available resources meant that the grip was intermittent and often almost non-existent. The seventeenth century was a time of considerable growth in the size of the bureaucracy.[50] In some areas, notably Siberia and northern Russia, the difficulty of recruiting only from the traditional landowning 'serving men' brought into it members of other social groups – sons of townsmen, churchmen or the better-off peasants. But the whole structure of administration remained primitive both in organization and in the numbers and quality of its members (it was not unusual for a *voevod* to be illiterate). Its traditional nature was underlined by the extent to which officials were still paid in grants of land as well as, or instead of, money.

For most of his reign Peter had no systematic plan for improving the governmental machine. The war with Sweden made more effective administration necessary to obtain the recruits, taxes and forced labour which it demanded. But for many years efforts to improve the administration were partial, hasty and unconsidered, the work of a man preoccupied by other pressing tasks. Nevertheless Peter had a number of basic ideas about the government of Russia and his own place in it which underlay all he attempted in this sphere.

He accepted without question the rightness and necessity of his own absolute power; and in the later years of his reign explicit statements of this kind, either by the tsar himself or by apologists such as Prokopovich, become more common. In 1716, for example, the *Ustav Voinskii* proclaimed that Peter 'is not obliged to answer to anyone in the world for his doings, but possesses power and authority over his kingdom and land, to rule them at his will and pleasure as a Christian ruler'. Nevertheless, this power was to be used only for the benefit of Russia. Far more than any of his predecessors, Peter felt a responsibility for ensuring this. From the early years of the eighteenth century onwards (the first example seems to be in the proclamation of 1702 which invited suitable foreigners to enter his service) his decrees frequently claim to serve the general good. Such repeated and explicit admission of the ruler's duty to secure this was something new in Russian history: the fact that he made it so frequently and sincerely is one of the strongest of Peter's claims to be considered in some sense an early example of 'Enlightened Despotism'.

How was this general good, which was superior to the interests of any particular class or group, to be achieved? Essentially, Peter believed, by all the different orders of society performing their distinct functions loyally and efficiently. This required careful regulation by the tsar and his advisers of the doings of both institutions and individuals. Peter never hesitated to interfere with the smallest details of the private life of his subjects if he felt this justified: his reign produced legislation forbidding peasants to weave cloth of less than a specified width, prohibiting the playing of cards for money and enforcing by fines the good behaviour of the faithful in church. The increase in the quantity of legislation was startling. In the second half of the seventeenth century an average of only thirty-six official decrees were issued each year, while in the first half of the eighteenth, thanks to Peter and the tradition he created, the number rose to 160. Of all the published material of Peter's reign perhaps seventy per cent was made up of laws intended to control and direct the tsar's subjects, or of calendars and similar government publications meant to inform them.[51] Much of this legislation was mere futile nagging, which was soon forgotten and had no practical effect. Almost every 'enlightened despot' in the second half of the eighteenth century (Joseph II's régime in the Habsburg territories is an outstanding example) succumbed at times to the temptation to behave in this way. Yet behind the flood of hasty and sometimes contradictory decrees can be seen a deep and genuine striving, however confused, towards the greatness and betterment of Russia.

For a long time Peter's efforts to improve the machinery of administration were tentative and experimental. Not until well into the second decade of the eighteenth century, when the war with Sweden was clearly won, did they become systematic and deliberate. Nevertheless, some important and lasting innovations were made even while the struggles with Sweden and the Turks were still uppermost in Peter's mind. The greatest of these, as far as central government was concerned, was the creation of the Senate in 1711. This was a body of nine officials originally set up to replace the tsar when he himself set out for the struggle with the Turks (the decree establishing it was issued on the day war was declared against the Ottoman empire) but which became a permanent institution with wide-ranging functions.

It was meant to supervise provincial administration and the collection of taxes, as well as acting as the highest judicial authority – a good example of the intertwining of justice with administration which was probably more marked in Russia than in any other European state. At first all its decisions had to be unanimous; but from 1714 the principle of majority decisions became accepted.

Peter regulated the Senate's work with great care. In 1711 at least six decrees on this subject were issued; and several others appeared in the years which followed. In 1714 it was ordered that different senators should be on duty each day in the senatorial chancery, preparing questions for discussion and making ready for meetings: each was to keep an official diary of his actions during these duty periods. Two years later the senators were ordered to work after dinner if necessary as well as before, while they were to hold meetings three times each week (from 1718 this became four or five times) and to be fined 50 roubles for every day of absence from sittings without good cause.[52] They were not to indulge in idle conversation while business was being transacted, or to interrupt each other or work in a disorganized way. Breaches of these provisions were to be punished by fines for the first and second offences, while a third would mean three days' imprisonment and a fine of 100 roubles. Such provisions show the tight rein on which Peter tried to keep even the most important of his subordinates, and the genuineness of his efforts to enforce high standards of efficiency. As far as the Senate was concerned, these efforts had almost as little success as those lower down the administrative hierarchy. Of the original nine members one was illiterate and unable even to sign decrees, while in 1715 two were severely punished for corruption. Nevertheless, at least in its capacity as a supreme court of law, it was a legacy of Peter's which was to endure for two centuries.

Another bequest of lasting significance was the creation of the *fiskals* in 1711. These hated officials, five hundred in all, were to ferret out offences of all kinds which weakened the government and the war effort – tax evasion, theft and embezzlement of public money. Their task was defined simply as that of 'secretly spying on all things'; and they were ordered to report to the Senate and, in especially important cases, to the tsar himself. Here again, however, Peter had to face the fact that no amount of regulations could compensate for the deficiencies of the men through whom he had to work. The *fiskals* themselves soon became notorious for their corruption and oppressiveness.

In provincial government the early years of the eighteenth century were a period of great strain and confusion. The demands of the tsar and the central authorities reached unprecedented heights. Popular discontent was intense; and the revolts of 1705–6 and 1708 showed how dangerous it might become. The old system was clearly unable to cope effectively with this situation. For this reason Peter created in 1708 eight enormous territorial divisions, the *gubernii*, to which in 1713–14 three more were added. Most of the *gubernii* were divided into provinces, which in turn were sub-divided into *uezdy*, relatively small and manageable units. Over each *guberniya* presided a governor and a vice-governor, who controlled both the military forces and the civilian administration of the area. Under them functioned a hierarchy of officials with specialized functions and titles which were often, revealingly, foreign – the *ober-kommandant*, the *ober-kommissar*, the *ober-proviantmeister* and the *landrichter*. All this was an important step in the process by which Russia, under Peter, was equipped with an elaborate framework of bureaucratic rule. Henceforth this was to act on society like a rigid corset, sustaining it but at the same time compressing the living flesh and distorting its growth. The changes of 1708, however, were merely the beginning of a long process of experiment and often ill-considered change in provincial administration. In 1713–14 a remarkable effort was made to subject the governors to control by elected councils of landowners in each *guberniya* and thus to introduce an element, however limited, of self-government into the structure; but this was ineffective and short-lived. In 1715 the *uezdy* were replaced by *doli*, new units each of which, in theory, contained exactly 5,536 tax-paying households. The artificiality of these units as compared to the natural and traditional character of the *uezdy* shows that Peter failed to understand the problem and how he was always attracted by simple and authoritarian solutions.

These constant changes produced little except confusion in the countryside. In themselves they were of only temporary significance. Side by side with them, however, went a development with great and lasting implications for the whole future of Russian society. This was the consolidation of the landowning class, through the deliberate and sustained action of the tsar, as

147

a group of hereditary state servants who must serve the ruler in the armed forces or the bureaucracy as a condition of retaining their social position and their lands.

The idea that service was owed to the ruler as a condition of holding an estate and serfs was by no means new. Peter, however, pushed this obligation to lengths hitherto unheard-of, changing its whole scope and nature. In the seventeenth century service had meant in effect relatively short periods of army duty, interrupted in a few cases by diplomatic or other special missions; and even this had not been rigidly enforced. Now it rapidly assumed a much more mixed and comprehensive character. The new navy, deeply disliked and hardly understood by many Russian landowners, began to compete with the army for their services. Work in the bureaucracy became a regular and systematic obligation for those unfit for or retired from the armed forces, though for long military service continued to carry greater prestige as the only truly 'noble' form of service. Even more important, service now became a lifetime commitment, a deeply onerous duty which took men from their families and estates for years or even decades at a stretch and inflicted on them real financial loss and personal suffering. The relatively easy-going atmosphere of Muscovite Russia had allowed many members of the gentry to bury themselves in their villages for long periods, immersed in local issues and indifferent to national ones and matters of high policy. This now became increasingly difficult.

The old service registers were revised and kept up to date more carefully than in the past: in 1711 those hitherto maintained by the *Razryadnyi Prikaz*, the seventeenth-century body responsible for the enforcement of state service by landlords, were transferred to the new Senate. Regular musters of young gentry were held so that none should slip through the official net. In 1722 the new post of *Heroldmeister* was created to supervise this work; and two years later its holder was ordered to draw up careful new lists of all those liable for service, bringing together for this purpose the records of the former *Razryadnyi Prikaz*, the Senate and the new War and Admiralty Colleges. Young men who evaded their liability for service were threatened with severe punishment. In 1714 a deeply unpopular attack was launched on the traditional rights and position of the landholding class when a decree forbade the division of landed estates between the sons of the owner in accordance with longstanding custom. Instead they were to pass undivided to one son (not necessarily the eldest), if there were no sons to a daughter, and failing both sons and daughters to some other relative. This did not amount to the creation of a system of entail in Russia, though it has sometimes been described as such and Peter seems to have been influenced by information from Saltykov about the existing law of entail in England. It applied to the lands held by townsmen as well as to those of the gentry and nobility, and the tsar's main motive in introducing it was not simply to prevent the division of estates for its own sake. He wished in the first place to safeguard the existence of a group of wealthy nobles with substantial landholdings; and also to force into state service young members of the traditional state-servant class by making it impossible for them to vegetate in the provinces on a share of their father's lands. 'Division of land among children after the father's death', proclaimed the decree in question, 'is a great hurt to our state, to both the interests of the government and those of the subjects', since 'everyone, being able to live without working, although poorly, will not serve the state or exert himself unless he is forced to, but tries to evade service and live in idleness.' Mackenzie, the British minister in St Petersburg, correctly attributed the new legislation to the tsar's desire 'to find a perpetual nursery of gentlemen for his fleet and armies.' The innovation was so unpopular that it could never be rigidly applied; and it was abandoned in 1730, a few years after Peter's death. But underlying it was the true Petrine spirit – admiration for effort and striving; contempt for the inert, the unambitious and the traditional. Peter's relations with the Russian landowning class centred around a sustained effort to induce and if necessary force it to live up to his own standards of activity and public spirit.

These intensified demands made the landowners more dependent than ever on the central government. They were now bound to the administrative machine and forced to absorb its ethos and values. Cut off from his roots in some particular estate or village, forced to think of and value himself in terms of his position in an official hierarchy, the Russian landowner rapidly came to adopt an outlook which was increasingly authoritarian and bureaucratic. He now thought more and more in terms not of local problems and peculiarities but of national needs and demands. Energetic and autocratic leadership from above, unquestioning obedience to those of superior official rank from below: to the noblemen moulded by long years of state service under Peter and his successors these seemed clearly the recipe for the solution of Russia's problems. The idea of service to an impersonal entity, to the state embodied in the ruler and the administrative machine, came to replace that of service given essentially to the tsar as a person which had been normal in Muscovite Russia. Once established, this attitude proved remarkably durable. It explains the consolidation in the first half of the eighteenth century of the military-bureaucratic autocracy which was to shape so much of Russian life for generations to come. Even an attempted reform, such as the provision of 1714 that in future officials should be paid only in money and not as hitherto also by grants of land, accelerated the changes in the character of both bureaucracy and landowning class which were now under way. It tended to increase the complete dependence of the official on the central government and to weaken what links had hitherto existed between government service and rural and agricultural life.[53]

In the last decade of his reign Peter embarked upon administrative changes more carefully considered and more successful than any attempted before. This was a period in which he consolidated much of what had been done piecemeal and without careful planning earlier in the reign. Thus the *Ustav Voinskii* of 1716 and *Morskoi Ustav* of 1720 were painstaking efforts to place the organization of the armed forces on a systematic basis, while the *Dukhovnyi Reglament* of 1720 was in many ways the logical culmination of Peter's religious policies over two decades or more. Yet these were also years in which there were significant administrative failures. Another remodelling of provincial administration in 1719, which broke up the eleven huge *gubernii* created between 1708 and 1714 into forty-five (later fifty) smaller and more manageable units, produced widespread chaos and never worked properly. An attempt to foster the growth of a more energetic and enterprising merchant class by entrusting municipal government in 1721 to elected representatives of the newly established guilds, in some ways an extension of the idea seen in the creation of the *Ratusha* in 1699, also had only limited effect. As always, Peter found it far easier to create new institutions, even to win wars, than to endow society with the vitality and spontaneity which could be the product only of slow organic growth. The Russian towns, lacking self-confidence and mostly small and poor, once more failed to live up to his expectations. The *Glavnyi Magistrat*, the new government department dependent on the Senate which was set up to supervise them, did nothing to strengthen their feeble desire for self-government. But two new departures of Peter's last years proved of great permanent importance; these were the administrative colleges established from 1718 onwards and the Table of Ranks of 1722.

Administration by colleges, small committees of ministers and high officials controlling more or less defined aspects of government activity, was a technique well established in many parts of Europe, notably in the German and Scandinavian states. As early as March 1715 Peter had discussed with the Senate the possibility of establishing something of the kind in Russia and thus simplifying the still very cumbersome *prikaz* system inherited from the past. By the end of 1717 the decision had been taken. In December of that year the presidents of the colleges which were to be set up in the near future were appointed. There is no doubt that Peter was strongly influenced by foreign example in his decision: of all his reforms this is one of those in which foreign influence is most obvious. In September 1715 he gave orders for the collection of information about the working of the collegiate system in Denmark; and in the spring of 1718, when detailed regulations for the new institutions were being drawn up, his agent Heinrich Fick sent him a detailed description of the Swedish colleges.[54] Those which took shape in Russia beginning that year, however, were not the result of any slavish imitation of foreign practice. They were inspired rather by a real desire to improve the quality of central government and to increase the personal control of the tsar over it. Of the total of eleven colleges three – those for foreign affairs, war and admiralty – were from the start regarded as more important than the others (a recognition of the strength of the external pressures and necessities which dominated so much of Peter's work). Of the others, three – the *Kamer-Kollegiya*, the *Shtats-Kontor-Kollegiya* and the *Revizion-Kollegiya* (which temporarily disappeared in 1722) – were concerned with financial affairs. Three more – the *Berg-Kollegiya*, the *Manufaktur-Kollegiya* and the *Kommerts-Kollegiya* – dealt with different aspects of industrial

151

and commercial life; while the *Yustits-Kollegiya*, whose powers were less clearly defined than those of any other, acted in many ways as a kind of ministry of the interior and the *Vochinnaya Kollegiya* (set up early in 1721) handled the affairs and interests of the landowning class. Each college was to consist of a president and vice-president, four or five counsellors and four assessors, supported by a staff of clerks, translators and copyists. They were to work under the guidance of the Senate, of which, it was ordered in 1718, their presidents should be members; but in 1722 this provision was limited to those for war, admiralty and foreign affairs. All this meant a marked increase in the size of the machinery through which Russia was governed. Different colleges varied greatly in size: in 1723 that for war had 353 employees, while the *Kommerts-Kollegiya* had a mere thirty-two. But the changes from 1718 onwards involved something like a doubling overall of the central administration, while by the last years of Peter's life the colleges together were handling and creating at least 200,000 documents each year.[55] Moreover central government was not merely bigger than ever before. It was also more rationally organised; for unlike so many of the *prikazy* which preceded them each college had jurisdiction, in its own sphere, over the whole of Russia without geographical limitation. The colleges also relieved the Senate of much of the burden of detailed administrative work which it had hitherto been carrying, freeing it to act as a court of appeal in legal matters and as a body concerned with the formulation of general policy and the drawing-up of new legislation. Inevitably the reform showed defects in practice. If the colleges were to work well, they needed a supply of trained and public-spirited men greater than Russia could provide. Several of them tended to become tools in the hands of their presidents. But there is no doubt of the tsar's deep personal involvement with the new structure. The *Generalnyi Reglament* of 1720, an elaborate document which finally established the colleges as an integral part of the machinery of government, was drawn up in no fewer than twelve different versions, of which nine were corrected or altered in draft by Peter himself. Like the *Ustav Voinskii* and *Morskoi Ustav* it aimed at the careful and systematic regulation of a large area of government activity, regulation of a kind lacking in the tsar's more hasty and unreflective early years.

The creation of the colleges did not exhaust Peter's creative energies in matters of administration. In 1721 the new post of *Generalprokuror* of the Senate was established by a decree which the tsar personally revised six times. Its holder had great powers. Though he was not a member of the Senate all matters submitted to its consideration were to go through his hands, and he was to preside at its meetings when the tsar was not present. All the *fiskals* were to be under his control, as was a body of procurators, his agents attached to the colleges. He was the greatest bureaucrat in Russia, the head of the formidable if still often creaky new administrative machine. He was also, more directly than any other official, to be the personal representative and agent of the tsar, 'our eye and attorney of state affairs'. P. I. Yaguzhinskii, the first holder of this great office, rivalled Menshikov as the most powerful man in the country after Peter himself. In the following year a new and significant post of *Reketmeister* was created, whose occupant was to investigate complaints of misbehaviour and unjust decisions by the colleges and report upon them to the Senate. Finally the rationalization and systematization which bulks large in much of Peter's activity during these last years found expression in the Table of Ranks issued in 1722.

This created an elaborate graded hierarchy in the armed forces, the administration and the court. In its final version it listed 262 different posts – 126 military and naval, 94 administrative and 42 attached to the court. Ranks in the armed forces were further subdivided into those in the infantry, artillery, guards and fleet, with those in the guards regiments counting as two grades higher than the same ones in other branches (so that, for example, a guards colonel had the same grading in the table as a major-general of infantry). All the officers and officials thus listed were, from field-marshal at one extreme to the lowly ensign at the other, classified in fourteen parallel grades. Those in the military and naval ones, and in the eight highest civil ranks, with their descendants, were to be recognized as the equals of 'the best and oldest nobility' and to enjoy the privileges of hereditary membership of the landowning class, essentially those of owning serfs and exemption from the newly levied poll-tax. Young men were to start their careers in the lowest grade and to rise by a combination of merit and length of service. The whole system was based upon the idea of rank as the reward of service, something to be achieved by effort and not passively accepted as the natural result of high birth. It would be a mistake, however, to see it as a deliberate effort to dilute the landowning ruling class with newcomers of humble birth. The basic assumption was that the ranks listed in the table would continue to be filled by members of this class, or at least by outsiders assimilated to it by successful careers in government service at a reasonably high level. For this reason, whereas all army and navy officers found a place in the table, the more humble ranks of the civil administration, clerks and copyists, were not included; and Peter turned down a suggestion from the Admiralty College for the inclusion of skilled workers such as shipwrights and blacksmiths.

Nevertheless the Table of Ranks gave some impetus to the replacement of the old nobility, proud of its descent and jealous of its privileges, by a new privileged class which reckoned social status essentially in terms of rank in the official hierarchy. This process had still a long way to go by 1722; but it was clearly developing. The old Muscovite titles of official rank had fallen into complete disuse by the early years of the eighteenth century, a process accelerated by the creation of the new and greatly enlarged regular army. The title of boyar was conferred on P. M. Apraksin in 1709, and the slightly less elevated one of *okolnichi* on another of Peter's subordinates, V. A. Yushkov, in 1711; but these appear to be the last occasions on which new grants of these traditional ranks were made.[56] New western titles such as Count and Baron and new official ranks such as privy councillor (*tainyi sovetnik*) and court councillor (*nadvornyi sovetnik*) symbolized the change, the rejection of Muscovite tradition and movement towards an aristocracy of service. Peter had always wished to open commissioned rank in the army to members of the non-privileged classes who showed the necessary qualities. His own rather ostentatious insistence on serving as a mere bombardier and accepting promotion in both services only when he merited it was intended to stress the importance of technical knowledge and practical experience as against high birth alone; and a series of decrees in 1714, 1719 and 1722 clearly envisaged the attainment of officer rank by those of humble origins. He could never disregard, and certainly did not wish to disregard, descent and family connections entirely when making appointments to important posts in the armed forces or the administration. The ranks and titles given to B. P. Sheremetiev in the early stages of the war with Sweden – commander of the cavalry, commander-in-chief, field-marshal – are an illustration of this. So are the careers of, for example, F. A. Golovin, who in the years before his death in 1706 was in effect foreign minister; F. M. Apraksin, governor of Archangel, admiral and finally head of the Admiralty College; G. I. Golovkin, who was in charge of foreign affairs for a number of years after 1706; or I. A. Musin-Pushkin, who was head of the *Monastyrskii Prikaz* after 1701, then senator and head of the *Shtats-Kontor-Kollegiya*. Peter was no egalitarian. When he needed a military or naval commander, a high official or a diplomat, his first instinct was to turn to the traditional ruling class as the obvious reservoir of talent to be drawn on for these purposes. Nevertheless the utilitarian ideal of rank and leadership based on merit was also one which the tsar found profoundly attractive throughout his life. The effect of the Table of Ranks, in other words, was essentially to consolidate a development which had long been in progress. Like the creation of the colleges a year or two earlier it was inspired to a considerable extent by foreign models, notably the Prussian *Rangordnung* of 1713. But it went further than any of these in the extent to which it bureaucratized the Russian ruling class, grading and valuing its members purely in terms of their official rank. Unlike most foreign schemes of this kind it gave no place to church dignitaries and inherited ranks in an aristocracy of birth. It thus reflected the rise in Russia of a new type of autocratic power working through a large and complex bureaucratic machine. Like the other great administrative documents of Peter's last years it was the product of long and elaborate consideration. It was discussed by the Senate and several of the colleges while the tsar, as well as controlling the whole complex process by which it was produced, himself drew up three different versions of it.[57] Once more the contrast with the hasty, laconic and rough-edged decrees on administrative matters of the first years of the century is unmistakable.

Peter's administrative reforms were inspired by high and genuine ideals – to serve the greatness and progress of Russia. This he hoped to do by improving the machinery of central government and strengthening its control of the provinces, by separating judicial from purely administrative functions, and by substituting the idea of legality or obedience to the tsar's decrees (*zakonnost'*) for that of mere obedience to custom or tradition. Yet the achievement fell far short of the ideal. In spite of strenuous effort and some considerable successes the gaps and deficiencies in the structure which he left to his successors are striking. The regulation of administration by law was difficult without some codification of the confused mass of official decrees and orders: and this was not carried out. Commissions were indeed set up for this purpose in 1700, 1714 and 1720, but bore no fruit. Though Peter decreed that no law was to be valid unless put in writing and signed by him, simple verbal commands of the ruler continued for long after his reign to be regarded as having the force of law. The separation of the judiciary from the administration proper remained little more than an aspiration. The *voevody* and the governors and vice-governors of the *gubernii*, as well as many lesser officials, retained important judicial functions, while cases involving serfs were normally settled by the landlords or their agents and never reached the official courts unless serious crimes or political offences were involved.

On a more material level, Peter's efforts were continually impeded by a lack both of money and of able and reliable men. Shortage of money meant irregularity and long delays in the payment of official salaries; even at the end of the reign there were proposals to pay administrators in the more remote and undeveloped parts of Russia, for example in the Urals, by grants of land. Poor and irregularly paid salaries, combined with a long tradition of more or less institutionalized bribery (decrees against this dated in Russia back to the later fifteenth century), doomed Peter to a long and losing struggle against official corruption. This struggle he waged, at least on occasion, with energy and ruthlessness. In 1721 a former governor of Siberia, Prince M. P. Gagarin, paid for his bribe-taking on the scaffold, as did the *Oberfiskal* Alexis Nesterov himself three years later. Peter, unlike his predecessors, tried to penalize those who offered bribes as well as those who accepted them. But it was a struggle doomed to defeat. Too many of the men through whom he had to work were unable to understand or sympathize with his aspirations. Many *voevody* and provincial governors were uneducated; and the mediocrity of so many of the subordinates upon whom he had to rely was one of the most frustrating of all the constraints under which he had to work. 'The Czar', wrote one of the best foreign observers, 'will always find the Obstinacy of his Subjects, and their natural Bent to Injustice and Extortion, an insurmountable Obstacle to the wise Ends he has proposed to himself'.[58]

Peter preferred, as has already been pointed out, to employ Russians of noble birth if possible in high administrative posts. Yet in his search for efficiency he was willing to entrust positions of influence not only to foreigners – for example H. J. F. Ostermann, the son of a Hanoverian pastor who in the last years of the reign was the most important director of Russian foreign policy; or Anton Devier, who in 1718 received the new and important post of *Generalpolizeimeister* of St Petersburg and who was born in Amsterdam, the son of a converted Portuguese Jew – but also to Russians of low birth. Menshikov, whose personal influence over Peter was at times immense, above all in the very difficult first years of the eighteenth century, may not have begun life, as his enemies alleged, by selling pies in the streets. But he was certainly of humble origins. The offices and honours which were heaped on him – Governor-General of Ingermanland, Karelia and Estonia, Prince of the Holy Roman Empire (a result of the emperor's desire to stand well with Peter) – were made all the more bitter to the old aristocracy by their consciousness of his low birth. Menshikov's greatest rival, at least in the later years of Peter's reign, P. I. Yaguzhinskii, who was to become *Generalprokuror* of the Senate in 1722, was the son of a Lithuanian, the sexton of the Lutheran church in Moscow. Even men of serf origins, if able and lucky enough, could rise high in the administrative hierarchy under Peter. Alexis Kurbatov, vice-governor of Archangel, and V. S. Ershov, vice-governor of the Moscow *guberniya*, are examples of this. But however wide the tsar cast his net socially and geographically he was never able to recruit the right type of administrator in sufficient numbers.

The shortcomings of his civilian officials, combined with his own impatient energy and continual demand for quick and visible results explain one of the most striking characteristics of the administration of Russia during the later years of Peter's reign – the extent to which it became dependent upon the army. To some degree this dependence had always existed. The repression of rebellion and the control of banditry could be achieved only by military force. Moreover, it had for long been normal to give administrative posts in the provinces to retired officers. Yet the extent to which, in the last decade of his life, Peter subordinated the highest civil institutions to military control and relied on military men in every aspect of government was something new, and to many contemporaries strange and even shocking. When in 1717, on his return to Russia, the tsar set up a special judicial tribunal composed of soldiers with wide-ranging powers to investigate corruption, the Hanoverian minister was struck by the fact that 'Things were come to that Pass in Russia, that the Members of a venerable Senate, composed of the Heads of the greatest Families in the Czar's Dominions were obliged to appear before a Lieutenant as their Judge, and be called to an Account of their Conduct'.[59] A year or two later the importance of the army was even more heavily underlined when Peter, in order to complete the census needed for the levying of the new poll-tax, sent regiments into the countryside and quartered soldiers in many Russian villages. In 1725 the War College was told that 'in the regiments there are no staff officers, as the greater part of them are with the census takers.'[60] Officers and non-commissioned officers of the indispensable guards regiments were, in the later years of the reign, attached to and often dominating almost every governing institution. Not even the Senate or the Synod escaped their influence. This pervasive military control of administration was to prove lasting, particularly in the provinces. The collection of the poll-tax, for example, was to be carried out by soldiers until 1763. It was only under Catherine II that much of the machinery of government in Russia escaped from the subordination to the army which Peter had imposed upon it.

The fact that powerful administrative organs could be so unresistingly subordinated to young officers, or even to sergeants, shows how completely they were the mere instruments of Peter's will, rather than independent, self-confident entities. The tsar had created them; he could change, adapt or even destroy them at will. So complete was their dependence on him that it is perhaps debatable how far they can be called institutions in the fullest sense. Peter's desire to create a system of government which was impersonal and regulated by law was genuine. Moreover, in his last years he seems to have envisaged involving the Russian nobility in government in other ways than as a mere source of officials. A decree of 1723 provided for the election by local landowners in each district of 'land commissars' (*zemskie kommissary*) to collect the poll-tax, while there was even a plan for the establishment of a council of nobles which would elect the presidents of some of the colleges. Here, as elsewhere in Peter's work, can be seen a conflict between his instinct to dominate, to direct and control all the life of Russia, and his genuine desire to encourage in his subjects greater initiative, self-reliance and self-confidence. But hopes and schemes of this kind were frustrated. The corporate consciousness of the Russian landowning class was slight; and for a long time after Peter's death what there was of it centred on the guards regiments far more than on any administrative machinery. For all his efforts Peter ruled through individuals rather than through laws or institutions. Great officials, and still more men with personal influence on him, such as Menshikov and Prokopovich, were more important forces in government than any of the new administrative creations.

. . .

NOTES

1. L. G. Beskrovnyi, *Russkaya armiya i flot v XVIII veke* (Moscow, 1958), p. 21.
2. M. D. Rabinovich, 'Formirovanie regulyarnoi Russkoi armii nakanune severnoi voiny', *Voprosy voennoi istorii Rossii XVIII i pervaya polovina XIX vekov* (Moscow, 1969), p. 225.
3. For the complex details of these different drafts, down to the last one during the tsar's lifetime, in 1724, see Beskrovnyi, *Russkaya armiya i flot*, pp. 25–9.
4. L. G. Beskrovnyi, 'Voennie shkoly v Rossii v pervoi polovine XVIIIv.', *Istoricheskie Zapiski*, XLII (1953), 289.
5. A convenient summary of the *Ustav* and the regulations which preceded it can be found in L. G. Beskrovnyi, *Ocherki po istochnikovedeniyu voennoi istorii Rossii* (Moscow, 1957), pp. 109–22.
6. A. Theiner, *Monuments historiques relatifs aux règnes d'Alexis Michaelowitch, Féodor III et Pierre le Grand* (Rome, 1859), p. 440; F. C. Weber, *The Present State of Russia* (London, 1723), I, 19–20.
7. For example he personally worked out certain signals for the use of his ships as early as 1694 and a code of instructions in 1696 for a new fleet to be built on the sea of Azov (G. Ya. Salman, 'Morskoi ustav 1720g. – pervyi svod zakonov Russkogo flota', *Istoricheskie Zapiski*, LIII (1955), 311).

8. P. Milyukov, *Gosudarstvennoe khozyaistvo Rossii v pervoi chetverti XVIII stoletiya i reforma Petra Velikogo* (2nd ed.; St Petersburg, 1905), p. 138.

9. See the detailed figures in G. A. Nekrasov, 'Voenno-morskie sily Rossii na Baltike v pervoi chetverti XVIIIv.', in *Voprosy voennoi istorii Rossii*, pp. 238–50.

10. F. F. Veselago, *Spisok Russkikh voennykh sudov v 1668 do 1860 god* (St Petersburg, 1872), *passim*. On the British contribution in general see M. S. Anderson, 'Great Britain and the growth of the Russian navy in the eighteenth century', *Mariner's Mirror*, XLIII, No. 2 (May 1956), 132–46, *passim*.

11. This, the accepted opinion, is however challenged by Salman, 'Morskoi Ustav', *passim*.

12. Much detail on the whole problem of the equipment of the army and navy can be found in Beskrovnyi, *Russkaya armiya i flot*, pp. 74–100.

13. For details of these local and limited demands for men see M. Klochkov, *Naselenie Rossii pri Petre Velikom*, I (St Petersburg, 1911), 105ff.

14. *Istoriya rabochikh Leningrada* (Leningrad, 1972), I, 26.

15. *Istoriya rabochikh Leningrada*, I, 36.

16. G. D. Kapustin, 'Guzhevoi transport v severnoi voine', *Voprosy voennoi istorii Rossii*, p. 162.

17. Klochkov, *Naselenie Rossii*, I, 158.

18. Klochkov, *Naselenie Rossii*, I, 170–3; W. Mediger, *Moskaus Weg nach Europa* (Braunschweig, 1952), p. 123.

19. Klochkov, *Naselenie Rossii*, I, 221, 227, 229.

20. Klochkov, *Naselenie Rossii*, I, 225, 233, 236.

21. *Istoriya rabochikh Leningrada*, I, 16.

22. S. M. Troitskii, 'Finansovaya politika russkogo absolyutizma vo vtoroi polovine XVII i XVIII vv.', *Absolyutizm v Rossii* (Moscow, 1964), pp. 294, 306.

23. N. P. Pavlov-Silvanskii, *Proekty reform v zapiskakh sovremennikov Petra Velikogo* (St Petersburg, 1897), p. 55.

24. Law was offered the title of prince, ownership of two thousand peasant households, and the right to build a new town of his own and to populate it with foreign artisans and craftsmen. (S. M. Troitskii, 'Le "système" de John Law et ses continuateurs russes', in *La Russie et l'Europe, XVIe–XXe siècles* (Moscow-Paris, 1970), pp. 52–3.

25. For more detail on these see the list in B. B. Kafengauz and

N. I. Pavlenko (eds.), *Ocherki Istorii SSSR; period feodalizma. Rossiya v pervoi chetverti XVIIIv; preobrazovaniya Petra I* (Moscow, 1954), pp. 101–2.

26. E. V. Spiridonova, *Ekonomicheskaya politika i ekonomicheskie vzglyady Petra I* (Moscow, 1952), pp. 84–6.
27. On these efforts to assist the growth of industry see Spiridonova, *Ekonomicheskaya politika*, pp. 92–100.
28. P. Milyukov, *Ocherki po istorii russkoi kultury*, 6th ed. (St Petersburg, 1909), Pt. I, p. 118.
29. For a detailed account of the beginnings of large-scale iron production in the Urals see B. B. Kafengauz, 'Stroitel'stvo pervykh ural'skikh zavodov', *Voprosy Istorii*, 1945, Nos. 5–6, pp. 44–73.
30. F. C. Weber, *The Present State of Russia* (London, 1722–3), I, 70.
31. A. Kahan, 'Observations on Petrine Foreign Trade', *Canadian–American Slavic Studies*, Summer, 1974, **8**, p. 225.
32. See the table printed by Ya. E. Vodarskii in *Istoricheskaya geografiya Rossii XII-nachalo XXv* (Moscow, 1975), p. 78
33. J.-G. Korb, *Diary of an Austrian Secretary of Legation at the Court of Czar Peter the Great* (London, 1863), I, 255–6.
34. Ustryalov, *Istoriya tsarstvovaniya Petra Velikogo*, IV, Pt I, 548–9.
35. N. A. Voskresenskii, *Zakonodatel'nyi akty Petra I* (Moscow, 1945), I, 33; Ustryalov, *Istoriya*, III, 511–12.
36. J. Cracraft, *The Church Reform of Peter the Great* (London, 1971), pp. 135ff.
37. Cracraft, *Church Reform*, p. 54. There is a useful discussion of Prokopovich and his significance in Simone Blanc, 'L'église russe à l'aube du "Siècle des Lumières"', *Annales*, XX (1965), 456–61.
38. T. Consett, *The Present State and Regulations of the Church of Russia Establish'd by the late Tsar's Royal Edict* (London, 1729), p. 18.
39. Cracraft, *Church Reform*, pp. 198ff., 209.
40. On Tessing and his activities see Bogoslovskii, *Pyotr Velikii*, IV, 294ff.
41. For a list of translations of this kind see *Istoricheskii ocherk i obzor fondov rukopisnogo otdela biblioteki Akademii Nauk*, I (Moscow-Leningrad, 1956), 152–55.
42. D. M. Lebedev, *Geografiya v Rossii petrovskogo vremeni* (Moscow-Leningrad, 1950), pp. 205–7.

43. The main ideas of Saltykov and Pososhkov are conveniently summarized in Kafengauz and Pavlenko (eds.), *Ocherki istorii SSSR*, pp. 634–42. There is a modern edition of Pososhkov's book (Moscow, 1937) edited by B. B. Kafengaus. See also L. R. Lewitter, 'Ivan Tikhonovich Pososhkov (1652–1726) and "The Spirit of Capitalism"', *Slavonic and East European Review*, 51 (1973), 524–53.

44. On these schools and their significance see M. Okenfuss, 'The Jesuit Origins of Petrine Education', in J. G. Garrard (ed.), *The Eighteenth Century in Russia* (Oxford, 1973), pp. 106–30.

45. *Entsiklopedicheskii Slovar'*, I. (1890), 164; for a brief account of the origins and early years of the Academy see A. Lipski, 'The Foundation of the Russian Academy of Sciences', *Isis*, XLIV (1953), 349–54.

46. *The Present State of Russia*, I, 4.

47. *The Present State of Russia*, I, 149.

48. Quoted in V. I. Lebedev, *Reformy Petra I. Sbornik dokumentov* (Moscow, 1937), p. 348.

49. D. D. Blagoi, *Istoriya russkoi literatury XVIII veka*, 2nd ed. (Moscow, 1951), p. 60.

50. For some figures see N. F. Demidova, 'Byurokratizatsiya gosudarstvennogo apparata absolyutizma v XVII–XVIIIvv.', *Absolyutizm v Rossii*, pp. 214–15.

51. N. I. Pavlenko, 'Idei absolyutizma v zakonodatel'stve XVIIIv.', *Absolyutizm v Rossii*, p. 416; S.P. Luppov, *Kniga v Rossii v pervoi chetverti XVIIIv.* (Leningrad, 1973), pp. 86–88.

52. G. Anpilogov, 'Senat pri Petre I', *Istoricheskii Zhurnal*, 1941, No. 4, 45.

53. N. F. Demidova, 'Byurokratizatsiya gosudarstvennogo apparata', pp. 229–30.

54. N. A. Voskresenskii, *Zakonodatel'nyi akty*, I, 542–9.

55. E. V. Anisimov, *The Reforms of Peter the Great: Progress through Coercion in Russia* trans. J. T. Alexander (Armonk, NY and London, 1993), p. 154.

56. S. M. Troitskii, *Russkii absolyutizm i dvoryanstvo, XVIIIv.* (Moscow, 1974), p. 41.

57. For a detailed discussion of the complex development of the Table between its first discussion not later than September 1719 and its final presentation to the Senate in January 1722 see Troitskii, *Russkii absolyutizm i dvoryanstvo*, Ch. 2.

58. Weber, *The Present State of Russia,* I, 80.
59. Weber, *The Present State of Russia,* I, 193.
60. Anisimov, *The Reforms of Peter the Great,* p. 162.

Chapter 6

OPPOSITION AND ITS REPRESSION: THE TSAREVICH ALEXIS

Bitter opposition to change, to new ideas, to foreign influences of all kinds, had been a force in Russia long before Peter was born. Xenophobia had been endemic in Muscovite society for generations. The *Raskol* of the 1650s and 1660s and its consequences were the clearest of all proofs of the ingrained conservatism inevitable in such an environment. But both Peter's tastes and many of his policies were so uncompromising a break with the past, so gross a challenge to convention and traditional ideas of propriety, that they could not but intensify his subjects' resistance to change. Consorting with foreigners, travelling abroad, working with his own hands at a bewildering variety of trades, wearing foreign dress, despising the traditional costume of his subjects and the beards so dear to almost all of them, disliking Moscow and the Kremlin, passionate in his love of the sea which the great majority of Russians had never seen, he flouted in almost all the externals of life the accepted view of how a tsar should behave. In his creation of a great army and the new navy, in the building of canals, harbours and the new capital, he imposed on Russia burdens unheard-of under his predecessors, burdens which no tsar of the true stamp, it was felt, would have asked his people to bear. Emotional rejection of foreign models and influences, genuine fear of the implications for Orthodoxy of many of Peter's policies, desperation engendered by the suffering resulting from the tsar's demands: all these generated opposition. In the extreme form of active revolt this showed itself relatively rarely. The streltsy outbreak of 1698, the rebellion in Astrakhan in 1705–6, the Cossack rising led by Bulavin in the following year and a peasant revolt in the Volga basin in 1709–10, which spread to a considerable area of central Russia, are the only important examples. But plots, abuse of the tsar as hopelessly corrupted by foreign influences, as an impostor, even as Antichrist, continued throughout much of Peter's reign, particularly in its first half. These were, besides, only the outward signs of a continual groundswell of discontent which seemed at times to threaten the overthrow of all the tsar's painfully won achievements. One aspect of the reign, therefore, a negative and often bloody but nonetheless fundamental one, was a constant struggle to crush opposition, to force on a recalcitrant society changes and sacrifices which it was deeply unwilling to make.

At the top, as at the bottom of Russian society, Peter imposed new burdens and affronted old prejudices. The conscripted peasant, torn from his village and family to endure a lifetime of military service or to sicken and too often die in the swamps of St Petersburg, had his parallel in the landowner forced into permanent state service and thus condemned to allow his estates to deteriorate through lack of personal supervision and his relatives to go for years without a sight of him. The deep-rooted hostility of the ordinary Russian to all imported novelties found some echo in the resentment with which members of noble Muscovite families saw the tsar bestow important posts on foreigners, or on Russians of humble birth. Class and personal resentments of this kind found to some extent a leader, or rather a symbol, in Peter's brother-in-law, A. F. Lopukhin, who in 1718 was to pay for this dangerous eminence with his life. But from the nobility and gentry, groups with a long tradition of state service which the tsar merely formalized and intensified, much less was to be feared than from infuriated and desperate peasants. Evidence of serious aristocratic resistance to Peter's reforms is in fact very slight. The unprecedented decision to send young nobles and gentry abroad in 1696 for naval training aroused only grumbling and ineffective complaints; and though members of two important families, the Sokovnins and the Pushkins, were involved in the Zickler conspiracy of 1697, this reflected their personal feelings rather than any general attitude of the Russian nobility. Though Peter's innovations might sometimes affront ruling-class sensibilities, they also opened much wider opportunities to able young members of that class than had ever existed before. In the enlarged and modernized army, in the new navy, in diplomacy, in the expanded and at least to some extent rationalized administrative machine, young men could now carve out careers in unprecedented numbers. Moreover, the more forward-looking and imaginative of them could also take pride in the fact that they were helping to guide Russia into Europe and the modern world, to develop her resources and make her for the first time a great force in the arena of international politics. A proud consciousness of this, coupled with an almost religious veneration of the emperor who led and inspired them, is often to be gleaned from what evidence of their feelings has survived.

The conservatism of official Orthodox tradition was a more intractable difficulty than anything Peter had to face from the nobility and gentry. In 1700 he attempted to weaken opposition of this type by his refusal to appoint a new patriarch; but he had to wait for almost two decades until he found, in Prokopovich, a leading cleric after his own heart, willing and able to aid effectively in the transformation of the church into an agency of government. As the scope of Peter's rather incoherent ambitions and the sharpness of the breach with tradition which they represented became obvious, in the 1690s and the first years of the struggle with Sweden, clerical alarm and opposition grew. The arrest and exile in 1696 of the monk Avraam have already been mentioned. Four years later the book-copyist Grigorii Talitskii was spreading allegations that Peter was Antichrist – allegations which, significantly, were favourably received by the Bishop of Tambov, by a number of priests and monks and by at least one high-ranking aristocrat, Prince I. I. Khovanskii. The fears and suspicions which Avraam, Talitskii and others voiced, moreover, were widespread among the population at large. To combat them Stefan Yavorskii, for several years Peter's chief subordinate in Church affairs, wrote his *Signs of the Coming of Antichrist and the End of Time;* but he was very far from being a whole-hearted partisan of change of the Prokopovich stamp.

The official church could be tamed and controlled. This objective Peter had largely achieved by the later years of his reign. The Old Believers were a different and in many ways more serious matter. It could be argued that Nikon, by the liturgical and ceremonial changes introduced in the 1650s and finally made official in 1667, had led the Orthodox Church in Russia into apostasy. If this were so, the 'Third Rome' (after Rome itself and Constantinople), the citadel of Orthodoxy, had fallen; and by definition there could be no fourth. The implication was appalling. The reign of Antichrist had begun; the end of the world was near. To the Old Believers the Russian state and the tsars from Alexis onwards, by supporting the apostate Nikon, had lost all claim to legitimate authority and the obedience of truly Orthodox men; in fact the state and the apparatus of government had become Antichrist. The liturgical reforms of the 1650s and 1660s thus brought a large section of the Russian people to refuse obedience to their ruler and his agents (a refusal symbolized by unwillingness to offer the customary prayers for the tsar). Once this became clear, the Old Believers began to align themselves with other oppressed or discontented groups. They and their doctrines became a nucleus around which serfs ground down by the demands of their lords, or Cossack groups fearing for their autonomy in face of the growing power of central government, could to some extent organize themselves. Thus in 1708 the Cossack leader Golyi, who continued the revolt begun in the previous year by Bulavin, claimed in a manifesto that 'we rebelled in order to defend the old faith, holy churches, and all monks, so that we shall not fall into the Greek faith [i.e., the innovations introduced by Nikon]'.[1]

Under the regency of Sophia the government had reacted to this dissidence with systematic ferocity. A decree of December 1684 ordered the hunting down of all *raskolniki* and their interrogation (in which torture played an active role). Those conspicuously absent from Church services, as well as those accused by gossip of adherence to the old practices, were to be arrested. If they were convicted of being Old Believers and refused to recant, they were to be burned at the stake. During the next few years, religious fanaticism in north Russia was carried to spectacular extremes. On a number of occasions (notably in two separate incidents at the Paleostrovskii monastery in Karelia) large groups of *raskolniki* burned themselves alive rather than endanger their hopes of salvation by falling into the hands of Antichrist and risking a recantation of their faith under torture.

In the 1690s official persecution and the hysterical intensity of feeling which it generated abated somewhat; and in his edict of 1702, intended to encourage the settlement of foreign experts in Russia, Peter proclaimed general religious toleration. He does not seem to have taken much interest in the liturgical and ceremonial issues which underlay the *raskol*. A ruler fighting a difficult and, at the time, unsuccessful war against a dangerous opponent, and in need of every man and every rouble he could wring from his own territories, was in no position to indulge unnecessarily in such luxuries as religious persecution. Cautious and limited compromises between the state and the still potentially fanatical force of Old Belief were therefore made. In 1703 the government agreed to leave in peace the *raskolnik* community centred on the monastery at Vyg in Karelia if in return it would supply iron ore for the new armament factories just set up in the Lake Onega area. This was the first of a series of such agreements. In 1709 a *raskolnik* group was allowed to return from the Baltic provinces, to which it had fled for greater safety, and settle in the Pskov district. In 1715 the Old Believers in the Vetka and Starodub areas of the Ukraine were rewarded for successful guerilla operations against the Swedish invaders in 1708–9 by orders that the Vetka colony should not be interfered with and by grants of land to the Starodub one.[2]

It should not be thought, however, that Peter felt any sympathy for the Old Believers or they for him. What they learned (no doubt often distorted by rumour) of his tastes and way of life, so impious and so shockingly foreign, could only strengthen their belief that he was indeed Antichrist. The new title of emperor (*imperator*), which was quite strange to the majority of Russians, helped to strengthen this belief. With one small change the title could be made, by the old Russian method of designating numbers by letters, to add up to 666, the number of the Beast in the Apocalypse. The allegation of one bishop that the Old Believers, 'wherever you find them, instead of being pleased with the good fortune of the Sovereign ... delight in his misfortunes', was only too justified. On his side the tsar could never look with any favour on dissident groups who loathed all he was trying to do and totally rejected his claim to legitimate authority; and after 1718 the tragedy of his son Alexis made him even more suspicious of conservative opposition of all kinds. In 1705, when *de facto* toleration of the Old Believers was becoming widespread, a heavy tax was imposed on all town-dwellers who refused to shave their beards. Its main object was fiscal: it was one of the many expedients to which Peter was driven in these desperate years to raise money for the war with Sweden.

Nevertheless it weighed especially heavily on the Old Believers, to whom even more than to the ordinary Russian the beard was an indispensable sign of true Orthodoxy. In 1716 a decree demanded that all Old Believers should register with the authorities and pay twice the normal rate of taxation for people of their social class. This also was a largely fiscal measure; but it was followed by others which were clearly intended to persecute. In 1718 it was proclaimed that all Old Believer laymen who refused to register themselves would be sent to hard labour for life. In 1724 all *raskolniki* other than peasants, if they retained their beards, were compelled to wear a special brass token, which was to be sewn onto their clothing. This was the culmination of a series of efforts to force Old Believers to wear distinctive marks of some kind: the token not only acted as a form of receipt for payment of the beard tax but made the wearer immediately identifiable as a member of a suspect group.

Peter's attitude towards this powerful and pervasive force in Russian society (whose numbers, in spite of repressive legislation, were probably increasing during much of his reign) was therefore inconsistent, even confused. Suspicion and fiscal pressure were combined with a considerable measure of *de facto* toleration. However, the Old Believers were not in themselves an active threat to his régime. They were by now divided into different sects; while the fact that they could for the most part show themselves openly only in remote and widely separated frontier areas made it difficult for them to act as a unified force. More important, their whole outlook stressed flight from the contamination of an irredeemably wicked world rather than organized effort to overthrow the forces of authority which they so much feared and hated.

Given the widespread dislike which so many of his policies aroused, his own fierce and impatient character and the tradition of autocracy which he inherited, it is not surprising that the repression and punishment of opposition should have bulked large during Peter's reign. This repression centred on the *Preobrazhenskii Prikaz*, the most enduring of all the tsar's new organs of administration and the most feared. It emerged in the mid-1690s (no precise date for its creation is known and probably there was never any written decree establishing it) from the administration of the Preobrazhenskii regiment. It was given jurisdiction over political offences, irrespective of where they were alleged to have been committed or the rank of the accused. By the beginning of 1697 it was responsible not only for organizing the Preobrazhenskii and Semenovskii regiments and safeguarding public order in Moscow, but also for crushing political opposition throughout Russia. It has thus a claim to be considered the first truly centralized organ of Russian government, the forerunner of the unsuccessful *Ratusha* of 1699 and the Senate of 1711. Its central position in the administrative structure was symbolized by the fact that its head, the ruthless and trustworthy Prince F. Yu. Romodanovskii, was given charge of the capital when Peter went abroad in 1697. In 1702 a decree ordered the sending to Moscow of all those accused of political offences and the transfer of their cases to the *Preobrazhenskii Prikaz*, and even after 1719, when the *Yustitz-Kollegiya* was established, it retained this exclusive jurisdiction over political cases. Its stability and longevity are in striking and significant contrast to the frequent changes which much of the machinery of administration suffered under Peter. That the tsar was interested in its work is also shown by his occasional active part in it. In 1698, after the streltsy revolt, he personally questioned Sophia and her younger sister Marfa and was present at other interrogations. In 1706 he showed a marked interest in the questioning of the captured Astrakhan rebels. A more adequate legal or quasi-legal foundation for the work of the *prikaz* was provided by a decree of the Senate of January 1714 which for the first time defined political crimes against the tsar. Two years later the *Ustav Voinskii* explicitly declared that the mere imagining of a politically disloyal or criminal action, or the desire to perform it, was to be punished in exactly the same way as its actual performance. One of the most potentially oppressive features of such legislation, designed to crush all opposition, was the vague and all-embracing way in which much of it was worded.

Though he could be very severe in his treatment of overt revolt (in addition to the streltsy put to death in 1698–99, 320 of the Astrakhan rebels were executed in 1706) Peter did not in general favour the death penalty for political crime. He preferred instead various forms of beating and exile. Of 507 cases tried by the *Preobrazhenskii Prikaz* in 1697–1708 of which details are known only 48 resulted in the death of the accused[3] (though admittedly many of these cases were trivial ones, the outcome merely of drunken loose talk or the malice of an informant). From 1707 onwards women, clerics and old men were exiled to monasteries in remote parts of Russia rather than to Siberia; though the fate of a man sentenced to exile with hard labour in Azov or Taganrog was pitiable. Nevertheless, the methods by which conspiracy, real or alleged, or even mere 'unseemly talk' were investigated are a telling illustration of the harsher side of Peter's autocracy. Of the 365 men examined by the *Preobrazhenskii Prikaz* in connection with the revolt in Astrakhan 45 died as a result of the tortures which they had to suffer. Individual cases make the point even better than figures of this kind. Thus when in 1699 a member of one of the streltsy regiments, named Volokh, was accused of having used insulting words about the tsar and of having said that two years before the streltsy had wished to kill him at Azov, his wife, called as a witness, was tortured no fewer than five times. On different occasions she suffered twenty, fifteen, twenty-four and again fifteen strokes of the knout and on the last occasion was also put to the fire. Both accuser and defendant were tortured twice; and since none of the three altered their evidence (the wife, Marfa, denied that her husband had said the words in question) the entire process was repeated in January 1701. In 1704 the case was still in progress and all three were tortured once more. Its final outcome is not known.[4]

The supreme illustration of both the strength and the pervasiveness of conservative opposition to Peter and of the ruthlessness with which it was crushed is the tragic story of the Tsarevich Alexis. Born in February 1690, he was the only surviving son of Peter by Evdokia Lopukhina (his younger brother, Alexander, died in infancy). At the age of little more than eight he was permanently separated from his mother, a fact which may well have deeply influenced the whole tragic course of his life, and brought up instead by Peter's favourite sister, Natalia. From the first the tsar was determined that his son should play an active role in the great work of change and modernization upon which he had embarked in Russia. In 1698–99 he decided to send the child to one of the German courts to be educated, though the idea, for reasons which are still not clear, was soon abandoned. From the summer of 1701 onwards German tutors – Martin Neugebauer and Heinrich Huyssen – subjected Alexis to an extensive course of instruction in languages, geography, mathematics, military exercises, dancing and other subjects. This training was explicitly based on that normal in the *Ritterakademien* of the period in the German world. The tsarevich, even at this early age, found studies of this kind deeply uncongenial. The early influence of his mother, his very limited contact with his father, above all his own innate tastes and sympathies, made Alexis totally unresponsive to Peter's ambitions. To him the Church and its traditional rites made a profound appeal. Ikons, vestments, the externals of piety, were always to him, as to almost all Russians, of deep significance. From childhood he was assiduous in attendance at church services and scrupulous in observance of fasts, while to have priests around him, or within easy reach, became almost a necessity.

Inherent in this situation was irreconcilable conflict between the fiery and demanding father and the weak but obstinate son. Many contemporaries believed that Menshikov, who had formal charge of the tsarevich's household, deliberately sharpened this conflict for his own purposes, ill-treating and bullying the son in order to safeguard his position as the closest associate of the father. Certainly at times he treated Alexis with remarkable lack of consideration. The imperial representative in Moscow reported in 1703 that the tsarevich had on one occasion been 'dragged by the hair on the ground' by the all-powerful favourite and that 'the Tsar said nothing about this'.[5] This wretched childhood left Alexis timid, secretive and lacking in self-confidence, characteristics which were coupled with an increasing tendency, notable even in the Russia of that age, to heavy drinking. More and more he feared, even hated, his terrible father and the demands he made. Increasingly he was surrounded by those (aristocratic conservatives such as A. V. Kikin and N. K. Vyazemskii, the priest Yakov Ignatiev, who was the tsarevich's confessor, and Alexis' own uncle, A. F. Lopukhin) who opposed all Peter was trying to accomplish and looked to the accession of Alexis for a reassertion of conventional values and traditional policies.

As early as 1704, after summoning his son to join him in the siege of Narva, Peter showed his severe displeasure with him. 'I may die today or tomorrow,' he wrote to Alexis, 'but know that you will have little pleasure if you do not follow my example. You must love all that serves the glory and honour of the fatherland; you must love true counsellors and servants, whether foreign or of our own people, and spare no effort for the general good. If my advice is lost on the wind and you will not do as I wish, then I do not recognize you as my son.'[6] In spite of disappointments, from early in 1707 Peter gave his son administrative work of importance in Smolensk and Moscow, in the raising of men and equipment for the Swedish war. In this Alexis completely failed to satisfy his stern taskmaster. 'I see', wrote the tsar in both sorrow and anger, 'that you go at too lazy a pace in these crucial days to concern yourself with business.' In October 1711 the tsarevich was married, by his father's command, to a foreigner and a Protestant, Princess Charlotte of Brunswick-Wolfenbüttel. The marriage reflected Peter's determination to strengthen Russia's influence in Germany and to assert the position of the Romanovs as a European ruling house. To Alexis, however, it was merely another unwelcome duty laid upon him, particularly as the marriage contract did not even oblige the bride to become a member of the Orthodox church. Finally in 1713, after a last effort to employ him in the supervision of shipbuilding on Lake Ladoga had also failed, he was given no further official posts and was allowed to live a completely private life in St Petersburg.

This position was unsatisfactory and unstable. Alexis was not politically active; but, given his inclinations as the heir to the throne, he inevitably became the symbol of resistance to Peter and his policies, the hope of those who disliked foreign influences, resented the demands which the tsar made on all his subjects, or envied the power of Menshikov. Such feelings were dangerously widespread. In 1712 even Stefan Yavorskii, then still Peter's main subordinate in religious affairs though never a wholehearted collaborator, referred to the tsarevich in a sermon as 'our only hope'. Peter's health was deteriorating: incessant work, endless travelling and heavy drinking meant that he was frequently ill. Hopes or fears of the tsar's death made the position of his son even more crucial; and at least as early as 1716 Alexis came to believe that Peter had not more than a couple of years to live. In October 1715 a crisis arose: in a long letter to the tsarevich, Peter complained that his joy in the victories which had been achieved over the Swedes was almost overcome by worry 'when I see you, the heir to the throne, who are so very useless for the conduct of state affairs'. Then followed the most heartfelt complaint: 'You will hear nothing of military affairs', even though, Peter insisted, 'order and defence' were the fundamentals of all political rule.

What he objected to, he went on to make clear, was not so much Alexis' failure to play an active personal role in the war as his lack of interest in a struggle so essential to Russia's whole future. The tsarevich's whole attitude was deeply unsatisfactory. 'How often have I not scolded you for this, and not merely scolded you but beaten you ... but nothing has succeeded, nothing is any use, all is to no purpose, all is words spoken to the wind, and you want to do nothing but sit at home and enjoy yourself.' This was, Peter went on, a last warning. His son might even now change for the better. 'But if not, understand that I shall deprive you of the succession and cast you off like a gangrened limb.' The letter ended with the warning that as the tsar had never spared himself he would not spare a useless son. 'Better a stranger who is able than someone of one's own blood who is useless.'[7] This letter betrays the bitterness, contempt and, perhaps most of all, blank incomprehension with which Peter viewed his heir. The father, indefatigably active, driven by a deep sense of responsibility and at the same time lacking both patience and imagination, simply could not understand a cast of mind so foreign to him. To Peter the situation was simple. There was a clear line of duty which Alexis refused to follow. By so doing he rejected and implicitly threatened everything which his father had struggled so hard to achieve.

Alexis replied to this letter by asking to be allowed to renounce his right of succession. But this in itself could not appease Peter. The tsarevich might change his mind: in any case he was certain to remain a focus for discontent. He must therefore either alter his attitude completely and collaborate actively in his father's policies, or renounce the world by entering a monastery. For the time being Peter did not force the issue; but at the end of August 1716 he wrote to Alexis once more, from Copenhagen, demanding that his son decide at once whether to take an active part in the war against Sweden or to become a monk.

This letter brought matters to a head. Already the idea of flight from a situation which he loathed had taken shape in the mind of the tsarevich 'I should be better off', he said in 1713, 'as a convict labourer, or in a fever, than here'; and when in the following year he went to take the waters at Karlsbad in Bohemia, Kikin had advised him to travel on from there to the Netherlands and Italy rather than return to Russia. Now Alexis travelled to Danzig as if to join the tsar; but from that city he fled to Vienna where, as he later claimed, Kikin and the Russian ambassador, Vesselovskii, had already prepared a welcome for him. For several months his whereabouts remained a mystery. Not until March 1717 was it learnt that he was living in a castle in the Tyrol placed at his disposal by the Habsburg government. To recover his runaway son was for Peter an urgent necessity. His relations with Austria were rapidly deteriorating, as the fears and resentments aroused by the Russian occupation of Mecklenburg reached their height. In hostile hands the tsarevich might become a dangerous weapon against his native country. There were reports that Alexis, on arrival in the Austrian capital, had asked the Emperor Charles VI for troops to use against his father and had said that he hoped also for British support. The tsar also felt that his prestige, and that of Russia, had been seriously damaged by his son's flight: it was this above all that he found unforgivable.

Charles VI and his advisers found themselves in an embarrassing situation. They deeply distrusted Peter and were reluctant to put Alexis, against his will, at the mercy of his father. But they were also alarmed by the threats of armed force which Peter used more than once to enforce their compliance with his demands. They therefore induced the tsarevich to move from the Tyrol to Naples (an Austrian possession since the European peace settlement of 1713–14 at the end of the war of the Spanish Succession) where he took refuge once more in the castle of St Elmo. His father's emissaries still pursued him. In August 1717 the Habsburg government agreed that P. A. Tolstoy, who had shown his great abilities as a diplomat while Russian representative in Constantinople from 1702 to 1714, should be allowed to go to Naples, present to Alexis a letter from his father, and negotiate with him if he still refused to return after reading it. Underlying this decision was the fear that Peter, if faced in Vienna by a blank refusal to cooperate, might use his forces in Poland to attack Silesia and perhaps even advance into Bohemia, where there was considerable unrest among the peasantry. Yet the Habsburg government stipulated that Tolstoy should see Alexis only in the presence of Count Daun, the governor of Naples, or his representative, and that the tsarevich should be assured that he would not be given up against his will.

The wretched Alexis showed himself no match for the skill and ruthlessness of Tolstoy. On the one hand he was scared by threats: the emperor, it was claimed, would not go on protecting him in face of Russian pressure (Weingarten, one of Daun's secretaries, was bribed by Tolstoy to deceive the tsarevich on this point). Peter would come to Italy in person to retrieve his errant son. Alexis might be separated from his mistress, the Finnish girl Afrosinia, who had accompanied him in his flight and who was now pregnant. This carried weight with Alexis, who was sincerely attached to the girl and hoped to marry her (his wife, whom he had treated very badly, had died in November 1715 after giving birth to a son). On the other hand inducements were held out to him. If he returned to Russia he would be forgiven by his father and allowed to live quietly on his estates and keep Afrosinia. Alexis knew that promises of this kind, even when made by his father or with his authority, were not to be relied on. Nevertheless, after ten days of discussion and intrigue, on 14 October he made the decision to return to Russia. The emperor and his ministers were uneasy at the turn events had taken, but Tolstoy saw to it that on the return journey from Naples the tsarevich should not linger in Vienna or have an audience with Charles VI. The emperor therefore ordered Count Colloredo, the governor of Moravia, to see Alexis as he passed through the province and make sure that he genuinely wished to go back to Russia. Tolstoy prevented a meeting between Colloredo and Alexis; and when an Austrian official succeeded in meeting the tsarevich, Tolstoy and members of his entourage made so tight a circle around Alexis that no private conversation was possible. In this hasty and semi-surreptitious way the runaway was brought home. He reached Moscow in February 1718.

Faced by his father's anger, he now collapsed entirely. He acknowledged his guilt in having fled from Russia and asked Charles VI for asylum, begged his father's forgiveness and by an oath on the Bible taken in the Uspenskii Sobor, the most important church in Moscow, renounced his rights of succession. His half-brother Peter Petrovich, Peter's baby son by Catherine, the Livonian girl whom he had married in 1712, was proclaimed heir to the throne. But the tsar remained unsatisfied. However many and solemn the renunciations Alexis might make, as long as he remained alive there must always be a threat to the continuance of Peter's own policies. Even if he became a monk, in the past a quite insuperable obstacle to any aspirant to the throne, this might no longer be enough.

'A monk's cowl', Kikin told him, 'is not nailed on a man. It can be laid aside again.' Alexis could rely on widespread sympathy from the Church and indeed from a large majority of ordinary Russians, while Peter Petrovich was only two years of age and might never reach manhood. (In fact he died in the following year.) If the tsar should die in the near future his policies and their consequences – conscription, forced labour, increased taxes, foreign customs – were likely to be swept away in a wave of conservative reaction of which the tsarevich would be the titular leader. With Peter's policies, moreover, would go the men who had applied them, from Menshikov downwards. There were thus a large number of powerful individuals with a direct personal interest in seeing that Alexis never came to power.

The result was a prolonged effort to identify and punish those who had encouraged the renegade in his flight and in his alleged hopes of overthrowing his father by force. This produced, between February and July 1718, a period of tension in Moscow and St Petersburg such as had not been seen since the punishment of the streltsy in 1698–99. These months were among the most difficult of Peter's reign. The Prussian, Austrian and Hanoverian representatives in Russia all believed that there was a real danger of very serious unrest: Pleyer, the Austrian minister, reported in June that a general revolt to undo Alexis' renunciation of the succession was possible. Earlier, in March, the French minister had concluded that the Russians hated all Peter's innovations and 'wait and hope only for the end of his life to plunge into the slough of sloth and crass ignorance.'[8] A new government agency, the Secret Chancellery (*Tainaya Kantselyariya*), with Tolstoy at its head, was set up to investigate the case against Alexis and his supporters. Established in St Petersburg at the end of March, it functioned in the new capital rather as the *Preobrazhenskii Prikaz* did in Moscow and continued to exist until 1726, though always on a smaller scale than the older institution. As in 1698–99, Peter took an active personal interest in the interrogations (frequently accompanied by torture) which went on throughout the spring and summer. The day after his renunciation of the succession Alexis was faced by a list of questions in his father's own handwriting which demanded full information about his accomplices. This was the first of seven such written interrogations. In an effort to improve his own position the tsarevich attempted, in a reply which occupied ten sides of paper, to throw as much as possible of the blame for what had happened on those who had advised him. Several of his associates – Kikin, the court official Ivan Afanasiev, Prince V. V. Dolgorukii – were now arrested. Evdokia, who for two decades had been officially the nun Helen in a Suzdal convent, had nothing to do with the flight of her son. But she had had a long-standing liaison, it was discovered, with a married officer, Stepan Glebov; and the bishop of Rostov, Dositheus, had prophesied that she would be once more recognized as tsarina and had openly wished for Peter's death. More menacing still, Peter's half-sister, Maria Alekseevna, had been in touch with Evdokia and Dositheus: her Miloslavskii descent aroused in the tsar's mind memories of the fears and humiliations of his adolescence. None of those arrested and denounced during this inquisition were in a position to do Peter any serious harm. There was no doubt of his deep unpopularity with much of the old Muscovite nobility and the Church; but even torture could produce no evidence of organized or effective opposition. He felt himself surrounded by hostility, however, menaced on all sides by treachery, even from those of whom he had formerly thought well. (Kikin had been one of the young men who took part in the great journey to the west in 1697; and Dolgorukii had been regarded by Peter as one of the best officers in his army.) He was thus confirmed in his belief that in the last analysis he could rely only on a small number of close and like-minded associates.

Alexis was finally doomed by Afrosinia, his real devotion to whom is one of the few attractive facets of his character. Faced by Peter with both written and verbal questions she confessed that her lover had never wished to give up the succession to the throne and during his flight had corresponded with possible supporters in Russia. He had also been determined to undo his father's most cherished achievements. 'When I am ruler', he had told her, 'I shall live in Moscow and leave St Petersburg as a mere provincial town. I shall keep no ships and an army only for defence, and I want to wage no wars with it. I shall be content with the old dominions: in the winter I shall live in Moscow and in the summer at Yaroslavl.'[9] These admissions painted a picture which now seems pathetic rather than threatening; but they doomed the tsarevich.

That Alexis had loathed his father's policies, that he had wished for his father's death: these facts were beyond doubt. That he had ever taken, or even seriously contemplated, any effective action against Peter was more difficult to prove. In particular it has never been shown satisfactorily that he asked for and was promised help from Charles VI in overthrowing his father and seizing the throne. This was the accusation which Peter was most anxious to press home. He made it in a manifesto published early in February, at the moment of Alexis' return. Four days before his death the tsarevich admitted it in writing. He did this only after torture; and it is not confirmed (though also not conclusively disproved) by the Vienna archives. It is, however, inherently unlikely that Charles VI, involved in a war with the Ottoman empire which did not end until late in July 1718, and faced by a Spanish attack on Sardinia, would have been willing or even able to involve himself in an adventure of this kind in Russia. All the evidence suggests that in 1717–18 the Habsburg government was understandably anxious to avoid hostilities with Peter. It has been conjectured that Alexis may have invented the story of a promise of imperial military support in conversation with Tolstoy during the return journey to Russia, hoping in this way to make his return, and the resulting renunciation of such possibilities, appear more praiseworthy: such pathetic and ineffective deceit would have been in character.[10]

After Afrosinia's revelations Peter proceeded to more severe measures against his son. On 30 June and 5 July Alexis, who had now been moved to St Petersburg, was knouted in the fortress of St Peter and St Paul. He received twenty-five strokes on the first occasion and fifteen on the second in an effort to extract further admissions. The tsar seems to have decided as early as May that his son must face a court of some kind and stand trial for his life. In mid-June, in a letter to church leaders, Peter complained that Alexis, in spite of his promises, had not completely revealed all his wrong-doing nor the names of all those who had encouraged him, a complaint which he had made several times since the beginning of the inquisition in February. He went on to ask what punishment 'the godless intention, following Absalom's example', of the tsarevich deserved. The reply given by fourteen metropolitans, bishops and abbots was in the circumstances remarkable for its courage. They argued that they were not in a position to pass judgment and urged Peter to be merciful. A special assembly of high officials, ministers, soldiers and other secular notables, 126 in all, showed less independence. On 3 July they signed unanimously a statement that the tsarevich's actions deserved the punishment of death. (Of the 126 only three were foreigners, a good illustration of the extent to which Peter had now become able to dispense with non-Russian advisers and subordinates.) On 7 July Alexis died. The precise cause of death has never been established. Officially it was an apoplectic stroke, though many other versions of what had happend were at once in circulation.[11] But whatever the exact circumstances, no contemporary doubted that the essential responsibility for the death lay at Peter's door, and posterity has echoed the verdict. The tsar felt his son's death as a relief. The very next day there were public celebrations of the anniversary of the battle of Poltava (though these were ended unusually early) and on 10 July Peter's name-day was, as usual, commemorated by drinking, fireworks and the launching of new warships.

In spite of the severity of Peter's interrogations and the tension generated by them during the spring and early summer of 1718, there were relatively few executions. Kikin and Bishop Dositheus were broken on the wheel. Avraam Lopukhin, the uncle of Alexis, was beheaded with four others at the end of the year. Glebov, who had aroused Peter's special fury, was impaled. The death-toll was small by comparison with the holocaust of 1698–99, though many suffered the lesser punishments of beating, imprisonment and exile. In particular the tsarevna Maria was imprisoned in the Schlüsselburg fortress and Evdokia immured for the next decade in a nearby convent. None the less the tsar had asserted with spectacular ruthlessness his uncompromising determination to continue on the course upon which he had embarked two decades earlier. Both Church and old nobility were now terrorized into submission (the assembly of notables which condemned Alexis included at least twenty-two members of old Muscovite noble families, several of them men whom he had thought of as sympathizers). Just as Poltava made clear the irruption of Russian power into a largely hostile Europe so the death of Alexis illustrated Peter's iron grip upon his own recalcitrant country.

Discontent did not die away after 1718. On the contrary, minor exhibitions of it seem to have increased sharply in Peter's last years. He himself became more and more preoccupied, even obsessed, by fears of domestic opposition, to which he had perhaps always attached more importance than it deserved. In 1718 the *Preobrazhenskii Prikaz* dealt with only 91 such cases: in the years which followed, the number rose steadily and by 1724 had reached 448.[12] It was always a small body. In 1727, two years after Peter's death, it had in Moscow a total staff of only thirty-two, including, significantly, two executioners, and ten in St Petersburg, one of whom was an executioner. But the moral effect it produced was out of all proportion to its size. Gloom and tension marked the end of the reign. In 1722 and 1723 harvests were bad, food scarce and prices high. Peasant flight, the most effective of all forms of resistance to the tsar's exactions, increased sharply. 'Everything', wrote the Saxon minister in September 1724, 'is going wrong, trade is coming to an end, there is neither navy nor paid troops, and everyone is dissatisfied and discontented.'[13] A war with Persia, where the Safavid dynasty was now in the last stages of a long decline, started in 1722 and posed problems. Derbent, Resht and Baku were taken, and the Persian provinces on the west and south shores of the Caspian annexed. But the Turks were hostile, the complexities of the situation in the Caucasus great and the losses of the Russian army by disease serious. The struggle was the only large-scale expression Peter was ever able to give to the ambitions for expansion into Asia which he had cherished throughout his reign (a large-scale expedition to Khiva and Bokhara in 1716–17 was annihilated in a Khivan ambush, and the Russian trade with India for which he had hoped remained a dream). In the long run his Persian war proved an expensive failure: by the early 1730s the cost of retaining the conquered provinces proved unbearable and they were abandoned. In the last years of his life, Peter's sense of isolation, of struggling alone against a dead weight of opposition and obscurantism, became greater than ever. Many of his associates of earlier years were dead; even Menshikov fell into disgrace and had to disgorge some of his immense wealth. In 1724 there was a last spectacular illustration of the power of corruption in Russian government and of Peter's still unquenched will to combat it, when William Mons, Catherine's chamberlain and the brother of Peter's former mistress, Anna Mons, was sent to the scaffold for offences of this kind. The affair, because of the involvement of his wife, saddened Peter's last months. 'I pity with all my heart this monarch', wrote the same Saxon minister in December 1723, 'who cannot find a single loyal subject apart from two foreigners who hold the reins of the empire; that is, Yaguzhinskii and Ostermann.'[14]

Yet none of this challenged Peter's power. Neither the most widespread discontent nor bribe-pocketing officials, neither bad harvests nor the costly new war, not even peasant flight, could shake his hold on Russia. His increasingly intense and self-confident autocracy is perhaps best symbolized by the fact that after 1722 the reverse of the rouble piece ceased to show, as hitherto, the traditional double-headed eagle. Instead it now displayed a cruciform monogram made up of four interlocked reproductions of the letter P in the Cyrillic alphabet.[15]

The question of the succession remained unsolved to the end. The death of Peter Petrovich in May 1719 left, by a curious revenge of fate, the infant son of Alexis, also called Peter, as the only surviving male member of the Romanov line. Was he to succeed on the tsar's death, as he unquestionably would have done in any west-European country? Or was the successor to be Peter's daughter Elizabeth, who did in fact become empress more than two decades later, in 1741? Or would perhaps one of Peter's nieces, Catherine, Duchess of Mecklenburg, or Anna, Duchess of Courland, next occupy the throne? The tsar never expressed any clear preference and made no effort to promulgate any formal rule governing the succession. The shapelessness and incompleteness of much of Peter's extraordinary achievement is illuminated by the fact that such a fundamental issue was left completely open. It illustrates his autocracy, and perhaps also his inability to come to a decision, that his only response to this situation, with all the dangers and uncertainties it involved, was to assume in 1722 the right to nominate as his successor whomsoever he chose. This was, raised to an imperial scale, the right over the succession to their own lands which he had conferred on the Russian nobles in 1714. Peter's assertion of it at this juncture shows a highly traditional concept of Russia as in some sense merely the tsar's personal estate. Prokopovich, in his *Pravda voli monarshei* attempted, with a great parade of Biblical and other quotations, to justify such a far-reaching assumption of authority. But Peter's action made depressingly clear how much Russian government and society still lacked the definite shape, the deep-rooted institutions, the effectively guaranteed legal rights now normal in western Europe.

In any case, the power Peter thus assumed was never used. No successor was named. It is questionable how much difference it would have made had he nominated one; for as soon as he drew his last breath the throne was at the mercy of court factions and the all-important guards regiments. The result was that his wife Catherine, who had not a shred of hereditary right, emerged, largely through the support of Menshikov, desperate to safeguard his position and perhaps even his life, as ruler of the empire. For four decades after Peter's death the Russian throne was to be the most unstable in Europe, the shuttlecock of factional struggles and palace revolutions. No man can bind the future. But this extreme dynastic instability and uncertainty underlines how overwhelmingly personal Peter's achievement was and the limitations to it which this set.

. . .

NOTES

1. *Bulavinskoe vosstanie (1707–1708gg.)* (Moscow, 1935), p. 466.
2. R. O. Crummey, *The Old Believers and the World of Antichrist: The Vyg Community and the Russian State, 1694–1855* (Madison, 1970), pp. 69–70. This paragraph and the following one draw heavily upon Professor Crummey's book.
3. N. B. Golikova, *Politicheskie protsessy pri Petre I* (Moscow, 1957), pp. 49–50.
4. Golikova, *Politicheskie protsessy*, pp. 66–67.
5. Quoted in E. Dukmeyer, *Korbs Diarium Itineris in Moscoviam und Quellen die es ergänzen* (Berlin, 1909–10), II, 96.
6. N. Ustryalov, *Istoriya tsarstvovaniya Petra Velikogo* (St Petersburg, 1858–63), vi, *Prilozhenie* 304–5.
7. Ustryalov, *Istoriya tsarstvovaniya Petra Velikogo*, VI, 346ff.
8. *Sbornik Imperatorskogo Russkogo Istoricheskogo Obshchestva* (St Petersburg, 1867–1916), XXXIV, 320.
9. Ustryalov, *Istoriya tsarstvovaniya Petra Velikogo*, VI, 240
10. R. Wittram, *Peter I, Czar und Kaiser* (Göttingen, 1964), II, 395.
11. For details of different more or less contemporary versions of the death of Alexis – that he had been beheaded, poisoned, stifled or had his veins opened – see E. Schuyler, *Peter the Great, Emperor of Russia* (New York, 1884), II, 345fn.; and O. F. Kozlov, 'Delo tsarevicha Alekseya', *Voprosy Istorii*, 1969, No. 9, 219–20.

12. N. B. Golikova, 'Organy politicheskogo syska i ikh razvitie v XVII–XVIII vv.', *Absolyutizm v Rossii* (Moscow, 1964), p. 258.
13. *Sbornik*, III, 387–88.
14. *Sbornik*, III, 366.
15. See the illustrations in I. Spassky and E. Shchukina, *Medals and Coins of the Age of Peter the Great* (Leningrad, 1974), Nos. 64, 66–7.

Chapter 7

PETER THE MAN: CHARACTER AND PERSONALITY

Throughout his life Peter's character was of a piece, changing little in essentials. He was consistent above all in the whole-heartedness with which he adopted and applied policies, in his belief in the rightness of his own judgment and his own scale of values. His faults were often glaring; but they were the faults of excess, of rashness, of haste and of too uncritical a self-confidence. They were seldom those of mediocrity, of indecision or of a shirking of responsibility.

Some of his leading characteristics have already been briefly mentioned – his almost boundless physical energy, his insatiable practical curiosity, and the genuine sense of personal responsibility for Russia and its people which he felt at least from his middle or later twenties onwards. The first of these marked him indelibly throughout his life. Faced with any situation which seemed to call for action, his overmastering instinct was to act at once, often almost without thought and in the most direct and personal way. Disturbed at dinner in January 1699 by the news that fire (the ever-present danger in a land of wooden houses) had broken out in the palace of one of the boyars, he sprang from table 'and running headlong to the place where he had heard the fire was raging, not only gave his advice, but actually employed his own hands in putting out the flames, and was seen labouring away among the very tottering ruins of the house'.[1] A quarter of a century later precisely the same impetuous response to an emergency was to precipitate his own death. But this urge to act, this will to be up and doing, went even deeper than such incidents indicate. It lay at the very roots of Peter's character. More than anything else it explains the impatience with which he regarded the passivity, the lack of ambition, of so many of his subjects. 'What do you do at home?', he irritably asked his companions on one occasion. 'I don't know how to stay at home with nothing to do.'[2] Few of his recorded remarks illustrate his character more simply or more clearly.

This lavish outpouring of physical energy, this obsessive activity, caught the attention of contemporaries more than any other aspect of his personality. 'That was a tsar, what a tsar!', said an unknown peasant of Olonets. 'He did not eat his bread for nothing but worked like a peasant.'[3] Peter's passion for working with his own hands took a wide variety of forms as well as the labour as a shipwright about which so much has been written. Throughout much of his life he tried to spend some time each day wood-turning (he took a lathe with him even on the disastrous Pruth campaign), and when his second marriage was solemnized the decorations included 'a sconce with six branches of ivory and ebon-wood' which he had himself made. 'He told me', the British minister in St Petersburg remarked, 'it had cost him about a fortnight's time and no one else had touched it; the piece is indeed curious for the workmanship, as well as the hand that made it.'[4] To the end of his life, and even after his health had clearly begun to give way, energetic handicrafts, such as metalwork involving much hammering of sheet-iron, continued to absorb a surprising amount of his time.

In Paris in 1717, as in London two decades earlier, he gave to many observers the impression of an energetic, intelligent and endlessly inquisitive visitant from what in many ways was still another world. A naive (and therefore all the more revealing) witness saw him then 'with short hair and no wig, with a plain face, large eyes, his body quite heavy and his behaviour gross . . . fleeing from being seen or visited by women, since he has neither seen nor received any that were not unavoidable during his visit to Paris of a month and thirteen days. [He is] thought to be well informed in literature, curious about all rarities and things worth seeing, making notes on all he sees and always carrying a pencil with him, seeking out practitioners of all the arts and trades and hiring them to go to his kingdom to establish themselves there, where a number have already gone.'[5]

A realization of the responsibility imposed upon him by the power which he wielded over Russia and its people took time to develop in him and become fully effective. During the later

1690s, however, the irresponsibility, even selfishness, of his early life began to disappear. It was replaced by a deep-seated feeling that he was a trustee obliged to foster the well-being and improvement of the country entrusted to his care. The manifesto of 1702 which invited foreigners to work in Russia stressed his desire to rule so that 'all our subjects, under our guardianship, will for the general good advance further and further towards the best and happiest condition'. This is the first clear statement from him of such an objective. Once adopted, however, this attitude stayed with him for life and became the driving force behind all his work. Almost two decades after the 1702 declaration he could speak in very similar terms, in a speech celebrating the signature of the treaty of Nystad, of the obligation laid upon him to work for the general good and the benefit of his country,[6] while it was precisely the lack in Alexis of any active public spirit of this kind which made the conflict between father and son so irreconcilable.

The combination of physical and mental energy with a profound sense of responsibility meant that Peter worked hard at the business of government, probably harder than any other monarch of the age. Of this there are convincing proofs. In the preparation of the *Morskoi Ustav* of 1720, for example, he laboured for five months, four days a week, from 5 a.m. to midday and from 4 p.m. to 11 p.m. A large part of the manuscript of this very long and detailed decree was written in his own hand and the rest corrected by him. The drafts of different schemes for the new collegiate organization of 1718–19 bear many insertions and corrections by him; and many important decrees – for example, that of 1714 on the indivisibility of estates, and that of 1722 fixing the duties of the *Generalprokuror*– were worked out in detail by the tsar in person. The more intelligent and far-seeing contemporary observers were often as much impressed by Peter's capacity for work as by that which he showed for drinking and crude horseplay. 'His Majesty might truly be called a man of business', wrote a Scottish doctor who had over a decade's experience of Russia and had seen much of the tsar during the Persian campaign of 1722, 'for he could despatch more affairs in a morning than an houseful of senators could do in a month. He rose almost every morning in the winter-time, before four o'clock, was often in his cabinet by three o'clock, where two private secretaries, and certain clerks, paid constant attendance. He often went so early to the Senate as to occasion the senators being raised out of their beds to attend him there.'[7]

All this paints a picture of seriousness, of sustained and constructive effort, which is in many ways very attractive. Peter's real devotion to duty becomes all the more admirable in the context of his constant disappointments with inefficient or corrupt subordinates, experiences which wrung from him the bitter though trite reflection that 'There is little truth in men, but much cunning.'[8] There were, however, striking blemishes on his character which, though they did not vitiate his good points, were none the less serious.

It is perhaps questionable how far he was, at bottom, a cruel man (though it was during his reign that a new and very brutal form of execution, by breaking on the wheel, was introduced into Russia). Except at moments of genuine crisis – in the destruction of the streltsy in 1698 and the punishment of Alexis and his associates two decades later – he showed, by the standards of his place and time, little taste for cruelty. His sparing use of the death penalty for political offences and his relatively moderate treatment of religious dissenters bear out this point. The sufferings which he inflicted on tens of thousands of humble and helpless people he never desired for their own sake. They were an inevitable result of his efforts to wrench Russia out of what he saw as stultifying conservatism and humiliating weakness. As such they had to be accepted and enforced. But they were always incidental to his real objectives.

If he was not cruel, however, he could certainly be violent, sometimes ungovernably so, in fits of rage. Physical assault, with cudgel, cane or even bare hands, on the unfortunate object of his anger was a commonplace; here again the urge to immediate and often unthinking action is visible. His huge stature (he stood about six feet seven inches tall) and the marked facial tic which afflicted him at moments of stress must have made this treatment even more frightening to the recipient than would otherwise have been the case. The most striking examples of this kind of behaviour again date from the very tense later months of 1698. Then on one occasion Peter struck Menshikov a blow so severe that blood 'spouted abundantly from the wound' and on another hurled Lefort himself to the floor and kicked him.[9] But behaviour of this kind, which was often followed by an immediate return of good humour, remained characteristic of Peter to the end. There is much force in the parallel which a great Russian historian has drawn between the tsar's associates and travellers admiring the view from the summit of Vesuvius while all the time awaiting the eruption of the uncontrollable forces under their feet.[10]

Allied with this lack of self-control was an unmistakable vein of coarseness, even grossness, in his tastes and much of his everyday behaviour. Some of this, for example the liking for dwarfs, giants and physical abnormalities of all kinds and for their display in pseudo-ceremonies, could easily be paralleled at other European courts in what was by present-day standards a highly insensitive age. In some respects he displayed unexpected sensibilities, as in his genuine fondness for gardens and gardening, at least in his later years (he appears to have had a particular liking for carnations). Yet we are left, in spite of his indisputable intelligence and range of interests, with the impression of a massive substratum of uncouthness. The obscene and blasphemous ceremonies associated with the 'Most Drunken Synod' are an example of this. The heavy drinking which continued to the end of his life was carried to lengths which even contemporaries, themselves far from abstemious, found astonishing or shocking. To be forced to take part in prolonged and brutish carouses with the tsar and his boon companions became from the 1690s a recognized hazard of the lives of foreign diplomats in Russia. In 1701, for example, a Prussian official begged not to be sent there as resident since 'he could not stand strong drink, especially in excess'; while in 1714 Frederick William I chose Count von Schlippenbach for a diplomatic mission to Peter partly because of his taste for drinking.[11] 'He's no proud man, I assure you,' wrote an English merchant from Archangel to his brother in 1702, 'for he'll eat or be merry with anybody . . . He's a great admirer of such blunt fellows as saylors are. He invited all the nasty tars to dinner with him where he made 'em so drunk that some slop't, some danced, and others fought – he amongst 'em. And in such company he takes much pleasure.'[12] The rigours of the tsar's hospitality are illustrated by an account given by the Hanoverian envoy of the entertainment offered by Peter, in the later years of his life, at the new palace of Peterhof, on the Baltic fourteen miles from St Petersburg. Each guest, already hardly able to stand after a long drinking-bout, was forced to empty a bowl containing a full pint of wine, 'whereupon we quite lost our Senses, and were in that pickle carried off to sleep, some in the Garden, others in the Wood, and the rest here and there on the Ground.' They were, however, soon awakened and forced to follow the tsar in cutting down trees to make a new walk to the seashore. At supper they drank 'such another Dose of Liquour, as sent us senseless to Bed'; but an hour and a half later they were roused once more to visit the Prince of Circassia (himself in bed with his wife), 'where we were again by their Bedside pestered with Wine and Brandy till four in the Morning, that next day none of us remembered how he got home.' At eight o'clock they were invited to breakfast, but given brandy instead of tea or coffee. This was followed by a fourth drinking-bout at dinner, after the guests had been forced to ride wretched horses, without saddles or stirrups, for the amusement of the tsar and tsarina. When the party sailed back to St Petersburg they were overtaken by a dangerous storm; and this allowed Peter to show at once the courage and leadership which made him a great monarch, taking charge and himself steering the ship. Yet when the party landed, 'after being tossed about seven Hours', they could find neither dry clothes nor beds and had to make a fire, strip naked and wrap themselves in sled-covers while their wet clothes dried.[13]

We are here not merely geographically distant from the courts of western Europe but in what was still, in many essentials, a different world. Nor did the tsar's taste for drunken jollifications pressed to almost grotesque lengths weaken with the passage of time. In the summer of 1724, only a few months before his death, a drinking-party to celebrate the consecration of a church at Tsarskoe-Selo, near St Petersburg, where Peter had just built a new palace, lasted for several days and consumed three thousand bottles of wine.

The simplicity of the tsar's own tastes; the fact that so much of his reign was spent in travelling, frequently outside Russia; a constant shortage of money and the imperative demands of the armed forces for what was available – all these combined to ensure that there was little elaborate or highly organized court life. Peter was certainly not indifferent to some kinds of outward appearance and some types of ceremony. This can be seen in his liking for firework displays and for complex ornamental waterworks. It is also very clearly visible in the elaborate triumphal processions, based on Roman models, which marked his most important victories. But for imposing buildings, rich furnishings, handsome clothes, elaborate meals, material luxury in almost any form, he had in general little use. In April 1694, when he accompanied his half-brother Ivan in the Easter procession, he took part for the last time in a traditional court ceremony in the Kremlim. Thereafter he made almost no use of the palaces there, several of which had been extensively redecorated, with the use of such new western luxuries as gilt leather, in the 1680s and early 1690s. Though handsome, the palace which he built at Peterhof was by the standards of western Europe relatively small and unpretentious, even though the grottos in the park attached to it were decorated with 10,000 seashells especially imported from Venice. Another at Strelna, also near St Petersburg, had scarcely been commenced at his death. The first Winter Palace in the city itself, begun in 1711, was a small two-storey wooden building which bore no relationship to the huge present-day structure of that name. Even the second Winter Palace which replaced it in 1716, though modestly attractive to judge by the plans (it was pulled down ten years later), was far from imposing by contemporary west-European standards. Like virtually every monarch of the age, Peter greatly admired Louis XIV, whom he regarded as a model of kingship. But he never contemplated creating a Versailles of his own.

So far as the mechanics of daily life were concerned, the simplicity of his tastes contrasted startlingly and impressively, in the eyes of many observers, with the powers he wielded. He never appeared, noted a foreigner admiringly, 'in a dress-suit of cloaths', except on important festivals and holidays: and 'when he was dressed, he wore the order of St Andrew; at other times he had no badge, or mark, of any order, on his person'. In St Petersburg he used an open two-wheeled chaise, attended by two soldiers or grooms and by a page, who often sat in the chaise with him and drove it. In winter he used a sledge drawn by a single horse, with the same small number of attendants.[14] His impatience with ceremony and complete lack of courtly manners frequently created surprise or embarrassment on his foreign travels – at the Prussian court in 1712, at that of Denmark in 1716, on his visit to Paris in the following year.[15] When his second wife, Catherine, made him a new coat of blue *gros-de-tours* material trimmed with silver braid he evidently thought the braid too extravagant and wore

191

this fine garment only once, at Catherine's own coronation in May 1724. Normally he wore merely a shabby old coat, into the pockets of which he was in the habit of stuffing official papers. Even his closest associates rarely dined or supped with him in St Petersburg; Menshikov alone was allowed to do this more than very occasionally. Finally, as perhaps the most convincing of all demonstrations of how far his tastes diverged from those of most of his fellow-monarchs, he neither hunted nor gambled.

The indifference to appearances, to luxuries and even to ordinary comforts, which marked much of Peter's behaviour can, however, be overstressed. He did not grudge expenditure on lavish public ceremonies when the occasion seemed to justify this. Thus, for example, when in August 1722 the small boat in which he had first learned to sail in 1688, and which he called the 'Mother of the Russian Navy', was brought to St Petersburg from Moscow, it was received with great ceremony. Three salvos were fired by the guns of the fortress and the assembled fleet, no fewer, it was claimed, than two thousand in all. This was almost certainly the most massive use of artillery for ceremonial purposes hitherto seen anywhere. (The day ended, typically, with a ten-hour banquet at which the tsar became drunk to a degree, according to observers well qualified to judge, scarcely precedented even for him.)[16] Peter also allowed his second wife, Catherine, to maintain a retinue much larger and a style of life much more expensive than his own. Her establishment included, among other forms of display, pages in red and green with trimmings of gold lace, and even an orchestra in green uniforms; here we see a foreshadowing of the ostentatious luxury which was to mark Russian court life in generations to come. In the same way Menshikov and some other favourites were actively encouraged to live in a luxurious style in St Petersburg.

More important politically was the tsar's willingness to spend money, and to encourage its expenditure by others, when this could heighten Russia's prestige abroad or popularize his policies at home. He was consistent in his concern that his country, and his own achievements, should present the best possible face to both foreign and domestic observers. In 1707, for example, he gave strict instructions to Menshikov, then in Poland, to keep up an appearance of pomp and luxury so long as he remained there in order to impress the population. He not only employed hack journalists such as Martin Neugebauer and Heinrich Huyssen to publicize his achievements in western Europe but also did his best to suppress the publication of hostile pamphlets and other material there.[17] Similar methods were used to influence domestic opinion. As soon as he heard of any important Russian victory Peter would demand reports of it 'which can be printed and distributed'. These would then appear either in the *Vedomosti*, a government news-sheet published very irregularly from 1703 onwards which is frequently referred to as the first Russian newspaper, or separately. Descriptions of the capture of Narva, and of the battles of Lesnaya and Poltava, were printed as placards and displayed in the streets of Moscow, St Petersburg and other towns, while 6,000 copies of the ratification of the peace of 1721 were produced for propaganda use of this kind For the great illiterate majority, official accounts of Russian successes were read out to the congregations in the churches after thanksgiving services.[18] The real effect of this kind of official propaganda is not easy to measure and may well have been very slight. The *Vedomosti*, apart from its extremely erratic appearance (in the whole year 1718 it was published only once) had by the end of the reign a print run of less than a hundred copies for each issue. But of Peter's wish to spread knowledge of his efforts and achievements there is no doubt.

Even the portraits of him painted at various times by western artists were pressed into service for similar ends. Two in particular, that by Kneller, painted when Peter was in England during the 'Great Embassy' of 1697–98, and that by Karl Moor, painted in Holland in 1717, seemed to the tsar to convey the idea of himself which he wished to disseminate; the result was that they were much more frequently engraved than other, and to the historian equally interesting, likenesses of the tsar (those produced by the Czech, Kupetskii, in 1711; by the Russian, Nikitin, in 1716; by Rigaud and Nattier in Paris in 1717; and by two foreign artists in Russian service, Tanauer in 1714 and Caravacque in 1722). Engravings made from them were widely distributed; and miniature copies were made, first by French and later by Russian artists, to be given away in considerable numbers as presents and rewards.[19] His posthumous reputation also preoccupied Peter. He dreamed of erecting a great memorial to himself, a lasting and visible perpetuation of his fame to posterity, though these plans were never realized while he was alive. A scheme for a great triumphal pillar surmounted by his statue and covered with bas-reliefs representing the main events of his reign (probably inspired by descriptions he had read of Trajan's column in Rome) had no result; and a projected bronze commemorative statue of him was not cast until after his death and was not mounted on its pedestal until 1800. Peter thus presents a picture of extreme simplicity in personal expenditure coupled with a willingness to tolerate, and even vicariously enjoy, the expenditure of those close to him and to spend quite lavishly where his own or Russia's prestige seemed to be involved.

Family affections and ties did not play a large part in his life. Two close relatives of his first wife were put to death in 1694 and 1698 when their conduct had aroused his suspicion, while his brother-in-law was executed in 1718 and one of his uncles exiled to Archangel. We do not even know with certainty how many children he had by his two wives.[20] His sister Natalia, only a year younger than he, remained until her death in 1716 his consistent admirer and supporter. But to Peter's achievements she contributed little: she probably understood many of his objectives only imperfectly. The same is true of his sister-in-law, the Tsaritsa Praskovia, wife of Ivan V, a formidable lady of the old Muscovite school who was also an admirer of the tsar until her death in 1723, and of his niece, the Duchess of Mecklenburg. All these meant something to Peter. It was to Natalia that the little Tsarevich Alexis was entrusted after his separation from his mother in 1698; and Praskovia took charge of Peter's young children by his second wife when their parents travelled to Germany in 1716. That second wife, Catherine, was, however, the only woman who was truly close to him (at least after he broke with his mistress, Anna Mons, in 1703) or on whom he seriously relied.

Catherine's story illustrates strikingly Peter's freedom in his personal life from the prejudices and proprieties accepted by other monarchs of the age. The daughter of a Lithuanian peasant, orphaned and destitute while still a child, she was taken to Moscow in 1703 after the Russian capture of Marienburg, where she had been in effect the servant of a Lutheran pastor. In Moscow, as a member of the household of Menshikov, she met and attracted Peter. Though illiterate, she was pretty and good-natured; her first child by the tsar was born in the winter of 1704–5. In 1707 they were married privately in St Petersburg; but it was not until four years later that the marriage was publicly avowed. Even then the fact that Peter's first wife, Evdokia, was still alive, and that there had been no divorce, made Catherine's status, and that of her children, extremely doubtful. By many contemporaries the marriage was seen, quite reasonably, as further evidence of the tsar's willingness totally to disregard conventional restraints of all kinds. 'I suppose', wrote the British minister to Russia to one of the Secretaries of State, 'you will have already heard that the Czar has married his mistress and declared her empress; it is one of the surprising events in this wonderfull age.'[21] Nevertheless the marriage was remarkably successful. Catherine bore her husband probably nine children, though of these only two girls (Anna, who in 1724 married Charles Frederick of Holstein-Gottorp; and Elizabeth, who was to become empress in 1741) lived beyond early childhood. Cheerful and comforting, she could soothe Peter when he was angry and encourage him when he was despondent. To be with him she braved difficult and uncomfortable journeys; she accompanied him on the disastrous Pruth campaign, to Pomerania and Denmark in 1716 and even to Persia in 1722. His letters to her show a domestic and even tender side which is hardly evident elsewhere in his correspondence.[22] He was not faithful to her physically. In that age, however, such fidelity was certainly not expected of a ruler; and none of his affairs (some of which were entered into with her knowledge) ever threatened the real hold of 'Katerinushka' on his affections. Her coronation in Moscow in May 1724, an almost unprecedented event, finally consolidated her official position. Peter placed the crown on her head with his own hands; and one motive for paying her this public honour was almost certainly to increase her chances of succeeding him should he die suddenly.

Apart from Catherine, the tsar's closest collaborator during much of his reign, and the one with whom the association proved most durable, was Alexander Danilovich Menshikov. After service in one of the 'toy regiments' and as Peter's personal adjutant, he accompanied Peter as a volunteer on the 'Great Embassy' of 1697–98. In spite of his humble birth, his intelligence, liveliness, almost brutal energy and capacity for the sort of rough merrymaking that Peter enjoyed, rapidly earned him not merely favour but also real affection from the tsar. After the death of Lefort the rise of the new favourite was

195

spectacular. Governor of the newly captured Schlüsselburg in 1702, he soon became Governor-General of Ingria, Karelia and Estonia and in 1705 a Prince of the Holy Roman Empire. In 1707 Peter gave him the title of Prince of Izhora, with the right to be addressed as 'Highness'; and in the following year made him governor of the St Petersburg *guberniya*. His influence over the tsar seemed so complete that even members of the old Moscow boyar aristocracy as important as Field-Marshal Sheremetiev now begged for his support. In 1708 he performed the greatest of all his services to Peter by the prompt destruction of Mazepa's headquarters. In the triumphal procession in Moscow after Poltava he rode in the place of honour on the tsar's right hand. His growing hold on Peter can be seen in the changing forms of address used in the tsar's letters to him – from the *Mein Herz* and *Mein Herzenchen* used until 1703 (it is doubtful whether these terms ever had the erotic significance which has been sometimes attributed to them), to *Mein Liebste Vrient* and *Mein Best Vrient* and finally the simple *Mein Bruder.*

Menshikov was in many ways an unattractive character. Ruthless, vindictive, above all intensely avaricious, he made a host of enemies. Indeed a good deal of noble opposition to Peter and his policies was inspired not so much by the tsar himself as by the favourite who seemed, in the eyes of so many Russians of good family, an arrogant and greedy upstart. In the spring of 1711, and again in 1714–15, serious accusations of peculation and corruption were brought against Menshikov. On the second occasion he was heavily fined; and perhaps only the support of Catherine averted a more severe penalty. In 1723–4 he was accused of concealing over 30,000 runaway serfs on his great estates in the Ukraine, and of illegally extending the boundaries of one of these estates. An investigation into these charges was still in progress at Peter's death. During the last decade or more of the reign, therefore, his old intimacy with the tsar was at an end. Yet no one took his place; and the memory of old friendship and past services was too strong to allow Peter ever to take really severe measures against a man who, for over a decade, had bulked so large in his life.

The blots on the tsar's character were thus considerable: irascibility, lack of self-control, grossness and insensitivity carried to the pitch of outright brutality. Yet against them must be set even greater virtues: courage, energy, self-sacrifice and a capacity for true and lasting friendship. Under all the crudeness, the impatience, the lack of feeling for outlooks or ideas different from his own, the cruelty under stress, can be seen an essential truthfulness and simplicity. Both Peter's faults and his good points were direct reflections of his deepest nature, undistorted by hypocrisy, calculation or artifice of any kind. Of no ruler in the history of Europe can it be said with greater truth that his work was the outcome of his own essential character.

. . .

NOTES

1. J.-G. Korb, *Diary of an Austrian Secretary of Legation at the Court of Czar Peter the Great* (London, 1863), *i, 219.*
2. V. O. Klyuchevskii, *'Pyotr Velikii sredi svoikh sotrudnikov'*, in his *Ocherki i Rechi* (Moscow, n.d.), p. 477.
3. V. O. Klyuchevskii, *Kurs russkoi istorii* (Moscow, 1904–10), IV, 308.
4. Whitworth to St John (Secretary of State), 2 March 1712, *Sbornik Imperatorskogo Russkogo Istoricheskogo Obshchestva* (St Petersburg, 1867–1916), LXI, 145.
5. Maria Sawizky, 'Unbekannte Aufzeichnungen über den Besuch Peters des Grossen in Frankreich', *Die Welt als Geschichte*, XVII (1957), 54
6. N. A. Voskresenskii, *Zakonodatelnyi akty Petra I* (Moscow, 1945), i, p. 156.
7. J. Bell, *Travels from St Petersburg in Russia, to diverse parts of Asia* (Glasgow, 1763), II, 359–60.
8. Klyuchevskii, 'Pyotr Velikii sredi svoikh sotrudnikov', pp. 480–81.
9. Korb, *Diary*, I, 182, 188.
10. Klyuchevskii, 'Pyotr Velikii sredi svoikh sotrudnikov', p. 488.
11. J. Krusche, 'Die Entstehung und Entwicklung der ständigen diplomatischen Vertretung Brandenburg-Preussens am Carenhofe bis zum Eintritt Russlands in die Reihe des europäischen Grossmächte', *Jahrbücher für Kultur und Geschichte der Slaven*, Neue Folge, VIII (1932), 182, 204.
12. British Library, Additional MSS 33573, f. 178.
13. F. C. Weber, *The Present State of Russia* (London, 1722–3) I, 93–5.

14. Bell, *Travels from St Petersburg*, I, 358.
15. S. F. Platonov, *Pyotr Velikii, lichnost' i deyatel'nost'* (Leningrad, 1926), pp. 98–102.
16. H.-J. Krüger, 'Aus dem russischen Tagebuch des Prinzen Ludwig Gruno von Hessen-Homburg (1723)', in *Archivalische Fundstücke zu den russisch-deutsch Beziehungen: Erik Amburger zum 65 Geburtstag* (Berlin 1973), pp. 37–8.
17. H. Doerries, *Russlands Eindringen in Europa in der Epoche Peters des Grossen. Studien zu zeitgenossischen Publizistik und Staatenkunde* (Berlin, 1939), pp. 33, 54–7, 59–61.
18. T. S. Maikova, 'Voennye "Yurnaly" petrovskogo vremeni', *Voprosy voennyi istoriya Rossii* (Moscow, 1969), pp. 384–5.
19. N. A. Baklanova, 'Otrazhenie idei absolyutizma v izobrazitel'nom isskustve pervoi chetverti XVIIIv.', *Absolyutizm v Rossii* (Moscow, 1964), pp. 498–9.
20. Lindsey Hughes, 'A Note on the Children of Peter the Great', *Study Group on Eighteenth Century Russia, Newsletter,* **21** (1993), 10–16.
21. Whitworth to St John, 23 May 1711, *Sbornik*, L, 433–4.
22. See the extracts, covering the years 1709–23, in E. Schuyler, *Peter the Great, Emperor of Russia* (New York, 1884), I, 441–5.

Chapter 8

'THE GREATEST MONARCH OF OUR AGE': PETER'S PLACE IN HISTORY

The heedless energy, the driving urge to immediate action, which had marked Peter's life also contributed to his death. Early in November 1724, en route by river from St Petersburg to the ironworks at Systerbeck, he saw a boat full of soldiers and sailors driven aground by the weather. Leaping into the water, he worked throughout the night, helping to save the lives of twenty men. This episode brought on a severe attack of fever; and new attacks of strangury and the stone, from which he had long suffered, soon added to the pain. Though he was only in his fifty-third year his health had for long been uncertain. Almost to the end he lived as he had in youth, indulging in bouts of heavy drinking with his cronies, incessantly encouraging and superintending new enterprises of all kinds. The good progress which had been made with the Ladoga canal, designed to connect St Petersburg with its hinterland, greatly pleased him when he inspected it in October; and as late as 27 January 1725 he proposed to travel to Riga in connection with the marriage of his daughter Anna to Charles Frederick of Holstein-Gottorp. By then, however, it was clear that he was seriously ill. By the beginning of February he was in intense pain; early in the morning of the 8th he died in St Petersburg. On 19 March the corpse was transferred with great ceremony to the cathedral of St Peter and St Paul, where it was finally buried in 1731. Nothing in the tsar's life was more fitting than this burial, not in the Moscow which for most of his life he had disliked and rejected but in the new capital, the visible symbol of the new Russia.

Throughout much of Europe, notably in Poland and Sweden, the news of Peter's death was greeted with relief, indeed pleasure. Russia, it seemed, might now rapidly relapse into the unimportance and weakness from which he had raised it. Within the country there were many at all social levels who hoped, now the great taskmaster was gone, for some lightening of the burdens which he had placed upon them. In the hasty and sometimes bitter argument over the succession which followed his death, the claims of Alexis's little son, in some sense the representative of the old traditional Russia, were strongly urged. Yet no one, foreigner or Russian, doubted for a moment that a remarkable man had just breathed his last. As a conqueror, still more as a lawgiver, he now seemed to equal the greatest figures of antiquity. Already in May 1724 an English newspaper had spoken of him as 'the greatest Monarch of our Age . . . whose Actions will draw after him a Blaze of Glory, and Astonishment, through the latest Depth of Time! and warm the Heart of Posterity with the same generous Reverence for the Name of this immortal Emperor, which we now feel at Mention of Alexander the Great: or the first, and noblest, of the Caesars.'[1] His Russian followers and partisans, better informed about the difficulties which he had had to face, felt equal admiration and a much greater sense of loss. 'He was your Samson, O Russia!', cried Prokopovich in the funeral sermon which he preached on 19 March.

He found you with little strength and left you, as his name signifies, strong as a rock, as a diamond. . . . Russia, he was your first Japhet! He carried out an enterprise hitherto unheard-of in Russia – the building and launching of ships, of a fleet new-born but yielding in nothing to old-established ones. . . . He was your Moses, O Russia! Are not his laws like the strong visor of justice and the unbreakable chains repressing crime? . . . O Russia! he was your Solomon, receiving from the Lord abundance of wisdom and reason! Do we not have sufficient proof of this in the intellectual disciplines which he introduced and in his efforts to point out and communicate to many of his subjects a great variety of knowledge, inventions and techniques before unknown to us? And what of the ranks and titles, the civil laws, the well-chosen regulations regarding social life, the welcome new customs and rules of conduct, the improvements introduced into our external appearance, so that we look at ourselves and are astonished to see our fatherland visibly changed and

become incomparably superior to what it was before? . . .
He was your David and your Constantine, O Russian
Church! . . . Drawn from the paths of ignorance, our
heart gives forth a sigh of relief![2]

Many of the young Russians whom Peter had made his helpers
and instruments shared these feelings. 'This monarch', wrote
one of them, I. I. Neplyuev, 'brought our fatherland into
comparison with others; he taught others to realize that we
too are people. In a word, whatever you see in Russia began
with him and whatever will be done in the future will draw on
this source.'[3]

These were the views of extreme partisans. Prokopovich,
until his death in 1736, was to be the most sincere and active
guardian of the Petrine heritage. More than anyone else it
was he who spread and consolidated the view of Peter as
the creator of a new Russia, of a new breed of Russian. This
extremely favourable, almost messianic view of Peter quickly
became a kind of orthodoxy both in Russia and in the world
at large. By the middle of the century adulation of the great
tsar had become a distinct strain in the Russian literature which
was then rapidly growing. From the 1760s Catherine II, the
greatest of his successors, repeatedly stressed that her reforms
were merely continuations and, where necessary, adaptations
of his. The erection in August 1782, in the Senate Square
in St Petersburg, of the great statue of Peter by the French
sculptor Falconet was merely the most striking physical symbol
of her efforts to appear to be continuing and fulfilling the
Petrine tradition.

It is now a truism to say that the view of Peter's reign
as marking a sharp transition from darkness to light, from
barbarism to civilization, is untenable. Such a view appealed,
in the eighteenth century and later, to the taste for the
dramatic which is inherent in every normal man. It also
encouraged hopes of rapid progress in the states of western
Europe under the guidance of intelligent, public-spirited and
energetic rulers, 'enlightened despots'. For these reasons it
attracted many writers. It was none the less one-sided and
inadequate. It tended to gloss over or ignore the failures
against the Turks, in Central Asia and, in the long run, against
Persia, which had to be set against the great success won in
Europe. It grossly underestimated the scope and effect of the

changes in Russian life which were already well under way long before Peter was born. Its view of the Russian people as sunk, until his advent, in depths of ignorance and superstition from which only his daemonic energy and unbending will could raise them, was unfair in view of the progress made before his reign had begun. Even more objectionable and unrealistic was the assumption that Russia had scarcely existed in any meaningful sense before it was discovered and influenced by Europe. Within a generation of Peter's death this had begun to be recognized and resented by some patriotic Russians. 'Those who proclaim that we were nothing but barbarians before Peter the Great . . . do not know what they are saying,' protested the poet Sumarokov, 'our ancestors were in no way inferior to us.'[4] This was a view as yet rarely made explicit; but it was one which future generations were to hear with increasing frequency and stridency.

The uncritically admiring attitude to Peter, so common by the end of his reign, also ignored the extent to which his work was incomplete at his death and the obstacles which it encountered in the mere geography, physical and human, of Russia. In a huge and thinly peopled country with very poor communications, the contacts of much of the population with the government were at best slight and intermittent. Ambitious innovating legislation was harder to enforce effectively than anywhere else in Europe; and the fact that so many of Peter's decrees were highly detailed and specific in their provisions merely accentuated the gulf between what the monarch ordered and what actually happened (or more often failed to happen) in some distant province. More important, the tsar's admirers ignored the fact that the results of much of his work were destructive rather than constructive. It was realized that he had superimposd upon Muscovite Russia a new system of rule, new modes of thought, even new assumptions, all of which were foreign or foreign-inspired. The importance of this, however, was grasped only slowly. Peter's insistence that the ruling class should adopt western dress and to some extent western customs, and even so far as possible receive a western-type education, had far-reaching implications. It meant that the division between lord and peasant, between rulers and ruled, between well-to-do and poor, was now more clearcut, more visible and more difficult to bridge. The entire cultural life of Russia was deeply affected by it. 'Fine' art (an import from Europe, hitherto largely unknown) was a world away from folk art; religious art, centred on the ikon, now became more and more distinct from secular art of all kinds. On the folk-tales and folk-poetry which were the only literature known to the great mass of the population was superimposed, after Peter's death but as a result of his work, a European-style literature of the upper classes and the two capitals. Distinctions of this kind existed everywhere in eighteenth-century Europe. But in Russia they were sharper than anywhere else; there their effects were to be uniquely pervasive and lasting. The great administrative reforms of the reign had, on a different level, some of the same results. By increasing the number of officials in Russia and making them cogs in an increasingly elaborate machine Peter undermined, indeed destroyed, the essentially personal character of authority which had been characteristic of Muscovite Russia. This was, in a sense, one of his greatest achievements. Yet by making the relationship between government and subjects increasingly impersonal and dependent on the workings of an unfeeling machine he was again dividing society, making it less of an organism.

These criticisms can easily be pressed to unfair and un-realistic lengths. No more than any other man could Peter foresee all the implications, many of them remote and indirect, of his own actions. In particular he did not foresee that with the whittling down under his successors of the obligation of the landowning class to perform state service, and its abolition in 1762, the serfdom which he had helped to extend would lose the justification which it had possessed in his eyes. From being part of a network of obligations to the state which embraced, at least in theory, all social groups, it now degenerated merely into the means by which a minority exploited a mass of unfree peasants; but this was hardly what Peter himself had intended. Nothing in him stands out more clearly than his deep concern for the well-being, the strength and the reputation of Russia. It was to this overriding objective that his own son was sacrificed. Peter was never an uncritical admirer of things foreign. To him the knowledge and techniques imported from the West were essential; but this was because they were the foundations upon which alone the new Russia of which he dreamed and for which he laboured must be built. He was well aware of his debt to foreign helpers: this awareness is seen in his proposal in 1721, at the moment of final victory over Sweden, to erect a monument to the memory of Gordon. But after the death of Lefort, all his closest associates were Russians; and as his reign progressed foreign influences in most aspects of Russian life (the navy and perhaps the founding of the Academy of Sciences are the only important exceptions) tended to decline.

It is impossible, moreover, not to admire the unsparing if often misdirected effort which, over three decades, he devoted to the achievement of a more powerful and more enlightened Russia. Perseverance in the face of setbacks; continual experiment with new institutions and methods; incessant travelling, often in considerable discomfort and sometimes over very long distances: all these present a picture of activity, both mental and physical, which no ruler in modern history can surpass. This passion to be doing marked every aspect of his own psychology and scheme of values. Criticism, if well-meant, he could bear, even when it was severe. What he could never abide was the terrible passivity, the lack of initiative, the placid and unquestioning acceptance of the traditional, which were so fundamental to the old Russia. This prodigal outpouring of energy was inspired by a deep sense of personal responsibility for the country entrusted to his care. He saw himself as the instrument of Russia's greatness, in a genuine sense the first servant of the state. His methods were too often ill thought-out and poorly adapted to the ends he had in view. Too often, at least in the first half of his reign, expedients were hastily adopted in a burst of unconsidered enthusiasm and as quickly abandoned when they failed to produce the desired results. Yet there was a consistency in his general objectives; and in his later years the means by which he strove to attain them became much more carefully considered and fully elaborated.

Nor were these objectives wholly material, a matter simply of more soldiers, more ships and more territory. He sincerely wished to make his subjects more enterprising and self-confident, to encourage them, at least for certain purposes, to show greater initiative and readiness for responsibility. Merchants and industrialists willing to become effective entre-preneurs, towns willing to take more control of their own destiny, landowners willing to elect their own representatives, all figured at different times in his plans and hopes. He created an apparatus of government without precedent in Russia for size and complexity. Indeed in a sense he created the Russian state itself: the concept of it as an entity distinct from the ruler, overriding the interests of any social group and even of the Russian people as a whole, is a creation of his reign. Yet he knew that legislation and new institutions by themselves could not achieve everything, that complete success demanded the active cooperation of the human beings upon and through whom he worked.

Few of the objectives for which he strove so hard and long were new. Almost without exception they were inherent in the history and geographical position of Russia and the necessities which these created. Greater military strength; a Baltic coastline; a more developed economic life: none of these was a new ambition. None was inspired by an irruption of novel ideas or foreign influences. All, and especially the first two, had a solid Muscovite tradition behind them, while even the transformation of church-state relations completed by 1721 had been foreshadowed to some extent by the great conflicts of the 1650s and 1660s. The navy was indeed a novelty; but though it was, together with the building of St Petersburg, the most personal of all Peter's major creations and the one with least foothold in Muscovite tradition, it was also the least important. In the structure and workings of Russian society great changes were made. Yet this was done by accelerating developments already under way as much as by introducing anything really new. The serfdom which Peter helped to extend and consolidate had been becoming more widespread and onerous for many decades before his reign. Though the Table of Ranks, and Peter's policies in general, made the privileged landowning class in Russia more open to men of talent and enterprise than ever before, they did not destroy, and were never meant to destroy, the position of well-established landed families and even of the old boyar ones.

Russia under Peter the Great can thus be regarded as undergoing, in the main, a process of forced and greatly accelerated evolution rather than of true revolution. Peter lacked almost completely the intellectual equipment of a modern revolutionary. He had no ideology, no articulated system of general ideas to guide his actions, no clear vision of a march of history irresistibly impelling Russia in a particular direction. First and last, he was a man of action. His abilities as a planner were far from negligible. They can be seen in the carefully elaborated large-scale legislation of the last years of his reign. But they were always less important than the urge to action, the desire to respond immediately to a difficulty or an opportunity. Sustained and well-considered policies he thus arrived at, when he achieved them at all, only after a long process of trial and error and of sometimes haphazard expedients. It was only relatively late in life that he acquired, for example, the breadth of view regarding the westernization of Russia which had characterized Golitsyn in the 1680s. Nevertheless, by altering so much the tempo of change, Peter altered to some extent also its nature. It is difficult to believe that, had he never existed, Russia would have remained for ever, or even for very long, without a Baltic coastline or real influence in Europe. Certainly the influence of foreign ideas and techniques in Russian life would have continued to grow. Almost certainly there would have been efforts to create a more effective and more centralized form of administration. But the speed with which these developments were carried through, the manner in which they were forced on Russia by the energy and determination of its ruler, the concentration within a generation or less of a whole set of far-reaching changes in many aspects of life, inevitably generated a widespread sense of dislocation and discontinuity. Most of the substance of Peter's work was not in the full sense revolutionary. But the 'furious man' whom Bishop Burnet had wondered at in 1697 displayed throughout his reign an ardour, a passionate energy and when necessary a ruthlessness, which gave much of what he achieved at least an aspect and style which to contemporaries appeared revolutionary.

. . .

NOTES

1. *The Plain Dealer*, 29 May 1724.
2. F. Prokopovich, *Sochineniya* (Moscow-Leningrad, 1961), pp. 126ff.
3. Quoted in H. Rogger, *National Consciousness in Eighteenth-Century Russia* (Cambridge, Mass., 1960), p. 257.
4. Quoted in H. Rogger, *National Consciousness*, p. 53.

. . . . .

GENEALOGICAL TABLE
AND MAPS

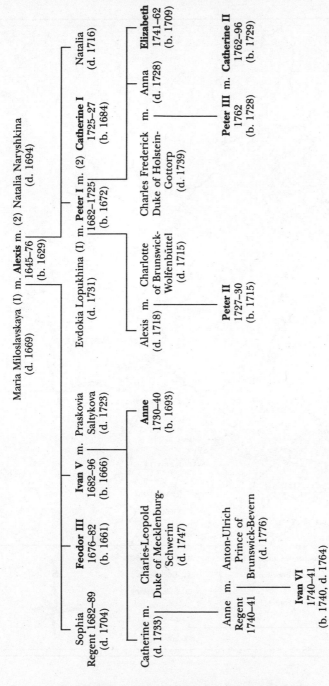

Maria Miloslavskaya (I) m. **Alexis** m. (2) Natalia Naryshkina
(d. 1669)   1645–76   (d. 1694)
                   (b. 1629)

Sophia
Regent 1682–89
(d. 1704)

Feodor III
1676–82
(b. 1661)

Ivan V m. Praskovia
1682–96   Saltykova
(b. 1666)   (d. 1723)

Natalia
(d. 1716)

Evdokia Lopukhina (I) m. **Peter I** m. (2) **Catherine I**
(d. 1731)   1682–1725   1725–27
                      (b. 1672)   (b. 1684)

Catherine m. Charles-Leopold
(d. 1733)   Duke of Mecklenburg-
            Schwerin
            (d. 1747)

Anne
1730–40
(b. 1693)

Anne m. Anton-Ulrich
Regent   Prince of
1740–41 Brunswick-Bevern
         (d. 1776)

Ivan VI
1740–41
(b. 1740, d. 1764)

Alexis m. Charlotte
(d. 1718) of Brunswick-
          Wolfenbüttel
          (d. 1715)

Peter II
1727–30
(b. 1715)

Charles Frederick m. Anna
Duke of Holstein-   (d. 1728)
Gottorp
(d. 1739)

Elizabeth
1741–62
(b. 1709)

Peter III m. **Catherine II**
1762   1762–96
(b. 1728)   (b. 1729)

The names of rulers are given in **bold** type, with their dates of rule.

1. The Romanov and Holstein-Gottorp Dynasties

2. Economic development and revolt during the reign of Peter the Great.

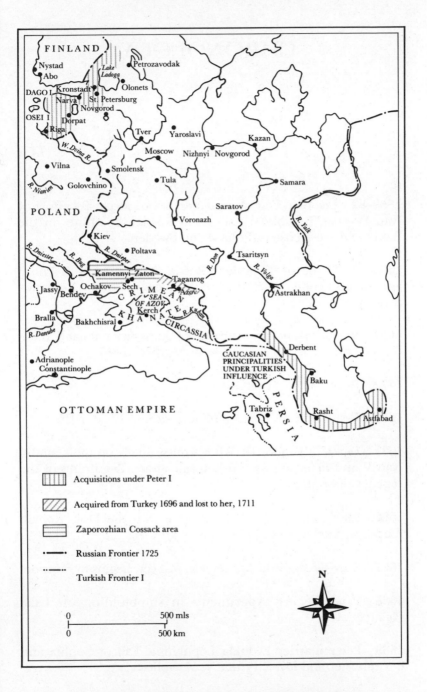

3. European Russia during the reign of Peter the Great.

CHRONOLOGY

1558–82 Livonian War. A sustained but unsuccessful effort by Ivan IV (the Terrible) to secure a Russian coastline on the Baltic at the expense of Poland and Sweden.

1605–13 'Time of Troubles': Russia threatened with Polish and Swedish conquest. Ends with the accession of the Romanov dynasty.

1667 Russia makes large territorial gains from Poland (confirmed and made permanent by a treaty of 1686).

1672 Birth of Peter the Great.

1676 Death of Tsar Alexis and accession of Feodor III.

1682 Death of Feodor III. After streltsy attack on the Kremlin Ivan V and Peter are established as co-tsars. Beginning of the regency of Sophia.

1686 Russia enters the Holy League with the Holy Roman Emperor, Venice and Poland.

1687 Slavo-Greek-Latin Academy in Moscow begins to function.

1688 Peter begins experiments in shipbuilding on Lake Pleshcheev.

1689 Peter marries Evdokia Lopukhina. Fall of Sophia and her minister and lover, Prince V. V. Golitsyn.

1693 Peter visits Archangel and has his first sight of the sea.

1696 Death of Ivan V. Capture of Azov, after an unsuccessful attack in the previous year. Building of a naval squadron there begins.

1697–98 'Great Embassy' to western Europe. Peter visits the Netherlands, England and Vienna, but secures no help against the Ottoman empire.

1698 Streltsy revolt breaks out and is savagely suppressed.

1699 Rapid growth of metal production in the Ural area begins.

1700 Peace is made with the Ottoman empire. Outbreak of war with Sweden and great Russian defeat at Narva. No successor is appointed when the Patriarch Adrian dies.

1703 Foundation of St Petersburg.

1705 Systematic conscription for the armed forces established; outbreak of rising in Astrakhan, which lasts into the following year.

1707 Great advance of Charles XII against Russia begins. Outbreak of Cossack rising in the Don area, which lasts into the following year.

1708 Effort at reform of local administration by the creation of the *gubernii* and their subdivisions (followed by further changes, notably in 1715). The Swedes are defeated at the battle of Lesnaya but are joined by Mazepa.

1709 Decisive Russian victory over Sweden at Poltava, followed by rapid rise in Russia's prestige and international standing.

1711 Outbreak of war with the Ottoman empire and Russian defeat on the Pruth. Creation of the Senate.

1713 Peace treaty with the Ottoman empire.

1714 Decree forbids subdivision of estates among the heirs when the holder dies.

1716 Flight of the Tsarevich Alexis to Vienna and Naples. Russian occupation of Mecklenburg provokes the hostility of Britain and the Emperor Charles VI. *Ustav Voinskii* (Military Code) issued.

1717 Peter's second journey to western Europe. He visits the Netherlands and Paris. Alexis returns to Russia.

1718 Death of Alexis. Creation of the administrative colleges begins. Unsuccessful peace negotiations with Sweden in the Åland islands begin.

1720 *Morskoi Ustav* (Naval Code) and *Generalnyi Reglament* (General Regulation) issued; increasing efforts being made to systematize the machinery of government.

1721 War with Sweden is ended by the treaty of Nystad. Peter assumes the title of emperor. *Dukhovnyi Reglament* (Spiritual Regulation) issued and the Synod set up.

1722 Table of Ranks issued. War with Persia begins. Peter assumes the right to nominate his own successor.

1724 Catherine, Peter's second wife (married privately in 1707), is crowned as empress.

1725 Death of Peter and accession of Catherine. Establishment of the Academy of Sciences in St Petersburg.

1727 Death of Catherine and accession of Peter II, son of the Tsarevich Alexis.

FURTHER READING

This is primarily a list of books and articles in English; but a small number of useful ones in French and German have been included, though inevitably the selection of these is somewhat arbitrary.

Two relatively old general studies in English are still well worth reading in spite of their age: B. H. Sumner, *Peter the Great and the Emergence of Russia* (London, 1950), which is a perceptive and balanced sketch, and V. Klyuchevsky, *Peter the Great* (London, 1958), a translation of a Russian original which gives a penetrating discussion of the social and economic changes of Peter's reign. Another important, and more recent, work translated from Russian is E. V. Anisimov, *The Reforms of Peter the Great: Progress through Coercion in Russia* (Armonk, NY, London, 1993): it is particularly good on the tsar's domestic policies and provides a comprehensive and balanced view of his work as a whole. L. R. Lewitter, 'Peter the Great and the Modern World', in the collection *Russia and Europe*, ed. P. Dukes (London, 1991), is a short sketch by the foremost British expert on the subject. I. Grey, *Peter the Great, Emperor of all Russia* (London, 1962) is essentially narrative and focused on the Great Northern War and foreign policy rather than on the changes within Russia. The most detailed narrative history in English is still the old E. Schuyler, *Peter the Great, Emperor of Russia* (2 vols, New York, 1884). Though its approach to the subject is now very dated and its coverage very uneven (it provides much more detail on the early years of the reign than on its later stages) it is based on extensive research and provides some picturesque detail. The most complete and balanced general account in any language is still R. Wittram, *Peter I, Czar und Kaiser* (2 vols, Göttingen, 1964), while the same author's *Peter der Grosse: Der Eintritt Russlands in die Neuzeit* (Berlin, Göttingen, Heidelberg, 1954) is only a sketch but very good within its limits. A general treatment in French is R. Portal, *Pierre le Grand* (Paris, 1961). Simone Blanc, (ed.), *Pierre le Grand* (Paris, 1974) is a short but well-chosen collection of extracts from illustrative documents and the writings of historians; L. Jay Oliva (ed.), *Peter the Great* (Englewood Cliffs, NJ, 1970) and M. Raeff (ed.), *Peter the Great – Reformer or Revolutionary?* (Boston, 1963) are similar but somewhat larger in scale.

On the Russia which Peter inherited and the growth of new cultural and other influences there, there is L. R. Lewitter, 'Poland, the Ukraine and Russia in the 17th century', *Slavonic and East European Review*, XXVII (1948–9), while R. Hellie, *Enserfment and Military Change in Muscovy* (Chicago, 1971) provides a stimulating discussion of the efforts to strengthen the country militarily and their very important social repercussions. The account of Russia provided by the most famous foreign traveller there of the seventeenth century, the Holsteiner Olearius, is available in S. H. Baron (trans. and ed.), *The Travels of Olearius in Seventeenth-Century Russia* (Stanford, 1967). On the, in many ways, still shadowy figure of the Tsarevna Sophia there are C. B. O'Brien, *Russia under Two Tsars, 1682–9: The Regency of Sophia Alekseevna* (Berkeley, 1952), and the more recent Lindsey Hughes, *Sophia, Regent of Russia, 1657–1704* (New Haven, London, 1990). G. Stökl, 'Russland und Europa vor Peter dem Grossen', *Historische Zeitschrift*, **184** (1957–8), and G. von Rauch, 'Moskau und die europäischen Mächte des 17. Jahrhunderts', *Historische Zeitschrift*, **178** (1954), are useful articles which set the scene for some of Peter's accomplishments. R. H. Warner, 'The Kozuchovo Campaign of 1694, or The Conquest of Moscow by Preobrazhenskoe', *Jahrbücher für Geschichte Osteuropas*, Neue Folge **13** (1965) is slight but throws some light on the young tsar's military preoccupations. The best discussion of Peter's famous journey to the west in 1697–8 is still R. Wittram, 'Peters des Grossen erste Reise in den Westen', *Jahrbücher für Geschichte Osteuropas*, Neue Folge **3** (1955). A more recent small book in English on some of its aspects, learned but badly organized, is G. Barany, *The Anglo–Russian Entente Cordiale of 1697–1698: Peter I and William III at Utrecht* (Boulder, Col., 1986), which is wider in coverage than its title suggests.

There is no comprehensive history in English of the Great Northern War. From the standpoint of Peter's great opponent there is much in R. M. Hatton, *Charles XII of Sweden* (London, 1968), while the later years of the struggle are treated in much diplomatic detail in J. F. Chance, *George I and the Northern War* (London, 1909), which is old and old-fashioned but still useful. A. Rothstein, *Peter the Great and Marlborough: Politics and Diplomacy in Converging Wars* (London, 1986) discusses Russia's relations with western Europe, and particularly with Great Britain, in the first decade or more of the war, though the author's touch is not always completely sure. L. R. Lewitter, 'Russia, Poland and the Baltic, 1697–1721', *Historical Journal*, XI (1968) provides a concise overall view of many aspects of the struggle, while the same author's 'Poland, Russia and the Treaty of Vienna of 5 January 1719', *Historical Journal*, XIII (1970) is more specialized. The relevant pages of W. Mediger, *Moskaus Weg nach Europa* (Braunschweig, 1952) has much information on many aspects of Russia's relations with the west during these years. The same author's *Mecklenburg, Russland und England–Hannover, 1706–1721* (2 vols, Hildesheim, 1967) is very detailed, as is E. Hassinger, *Brandenburg-Preussen, Schweden und Russland, 1700–1713* (Munich, 1953). B. H. Sumner, *Peter the Great and the Ottoman Empire* (Oxford, 1949) is short but very much to the point and still much the best account of its subject in any west-European language, while there is an important account of the disastrous Pruth campaign by a Turkish historian in A. N. Kurat, 'Der Prutfeldzug und der Prutfrieden von 1711', *Jahrbücher für Geschichte Osteuropas* **10** (1962). On the dramatic affair of Mazepa the most balanced account in English is still probably that in W. E. D. Allen, *The Ukraine: A History* (Cambridge, 1940). P. Englund, *The Battle of Poltava: The Birth of the Russian Empire* (London, 1992), is a graphic account of the Swedish campaigns of 1707–9, but written entirely from the Swedish standpoint. Some aspects of the sudden rise in Russia's international importance and the attention given her in western Europe can be followed in the appropriate sections of M. S. Anderson, *Britain's Discovery of Russia, 1553–1815* (London, 1958) and A. Lortholary, *Le Mirage russe en France au XVIIIe siècle* (Paris, n.d.). The creation of permanent diplomatic links with western Europe which was one of the most important aspects of this change is covered in Avis Bohlen, 'Changes in Russian diplomacy under Peter the Great', *Cahiers du monde russe et sovietique*, VII (1966).

Much the greater part of the specialized writing on the growth of the armed forces under Peter is in Russian; but in English there is an excellent account in the relevant chapter of J. H. L. Keep, *Soldiers of the Tsar: Army and Society in Russia, 1462–1874* (Oxford, 1985). On the economic growth which provided one of the essential foundations for Russia's new international status there is the ambitious and large-scale A. Kahan, *The Plow, the Hammer and the Knout: An Economic History of Eighteenth-Century Russia* (Chicago, London, 1985), which is full of detailed information, much of it in quantitative form, though some of its claims and arguments have been challenged. Simone Blanc, 'The Economic Policy of Peter the Great', in W. L. Blackwell (ed.), *Russian Economic Development from Peter the Great to Stalin* (New York, 1974), is a perceptive short sketch, while A. I. Pashkov (ed.), *A History of Russian Economic Thought* (Berkeley, Los Angeles, 1964) contains much information in the chapters relevant to this period. The most important of the 'projectors' who supported and amplified Peter's efforts at economic growth is discussed in L. R. Lewitter, 'Ivan Tikhonovich Pososhkov (1652–1726) and "The Spirit of Capitalism"', *Slavonic and East European Review*, 51 (1973). The basic work in English on Peter's religious policies remains J. Cracraft, *The Church Reform of Peter the Great* (London, 1971). There is a short discussion of what remains their most curious and mysterious aspect in R. Zguta, 'Peter I's "Most Drunken Synod of Fools and Jesters"', *Jahrbücher für Geschichte Osteuropas*, Neue Folge 21 (1973), while M. Cherniavsky, 'The Old Believers and the New Religion', *Slavic Review*, XXV (1960) throws light on one aspect of the opposition to the tsar. The intellectual history of the period is a difficult subject, large, complex and many-faceted; and much of the most important writing on it is in Russian. In spite of its age P. Miliukov, *Outlines of Russian Culture* (3 vols, Philadelphia, 1942), which is an abridged version of a Russian original first published in the 1890s, may still be useful as a starting-point for the English-speaking student. The most obvious and important material sign of changing attitudes in Russia was the building of St Petersburg; and on this and new cultural forces generally there is much interesting information in J. Cracraft, *The Petrine Revolution in Russian Architecture*

(Chicago, London, 1988), which is much wider in coverage than its title indicates. Briefer and more limited in scope but still useful are the early pages of J. H. Bater, *St Petersburg: Industrialization and Change* (London, 1976). Of the activity of foreign artists and architects in Russia, which contributed so much to the creation of the new capital, there is a useful summary account in L. Réau, *Pierre le Grand* (Paris, 1960). A fundamental aspect of intellectual progress is discussed in the early pages of G. Marker, *Publishing, Printing and the Origins of Intellectual Life in Russia, 1700–1800* (Princeton, 1985), while an initiative which Peter did not live to see come to fruition is covered in A. Lipski, 'The Foundation of the Russian Academy of Sciences', *Isis*, XLIV (1953). On education M. J. Okenfuss, 'The Jesuit Origins of Petrine Education', in J. G. Garrard (ed.), *The Eighteenth Century in Russia* (Oxford, 1973) is a challenging article, while the same author's 'Russian Students in Europe in the Age of Peter the Great', also in this collection, is a useful study, as is his 'Technical Training in Russia under Peter the Great', *History of Education Quarterly*, XIII (1973).

On administrative development, one of the most complex and constantly-changing aspects of Peter's reign, there are the relevant pages of G. L. Yaney, *The Systematization of Russian Government: Social Evolution in the Domestic Administration of Imperial Russia, 1711–1905* (Urbana, Chicago, London, 1973), and of the more recent J. P. LeDonne, *Absolutism and Ruling Class: The Formation of the Russian Political Order, 1700–1825* (New York, Oxford, 1991). The most detailed study in English, however, is C. Peterson, *Peter the Great's Administrative and Judicial Reforms: Swedish Antecedents and the Process of Reception* (Stockholm, 1979) which, as its title suggests, is very informative on the debt which the creation of the new administrative colleges in particular owed to foreign example. There is a useful summary discussion in Simone Blanc, 'La Pratique de l'administration russe au XVIII siècle', *Revue d'Histoire Moderne et Contemporaine*, **X** (1963). The changing nature and position of the Russian nobility (if the word is applicable) is discussed in R. O. Crummey, 'Peter and the Boiar Aristocracy, 1689–1700', and Brenda Meehan-Waters, 'The Russian Aristocracy and the Reforms of Peter the Great', both of which are in a special issue of the *Canadian–American Slavic Review*, **8** (1974) devoted to different aspects of Peter's reign. It also contains S. Benson, 'The Role of Western Political Thought in Petrine Russia', a useful article. There is an interesting and perceptive analysis of the changing nature of the Russian monarchy as a largely unintended result of Peter's work in M. Cherniavsky, *Tsar and People: Studies in Russian Myths* (New Haven, London, 1961). One aspect of opposition to the tsar is illustrated in R. O. Crummey, *The Old Believers and the World of Antichrist: The Vyg Community and the Russian State, 1694–1855* (Madison, 1970); while the ruthless crushing of all forms of resistance is brought out in J. Cracraft, 'Opposition to Peter the Great', in E. Mendelsohn and M. S. Shatz (eds), *Imperial Russia, 1700–1917: Essays in Honour of Marc Raeff* (De Kalb, Ill., 1988). Peter's posthumous reputation, an interesting and important subject in its own right, is covered in detail, so far as his own country is concerned, in N. V. Riasanovsky, *The Image of Peter the Great in Russian History and Thought* (New York, Oxford, 1985).

The most interesting guides of all, in many ways, to these years in Russia are provided by the accounts of the country written by foreigners with experience of it. Two in particular are very illuminating: J. Perry, *The State of Russia under the Present Czar* (London, 1716; reprinted London, 1967) (the author was an English engineer who worked in Russia for many years); and F. C. Weber, *The Present State of Russia* (2 vols, London, 1722–3; reprinted London, 1968) (the author was Hanoverian minister in St Petersburg).

INDEX

Although Russian technical terms, titles, etc., have normally been briefly explained when they first occur in the text, an explanatory word or phrase has also been added in the Index where this seemed appropriate.

Baltic, 57–8; considers English mediation, 58; wins battle of Poltava (1709), 64; increased international standing, 65–8; war with Ottoman empire (1711–13), 70–4; hopes for help of Balkan peoples, 70–1; defeated on river Pruth (1711), 71–2; signs treaty with Ottoman empire (1713), 74; and 'Northern Crisis' (1716), 75–7; and treaty of Vienna (1719), 78; negotiates with Sweden (1718–19), 80; makes peace with Sweden (1721), 81–2; assumes title of emperor (1721), 83; hopes for marriage alliance with Bourbons, 86; seeks alliance with France, 85–6; reforms inspired by war needs, 91–3; passion for the navy, 99; conscription for armed forces, 102–3; demands forced labour, 103–4; importance of coercion in achievements, 106–7, 114–15, 116; struggles to raise money for war, 107–8; and to accumulate precious metals, 108; introduces soul tax (1718), 108–9; attempts to make Russia richer, 110–11, 114; protectionist policies, 111; wishes to encourage private initiative, 112–13; feels responsibility for Russia, 113; attempts to improve agriculture, 117; attempts to create a merchant marine, 117–18; economic achievements, 119–20; religious attitudes, 120–1; and 'Most Drunken Synod', 121–2; taxes the Church, 123–4; subjects Church to state control, 124–8; establishes Synod, 125; weakens church, 126–8; emphasis on technical knowledge, 128–9; encourages translation of foreign books, 129–30;

and the Russian language, 130; encourages mapping of Russia, 130–1; wishes to foster education, 132; creates Academy of Sciences, 134–5; buys books and works of art, 135–6; encourages writing of Russian history, 136; builds St Petersburg, 136–9; attempts to improve status of women, 139–40; his work divides Russian society, 140–2; attempts to improve administration, 144–7; ideas about government and society, 144; increase in legislation under, 145; creates Senate and *fiskals*, 145–7; creates *gubernii* and *uezdy*, 147; makes landowners a service class, 147–50; forbids division of landed estates (1714), 148–9; remodels local government (1719), 150; establishes administrative colleges (1718), 151–2; establishes Table of Ranks (1722), 152–3; creates office of *Generalprokuror*, 153; deficiencies of his administrative work, 155–6; struggles against official corruption, 156; employs foreigners and men of low birth, 157; strength of military influences under, 157–8; his unorthodox behaviour as tsar, 164; little aristocratic resistance to, 165–6; religious opposition, 166–9; attitude to Old Believers, 167–9; opposition of Old Believers to, 168; and treatment of political crime, 169–71; conflict with son Alexis, 172; admonishes Alexis (quoted), 172–3; faces danger of serious unrest (1718), 177; interrogates Alexis, 177–8; responsible for death of Alexis, 180; hopes for expansion in Asia, 181; strength of autocracy of, 181;